To Whom Does Christianity Belong?

To Whom Does Christianity Belong?

Critical Issues in World Christianity

Dyron B. Daughrity

Fortress Press
Minneapolis

TO WHOM DOES CHRISTIANITY BELONG?

Critical Issues in World Christianity

Understanding World Christianity Series

Cover image: Philippines/Photo: Dondi Tawatao/Getty Images. Embodied Grace/
Photo: Lenny Foster. Indian Christians offer prayers/AP Photo/Photo: Mahesh
Kumer A.

Cover design: Alisha Lofgren

Library of Congress Cataloging-in-Publication Data

Print ISBN: 978-1-4514-7227-1

eBook ISBN: 978-1-4514-9658-1

The paper used in this publication meets the minimum requirements of American
National Standard for Information Sciences — Permanence of Paper for Printed
Library Materials, ANSI Z329.48-1984.

Manufactured in the U.S.A.

This book was produced using PressBooks.com, and PDF rendering was done by
PrinceXML.

In loving memory of

Brother Grover C. Ross (1908–1999)

and

dedicated to

Jerald Wayne Daughrity

Varen Ross Daughrity

Ross Dyron Daughrity

Contents

Introducing the Fortress Series
"Understanding World Christianity"

The idea of a major project on world Christianity is timely. According to research from Pew, approximately two-thirds of the world's nations and territories are Christian majority.[1] Christianity continues to widen its global net, claiming the allegiance of well over two billion people. Of the ten largest national Christian populations—the United States, Brazil, Mexico, Russia, Philippines, Nigeria, China, DR Congo, Germany, Ethiopia—only two are from the Western world. Around one-sixth of the *human* population holds membership in the Roman Catholic Church. The modern Pentecostal/Charismatic movement—only a century old—claims roughly 600 million people today. As Pew reports, "Christians are also geographically widespread—so far-flung, in fact, that no single continent or region can indisputably claim to be the center of global Christianity. A century ago this was not the case."

Of the eight cultural blocs of the world, Christianity is the largest religion in six of them: Latin America and the Caribbean, North America, Western Europe, Eastern Europe, Africa, and Oceania.

1. See Pew Forum's study "Global Christianity—A Report on the Size and Distribution of the World's Christian Population," December 19, 2011. Located at http://www.pewforum.org/ 2011/12/19/global-christianity-exec/.

Only in Asia and the Middle East is Christianity not the religion most people adhere to. However, some of the most important developments in world Christianity are happening in Asia, and the Middle East will forever be the land of Jesus—where the gospel was unleashed. Furthermore, Islam—by far the most dominant Middle Eastern faith—can scarcely be understood apart from the history it shares with Judaism and Christianity. Christianity's influence in the world is profound, and there is little reason to think it is abating.

In the 1960s, esteemed church historian Stephen Neill began noticing that—for the first time in human history—there existed a truly *world* religion: Christianity. Neill was ahead of his time. Due to his globe-trotting on behalf of the World Council of Churches, he was able to observe rather intimately how deeply Christianity was taking root in Africa and Asia, seemingly against all the odds. While the leviathan structure of European colonialism was collapsing, Christianity defied all predictions by indigenizing. Many thought that when the colonial administrators and missionaries left, Christianity would wither. But the opposite happened. When the Europeans and North Americans got out of the way, these people integrated the gospel into their cultures, into their own lands, on their own terms. And today, we are front-row observers to these events, many of which are still unfolding. Christianity is changing civilizations as civilizations change Christianity. These stories are fascinating, they are important, and they need to be told.

The Understanding World Christianity project addresses head-on the fact that many churches, colleges, and seminaries are struggling to come to terms with the reality that Christianity is now a worldwide faith, not just a Western one. There is a popular and hardened conception that Christianity is dependent upon the nations of Western Europe and North America. Some variants of the story prolong the worn-out narrative that Asia and Africa are being, somehow, held hostage by the white man's religion, and that Christianity has everything to do with colonialism and imperialism, and nothing to do with indigenization, freedom, and self-assertion. Thus many students even take degrees in Christianity under a long-outdated curriculum: Christianity is born in the Middle East, Constantine makes it a Western faith, the Enlightenment ushers in a modern era, Christianity fades, and now we inhabit a *postmodern* world.

This Eurocentric paradigm is obsolete, for many reasons. First of all, Christianity has expanded terrifically. No longer is it centered in the West. It is now broadly spread out across the world, especially in Africa and Latin America. Second, the important modern European thinkers—Bonhoeffer, Tillich, Barth—who are typically required reading in Western seminaries do not adequately represent the world's Christians. Christianity is so much more diversified now. We are in great need of hearing the southern voices such as John Mbiti, Kwame Bediako, Oscar Romero, and M. M. Thomas. The Western academy needs to think more globally, given the striking changes the Christian faith has undergone in the last century. Third, in what some call an era of globalization, we are much more exposed to the non-Western world. Media, immigration, and increased international travel have made cultures intersect and cross-pollinate, creating a hybridity that was not so obvious a generation or two ago. This is especially the case for people who live in cities. Los Angeles, Dallas, Chicago, New York, and Miami are excellent examples of this diversification process, which has a trickle-down effect throughout America's smaller cities, towns, and villages. A woman in small-town New Mexico could very well have an Indian physician, a Vietnamese priest, and a Guatemalan housekeeper. These situations are increasingly common for the average American.

Thankfully, a corpus of research on Christianity's *global* history is proliferating, and there is a growing awareness that Christianity never was the exclusive possession of the Western world, and certainly is not today. In spite of the gains that have been made, there are fundamental questions that remain unaddressed or underaddressed. For example, what is the *meaning* of global Christianity? How will the drastic changes to Christianity's geography impact theology, mission, and ministry? Indeed, what does this new body of research have to say to the church? What can Christians do with this information? How must missionary work be reconceived? These are practical questions begging further investigation. It is critical that Christians respond to global Christianity in sensitive and thoughtful ways. The Understanding World Christianity series will equip specialists, leaders, and students with up-to-date, on-the-ground information that will help them get their heads around the stories and the data.

In the parable of the Sower, Jesus described a scene where seed was scattered on various types of soil. Some seed was unproductive, but some produced bountifully. Similarly, at the beginning of the twenty-first century, Christianity flourishes in surprising places. The continent of Africa is half Christian. China and the former Soviet Union are opening up to Christianity after decades of oppression. The 266th pope is from Buenos Aires. Korea is home to some of the largest Christian congregations in the world. Meanwhile, in Christianity's old heartland—Western Europe—it appears faith is receding. Who could have foreseen these astonishing developments a century ago?

In the early years of the faith, when Christian gentiles began to outnumber believing Jews, the faith began to take on a decidedly different identity. Led by the apostles' ambitious missionary work, the early church adapted capably, and grew exponentially. Peter and

Paul profoundly shaped "the Way" by fashioning it into an institution open to all people, all nationalities and ethnicities alike. It was a blended family par excellence, albeit with considerable growth pains. Today we stand at a similar crossroads. The Global South has become the new heartland of a faith that was anchored in the West for centuries. The composition of Christianity—easily the world's largest religion—is changing, right before our eyes.

An important question remains, however. Is it a *fait accompli* that Christianity will continue to move south, with little for the Western churches to do but watch?

Scholars such as Robert Wuthnow contend there is much that the churches in the Western world can do, and in fact are doing. In *Boundless Faith: The Global Outreach of American Churches*, he shows that American churches now spend $4 billion annually on overseas ministry, more than ever, and "full-time missionaries serving abroad has increased steadily." In contrast to paternalistic models of the past, where the sending church was the clear authority, mission work today follows a collaborative paradigm, "through direct partnerships with overseas congregations, engaging in faster and more efficient transcultural communication, interacting with a sizable population of refugees and immigrants, and contributing to large-scale international humanitarian and relief organizations."[2] Our mental maps of missionaries flowing from the West to the rest must be updated, as Brazil, Korea, and Nigeria are now sending nations with robust missionary programs. India, Vietnam, and the Philippines provide hundreds of Roman Catholic priests to serve in the United States. Indeed, Christians from the Global South are globally engaged, and North American churches are wise to partner with them.

2. Robert Wuthnow, *Boundless Faith: The Global Outreach of American Churches* (Los Angeles: University of California Press, 2010), 1–2.

The Understanding World Christianity series will contribute to this robust conversation in key ways. It will interpret these monumental changes for a larger audience. It will engage critical questions arising from a global, interconnected Christian faith. And it will draw upon some of today's best specialists—familiar with Christianity on the ground in their respective geographies—in order to create authoritative and readable composites of what is happening. Authors for the series come from a range of ecclesial backgrounds, including Orthodox, Roman Catholic, mainline Protestant, Evangelical, and Pentecostal.

The new era of world Christianity is impacting global politics, higher education, Christian ministry paradigms, and countless charitable organizations. This project will help professors, pastors, students, and professionals understand that with the global spread of Christianity comes a new opportunity for sharing the ongoing story, informed by sensitivity to local and contextual differences. As our world flattens and as Christians globally become more interdependent, a rich complexity is developing. Worldviews are shifting, societies are transforming, and theologies are being rewritten. This project will help Christians to navigate through the differences more carefully and more thoughtfully.

Preface

The idea for this book began at an American Society of Church History conference in New Orleans in 2013. I convened a session entitled "To Whom Does Christianity Belong? Christianity and National Identity in Asia, Africa, and Latin America."[1] The papers dealt with various aspects of Christianity in India, Nigeria, and Brazil, competently introduced and responded to by Scott Sunquist.

Following the presentations, questions and comments were delightfully spirited, and proved a little provocative. One audience member asked a series of questions that unleashed a fascinating exchange: "What *is* Christianity? Is it a European export? Should it still even be considered a Western faith? To whom does it belong? Where is at its most authentic? And who gets to decide?"

In other words, is Christianity in India, Nigeria, and Brazil as genuine—or as orthodox—as the older, European manifestations of the faith? In the case of India, is Christianity there simply a cultural leftover from the days of Portuguese colonialism or British imperialism? Are Indian Christians somehow less Indian when they embrace Christianity? Is Christianity *actually* a Western European religion?

---

1. Other participants in the session were Scott Sunquist, Todd Hartsch, and Corey Williams.

If a Nigerian becomes a Christian, does that mean she is essentially adopting a British faith since the missionaries were largely from Britain? Most Brazilians are Christian; but is their faith *actually* European? For how long will Christianity be associated with missionaries and colonial leaders?

And that brings up a deeper, older question: who brought Christian faith to the Europeans? For how long must Christianity be associated with the cultural milieu of the person who brought it to another culture? When does the cord get cut? When do societies reach a point where they can consider their religion properly *their own* rather than associating it with the people who brought it to them or forced it upon them?

Myriad questions were precipitated by the wonderfully insightful comments of our audience that day. As a panel, we were pleasantly surprised, but caught off guard when we realized how deep these critical questions were going, and how they were striking at the very core of Christian faith.

There was one important question that day that I could not get out of my mind, and it motivated the writing of this book: "What *is* Christianity, anyway?" It seemed like a perfectly sensible question with a fairly straightforward answer. But when I tried to answer the question I began to understand what was in plain sight: Christianity is extremely complicated. Who gets to define it? Who is in the circle? Where does Christianity originate? With God? With Judaism? With Christ? With Paul? Where is the "center" of Christianity? Is it best conceptualized as a Western European religion that has shaped Western culture, laws, and values for two millennia?

Has the "center" of Christianity actually moved to the Global South in recent decades? Perhaps the *center* is in Brazil—which has the largest population of Catholics *and* Pentecostals in the world? Or is the *center* best understood as being in the United States with all of its power, prosperity, and influence? Or is the *center* of Christianity in Jerusalem, where it began, but where very few Christians reside? Perhaps the quintessential Christian is an Italian Catholic, living in Rome—worshiping near the seat of the largest Christian denomination. And authentic Christianity radiates out from there, losing a bit of its authenticity and prestige the farther one gets from the core.

Or, perhaps, we are missing the point by thinking of Christianity as being *based* here or there. Indeed, there are implications to basing the Christian faith in one place and not in another. When the holiness of a *place* is emphasized, there is a sense that certain cities bear a higher measure of holiness, and thus uniquely *belong* to Christianity. Throughout Christian history, many thousands fought and died in order to reclaim Jerusalem—the city of Jesus' crucifixion, death, and resurrection. Or perhaps since Christianity now languishes in Western Europe and thrives elsewhere, the argument can be made that Los Angeles, Sao Paulo, Kinshasa, Lagos, Nairobi, or Seoul are the *new* centers?

There are other implications in christening this or that city, nation, or denomination as being the *center* of Christianity. And unfailingly these implications have to do with ownership. Who owns Christianity? Who gets to define its doctrine and praxis? When and if we decide where Christianity is *based*, then we must listen very carefully to the voices coming from that crucial point, that *axis mundi* for Christians.

An example here would be the Christians of Armenia, the world's first national church. The Armenian Church has been considered heretical throughout the history of Christianity, due to its opposition to the Christology endorsed at the Council of Chalcedon (A.D. 451).

They have maintained their faith throughout the centuries in spite of terrible odds and many rounds of persecution. Are they *in*? Are they Christians or not? Even the question is preposterous. These people have held on to Christianity through trouble and war on a scale few nations will ever see.

Perhaps we consider a *person* to be the center of Christianity. Of course Jesus Christ is, fundamentally, the reason for Christian faith, but who is the correct interpreter of his life and its meaning? In the West, that honor probably goes to Augustine. However, in the sixteenth century, Luther became the chief interpreter of Augustine for Protestants. And so who becomes the chief interpreter of Luther? What did Luther *really* mean? And what about the churches of the East who scarcely know of Martin Luther? To them, he is merely an Augustinian monk in the sixteenth century who happened to cause turbulence in the Western church, but had little impact on the Eastern churches.

Does any of this even matter to a Pentecostal Christian in, say, Rio de Janeiro who believes that the power of the Holy Spirit is available for all who believe, just as it was to the earliest followers of Jesus? Jesus said in John 14:12, "Whoever believes in me will do the works I have been doing, and they will do even greater things than these." Did Jesus really mean that? Can disciples today raise the dead and heal the blind?

Who gets to interpret whom? And whose interpretation is best? Are the professional social scientists and historians the chief interpreters today since they seem to understand this complicated academic discourse best? They know where Christianity is strong and growing, and where it is declining. They understand that theology changes according to culture. Historians track all of these developments, and theologians interpret what this all says about God.

Thus, are we to turn to academicians for an answer to the question, "To whom does Christianity belong?"

Typically, practicing Christians will choose to locate the authority of Christian faith in the individual or in the institution. Protestants often argue that Christianity is within you and you must be the judge of your own actions. There are exceptions to this stereotype, but it is certainly representative of many Protestants, who make up 40 percent of the world's Christian population. However, for Roman Catholic and Orthodox Christians, authority is located in the institution: the church, the body of Christ on earth, led by a properly sanctioned clergy.

So to whom does Christianity *really* belong? To the institution or to the individual? It is a puzzle. And one's answer will probably be determined by the church one attends, if one attends a church.

Perhaps, however, we scrap the question altogether. Perhaps we *should* scrap it, but not until we have at least considered it. This volume is an attempt to deal with that vital question with all of its implications. And when we at least ask the question, we begin to see the complexity and beauty of that vast religion to which many of us cling with all of our heart, soul, mind, and strength.

Acknowledgements

I would like to thank the many people who have directly and indirectly helped to bring this book to light.

First, at Fortress Press, I am deeply grateful to Will Bergkamp. His leadership and support have been vital in getting the Understanding World Christianity project up and running. Sincere appreciation goes to my diligent editor, Lisa Gruenisen, for valuable input.

Many thanks go to my colleagues at Pepperdine. The Religion Division is a very hospitable place to research and teach, and I extend my thanks to the men and women who serve faithfully. I make special mention of Tim Willis, Rick Marrs, and Lee Kats. They have provided unfailing support and encouragement conducive for scholarship.

I thank my many students who continually inspire me. They are so competent, so gracious, and so busy. Yet they manage to find time to come to my office, gather in my home, send occasional updates, and show kindness in countless ways. I have sheer joy watching them flourish as students and thrive after graduation.

I thank my colleagues in various scholarly societies such as the American Academy of Religion, American Society of Church History, the Yale-Edinburgh Group, the World Council of Churches, and the Center for Studies on New Religions. Thanks also to the many friends and colleagues all over the world who are working together to expose more people to the fascinating field of World Christianity. I make special mention of Philip Jenkins and Lamin Sanneh for inspiring so many of us.

Most of all I thank my immediate family: parents Jerald and May Dell, brother Varen, and children Clare, Ross, Mande Mae, and Holly Joy—born January 3, 2015. My greatest debt is to my wife, Sunde.

Now unto him that is able to do exceeding abundantly above all that we ask or think, according to the power that worketh in us, Unto him be glory in the church by Christ Jesus throughout all ages, world without end. Amen. (Eph. 3:20–21, KJV)

Dyron B. Daughrity
Malibu, California
January 30, 2015

PART I

Introduction

1

———

To Whom Does Christianity Belong?

Luke 14:23

Then the master told his servant, "Go out to the roads and country lanes and compel them to come in, so that my house will be full."

In the earliest years of Christianity, there was profound conflict over how to interpret Jesus' teachings, his life and death, and how his followers should respond. It was unclear whether Jesus was opening the way for gentiles to become part of the Jewish story or not. On several occasions the Gospel writers describe a scene where the apostles are confused and do not understand the meaning of what Jesus is saying.

One of the most difficult teachings had to do with Jesus' following. Who gets to be a follower of Jesus? Were his teachings just for Jews? Can gentiles join? It was not clear. It took the apostles some time to form a consensus, and had it not been for James—Jesus' brother—Christianity might have turned into a mere Jewish sect. We do know that the apostle Peter struggled during his lifetime over whether to allow gentiles into the club of Jesus followers, and what that might look like. The apostle Paul worked enthusiastically to bring gentiles into the movement through his impressive missionary travels across the Mediterranean world.

A Banquet and a Sower

It was no easy task to figure out what Jesus meant by some of his parables. For example, in the parable of the Great Banquet there is a scene where a man prepares a great feast but none of the invitees show up. They are too busy. Offended, the man instructs his servants to invite "the poor, the crippled, the lame, the blind."[1] When they came, the man urged that his servants go out into the countryside to find anyone else who could attend, "so that my house will be full."

What does this parable mean? Typically it is explained that the banquet represents the new era that Jesus inaugurated, the "new testament" or "new covenant." The original guests were the Jewish leaders, but they did not come. Later, the outcasts get invited, meaning the marginal within Jewish society and even gentiles.

As we know, the marginal ended up in the house, sitting around the table. Within a short period of time, in fact, Christianity had more gentiles than Jews. But the transition was not without its problems. Acts 15, the famous Jerusalem Council, is a clear example. The apostles struggled with what Christian belief entailed. Must gentiles become like Jews in order to be followers of Christ? Should they become circumcised? Must they refrain from certain foods, as the Torah commands? Should they abide by the same sexual ethics as Jews, in spite of the fact that they come from very different worldviews?

---

1. The parable occurs in Matthew 22 and Luke 14. This quotation comes from Luke's account (v. 13).

In other words, "To whom does Christianity belong?" To the Jews or to the gentiles? The conclusion of that first Christian council was summed up by James: "It is my judgment, therefore, that we should not make it difficult for the gentiles who are turning to God."[2] Their conclusions were written down in a letter addressed to the gentile believers. Paul and some others were commissioned to deliver it to the churches.

With the stroke of a pen, Christianity was well on its way to becoming a gentile faith. No longer did it belong solely to Jews. That letter, sanctioned by the first Christian council, opened the floodgates when it was delivered to believers in Antioch, where the word *Christian* originates. The gentiles pulled up to their place at the table. And they were given their slice of the pie—a pie that had belonged to the house of Israel for a very long time.

A very similar process is going on in Christianity today. For centuries, Christianity has been associated with European civilization. And for good reason. Most Christians were Europeans. However, in the last century, that situation has changed dramatically. Christianity has become a religion that is more associated with the Global South, while Europeans continue to distance themselves from it.

And similar to that letter penned at the Jerusalem Council, the implications are huge. A whole new group of people will come to the banquet. So many people have come that now Christianity seems to be entering a new phase. The African, the Asian, and the Latin American masses have come to the banquet and they are changing the identity of Christianity in ways unimaginable only a few decades ago. As a result, much of the baggage associated with European Christendom is being shed. The state church idea is nearly dead. Missionaries are sent *to* Europe rather than being sent *from*

2. Acts 15:19.

Europe. Young Europeans know little of Christian identity while entire civilizations in the Global South have adopted a Christian identity as their own.

In another story from Jesus, the parable of the Sower, Jesus describes a farmer sowing seed.[3] Some of the seeds were quickly devoured by birds. Some fell onto rocky places or onto soil that was too shallow. Some seeds ended up in the thorns, which eventually choked the plants. Of course some seed fell onto good soil and took root, producing a harvest. And the sheaves are coming in bountifully.

Christian seed was sown in the Global South, and for complex reasons the soil once thought to be barren has turned into a rich and plentiful garden. Christianity is strong and flourishing in surprising places. Who would have thought that the "Dark Continent" would rather quickly endorse the Light of the World? Why did China and the former Soviet Union open to Christianity after decades of official atheism? Who could have anticipated a pope from Buenos Aires? How did Korea become home to some of the largest Christian congregations in the world? Why is the seed suddenly bearing so much fruit?

Likewise, why are so many sprouts choking in formerly Christian Europe? Why have they, seemingly, gone to the birds?

To whom does Christianity now belong? Can we still properly call it a Western religion? Or is it now better described as a Global South phenomenon? The religious studies courses that offer Christianity as a Western faith need to be revised. The old models—perpetuated still in Western universities—are obsolete. Christianity has gone global. It no longer makes sense to teach it as a Western faith. A new teaching model, one that takes into consideration Christianity's global presence, must emerge.

3. See Matthew 13, Mark 4, and Luke 8.

What Happened?

While Christianity still has a presence in the West—particularly in the United States—it is probably *better* described as a Global South phenomenon today. Several key statistics illustrate why.[4]

- Globally, religion is on the rise. In 1970, around 80 percent of the world's population was religious, but by 2010 that number had risen to nearly 90 percent.

- In 1970, around 40 percent of all Christians were from Asia, Africa, or Latin America. By 2020, that figure will be around 65 percent.

- Pentecostal and Charismatic Christians are growing about four times faster than other Christians. In 1970, Pentecostals/Charismatics claimed around 5 percent of the world's Christians; in 2010 that number was around 26 percent.

- Christianity's spectacular growth in Africa continues, from 143 million in 1970 to an estimated 630 million in 2020. About one out of every three of these Christians will be Roman Catholic.

---

4. The statistics in this section come from the work of David Barrett and Todd M. Johnson. In particular, I am using the "Key Findings of Christianity in Its Global Context, 1970–2020" by Gina A. Bellofatto and Todd M. Johnson, *International Bulletin of Missionary Research* 37, no. 3 (July, 2013): 157–64. The full report can be downloaded for free at http://wwwgordonconwell.com/netcommunity/CSGCResources/ChristianityinitsGlobalContext.pdf. Todd Johnson was the primary research associate of David Barrett—the scholar who led the work of the *World Christian Encyclopedia* (Oxford: Oxford University Press, 2001) for many years. That work has evolved into the World Christian Database, which is housed at Gordon-Conwell Theological Seminary and is supported by Brill Publishers. The World Christian Database has been described by eminent sociologist Rodney Stark as "the very best" source for statistics on worldwide religious affiliation. See Stark, *The Triumph of Christianity* (New York: HarperOne, 2011), 388 and 493n6. Similarly, Robert Wuthnow discusses Barrett and Johnson's work in *Boundless Faith: The Global Outreach of American Churches* (Los Angeles: University of California Press, 2009), 41. His conclusion is that "Barrett's particular set of statistics comes as close to being 'official' as any such statistics could be." He refers to Barrett and Johnson's work as being "the most authoritative source." He also cites an important independent study of Barrett and Johnson's statistics (by Becky Hsu, Amy Reynolds, Conrad Hackett, and James Gibbon) that "largely confirmed the validity of Barrett's statistics."

- Christianity is the fastest-growing religion in Asia right now.

- In Europe, Christianity is in decline as many embrace agnosticism or atheism.

- Christianity in Latin American continues to rise. As many people convert to Pentecostalism, the Roman Catholic Church has adapted in creative ways. The election of Pope Francis from Argentina has energized Catholicism there.

- Christianity is declining in the United States. Agnosticism is growing nearly four times faster than Christianity in North America. In 1970, around 91 percent of North Americans were Christian. That number will be around 77 percent in 2020.

- The "reverse missions" phenomenon continues apace—Global South churches are sending missionaries to the North.

- Nearly half of the world's migrants are Christians. And these people take their faith with them. Many of them function as missionaries.

These "key findings" certainly provide much food for thought, but what is striking is just how unfathomable these statistics would have been just a century ago. The demography of world religion, and especially world Christianity, has changed dramatically. One thing is certain, however. It is not clear any more what we mean by Christianity in this new and globalized context. When gentiles began to outnumber Christian Jews, the faith began to take on a drastically different identity. That same process is underway as the Global South becomes the heartland of a faith that was so solidly Western for so long.

"Global Christianity" or "World Christianity"?

We have seen that Christianity experienced a major paradigm shift in recent years. While it may look like this change happened very recently, the fact is that the seeds were planted decades ago. In the case of the Roman Catholic Church's global expansion, the seeds go back to the rise of the Spanish and Portuguese empires. The Jesuits (or, the Society of Jesus), founded in 1534 by Ignatius Loyola, took Christian teaching to the ends of the earth with their epochal missionary work. Most impressive of them all was Francis Xavier—truly one of the great missionaries of all time. Protestant missionaries did not begin in earnest until the early 1700s. Nevertheless, the fact that sub-Saharan Africa, Latin America, and pockets of Asia are strongly Christian has much to do with the countless missionaries who went abroad during those years. The European powers were rising in influence and expanding globally, and Christianity traveled with them.

While *global Christianity* and *world Christianity* are concepts that go back at least to the era of Jesuit missions, general usage of those expressions is rather recent. In his excellent book *Boundless Faith*, sociologist Robert Wuthnow competently explains where the expressions come from.[5] In 1943, a Methodist pastor named Walter A. Graham gave a lecture in Baltimore on "Global Christianity at Work." In 1979 the *Washington Post* used the expression in a story about a papal visit. The *New York Times* did not use the phrase until 1994. The following year, a book by F. J. Verstraelen was published containing the expression in its title: *Missiology: An Ecumenical Introduction, Texts and Contexts of Global Christianity.*[6] It was Philip

---

5. Wuthnow, *Boundless Faith,* chapter two, "The Global Christianity Paradigm."
6. F. J. Verstraelen, *Missiology: An Ecumenical Introduction, Texts and Contexts of Global Christianity* (Grand Rapids, MI: Eerdmans, 1995).

Jenkins's highly influential 2002 book *The Next Christendom: The Coming of Global Christianity* that blew "global Christianity" into the mainstream of scholarship.[7] Wuthnow writes, "It is difficult to overestimate the significant of Jenkins's contribution to the idea that a new paradigm was required for understanding Christianity."[8] Jenkins's book attracted major attention as many important newspapers reviewed it favorably and it collected numerous awards. This book more than any other helped to birth a new subfield in religious studies: global Christianity.

The phrase *world Christianity* has a longer history. Wuthnow found that the first book published using the expression in the title was in 1929. It was Francis John McConnell's *Human Needs and World Christianity*.[9] *World Christianity* was used occasionally by major newspapers up to the 1990s, but it was Yale historian Lamin Sanneh who began to popularize it for a larger audience.

Importantly, Sanneh began to argue that there are critical differences between the two expressions *world Christianity* and *global Christianity*. In his 2003 book—one year after Jenkins's *Next Christendom*—he made the distinction clear:

> "World Christianity" is the movement of Christianity as it takes form and shape in societies that previously were not Christian. . . . World Christianity is not one thing, but a variety of indigenous responses through more or less effective local idioms, but in any case without necessarily the European Enlightenment frame. "Global Christianity," on the other hand, is the faithful replication of Christian forms and patterns developed in Europe. . . . It is, in fact, religious establishment and the cultural captivity of faith.[10]

---

7. Philip Jenkins, *The Next Christendom: The Coming of Global Christianity* (Oxford: Oxford University Press, 2002).
8. Wuthnow, *Boundless Faith*, 34–35.
9. Francis John McConnell, *Human Needs and World Christianity* (New York: Friendship Press, 1929).

Clearly, Sanneh has a problem with using *global Christianity* to refer to indigenous Christianities that begin without significant Western input. For example, the manifold African indigenous churches that are mushrooming across the continent have little to do with Europe. Sanneh would never call these movements part of the "global Christianity" paradigm because they were not European church plants. In all his work, notably in his magisterial *Translating the Message*, he has shown that the new Christianities proliferating globally, especially in Asia and sub-Sahara Africa, are indigenous responses rather than extensions of churches or missionaries from the Western world.[11] Central to his argument is language: the mother tongue appropriation of the gospel dignifies cultures as the message of Christ gets translated into local vernaculars.

The debate over whether this new subfield should be called *global Christianity* or *world Christianity* plays out in books, articles, research centers, and the like. Some scholars line up behind Jenkins's preference, others follow Sanneh. Jenkins has written that he sees the distinction "difficult to draw in practice." Even when there can be a distinction detected—between a more homegrown world Christianity versus an imported global Christianity—"the two forms often mutate and merge into each other." Jenkins concludes, "I will therefore continue to use 'global' Christianity in a broad and nonjudgmental sense."[12]

Sanneh sees more at stake, however. He writes,

> The term "global Christianity" carries vestiges still of that root imperial phase by suggesting that growing communities of professing Christians

10. Lamin Sanneh, *Whose Religion Is Christianity? The Gospel beyond the West* (Grand Rapids, MI: Eerdmans, 2003), 22.

11. Lamin Sanneh, *Translating the Message: The Missionary Impact on Culture* (Maryknoll, NY: Orbis, 1989). The book was expanded in 2009.

12. Philip Jenkins, *The Next Christendom,* rev. and expanded ed. (Oxford: Oxford University Press, 2007), xiii.

around the world are evidence of the economic and political security interests of Europe, that churches everywhere are a religious expression of Europe's political reach, or else a reaction to it. "Global Christianity" as an expression also carries connotations of parallels with economic globalization.[13]

In my own work I have used the terms somewhat interchangeably. However, Sanneh's rationalization makes sense. Indigenous churches in the Global South often bear little resemblance to the European denominations planted globally in the heyday of colonialism and European hegemony. The issue does require sensitivity.

While Sanneh prefers *world Christianity* and Jenkins prefers *global Christianity*, scholars of Christianity emphasize different aspects of what we see happening globally. For example, Wuthnow speaks of Christianity's "boundless" nature. Similarly, in my own work, I have emphasized what I call the "borderlessness" of Christianity.[14]

We would be remiss if we did not discuss the work of Andrew Walls, described by *Christianity Today* as "the most important person you don't know."[15] Walls is deeply respected by virtually everyone studying world Christianity today. He is the fountain out of which the likes of Sanneh and Jenkins flow, and they both admit it.

Walls is a Scottish, Oxbridge-educated scholar who moved to Sierra Leone in 1957 to serve as a church history professor in a colonial college. What he witnessed in Africa changed his worldview. While "happily pontificating" on early Christianity, he came to realize he "was actually living in a second-century church."[16] Africans

---

13. Sanneh, *Whose Religion Is Christianity?*, 23.

14. Dyron Daughrity, *The Changing World of Christianity: The Global History of a Borderless Religion* (New York: Peter Lang, 2010).

15. Tim Stafford, "Historian Ahead of His Time," *Christianity Today*, February 8, 2007, http://www.christianitytoday.com/ct/2007/february/34.87.html. See also William Burrows, Mark Gornik, and Janice McLean, eds., *Understanding World Christianity: The Vision and Work of Andrew F. Walls* (Maryknoll, NY: Orbis, 2011).

16. Stafford, "Historian Ahead of His Time," 2.

were rapidly turning to Christ, and he was a front-row observer. He began to see that the Christianity his British compatriots had established was becoming translated and assimilated into the local context in creative, unpredictable ways. Africa was becoming the Christian heartland of the world, but it was complex, uncontrolled, vibrantly new, and unsettled. When the British began leaving Africa en masse in the 1960s, the Christian movement accelerated, diversifying in the process.

Walls made a career out of analyzing how Christianity gets translated and indigenized in new cultures. In his view, this is the genius of Christianity: its translatability. Walls's ideas overhauled the field of church history to the point that most classic models are now obsolete. No longer can the history of Christians be told in an exclusively Western framework, that is, from Acts to Augustine to Aquinas to Luther to Wesley to Barth. Now, church history must be told in all of its vast geography and extreme diversity.

Walls broadened the academic study of Christianity by making us think globally, even when dealing with our own personal, local faith traditions. In his watershed essay, "Eusebius Tries Again: Reconceiving the Study of Christian History" he writes,

> The "church" that is the subject of "church history" is implicitly defined as the church we ourselves know—our tradition as it has developed. In principle, there is no harm in this focus, provided we know what we are doing, and provided also we do more than this. It is natural and right to seek to understand one's own tradition; it means to know who one's ancestors are. But there are lurking dangers, both historical and theological. One is that we think by the study of our own tradition we are doing church history. We are not—we are doing our church history. If this is the only lens through which we study Christian history, we have bypassed the story of the whole people of God in favor of "clan history." Such an approach reduces the area in which we look for the works of God, whereas the promises of God are to all who trust them. The Lord of Hosts is not to be treated as a territorial Baal.[17]

Walls's recommendation is nothing less than a "Re-conception of the Syllabus." I am one of many in a new generation who have taken Walls's advice seriously, and most of the history that I write, I like to believe, respects the "whole history of the people of God." Walls's writings have forced scholars to hybridize the local with the global. While all disciples of Jesus practice their faith in their own parochial, local way, the inescapable fact remains that Christianity is today a *world* religion.

Christianity has thus become a major field of interest in the academic setting. Anthropologists, sociologists, historians, theologians, and political scientists inevitably have to deal with world Christianity, simply because its presence is felt all over the world. Of the world's eight cultural blocks, the Middle East, Asia, Africa, Latin America, North America, Western Europe, Eastern Europe, and Oceania, Christianity is the largest in six of them. And in the two cultures where it is not the largest faith—Asia and the Middle East—we can quickly reason that Christianity *used to be* the largest in one (Middle East) and is making huge strides in the other (Asia).

The study of world Christianity has a bright future. Philip Jenkins has decried the dearth of courses on Christianity in religious studies programs. He notes that while it is important to study Islam, Buddhism, Hinduism, and Judaism, Christianity "receives nothing like the attention it merits in terms of its numbers and global scale. Whatever the value of Christian claims to truth, it cannot be considered as just one religion out of many; it is, and will continue to be, by far the largest in existence."[18]

To bring this chapter back around, we must ask once again, "To whom does Christianity belong?" I asked a colleague that question

---

17. Andrew Walls, "Eusebius Tries Again: Reconceiving the Study of Christian History," *International Bulletin of Missionary Research* 24, no. 3 (July 2000): 107.
18. Jenkins, *The Next Christendom*, 255.

recently and he answered quickly, "It belongs to God." Maybe so. However—to borrow imagery from the parables we cited earlier—the seeds have been scattered, but the house is not yet full.

A Quick Preview

This book will help readers understand what is happening in world Christianity today. We attempt to answer the question "To whom does Christianity belong?" by exploring what Christianity looks like in all of its splendid variety. We will investigate how the global explosion of Christianity happened, and what this might mean for a faith that was associated with the Western world for so many centuries. We will look at some of the major changes happening in Christianity: doctrine, demographics, and practice. The book will equip readers in order to help them answer the title question on their own, although, in the conclusion, I will try to answer the question myself.

I have organized the book into four major parts. The first part is introductory. This present chapter and the next one orient readers to fundamental issues in the study of world Christianity. In this chapter we unpacked some of the key terms, key thinkers, and key developments in the burgeoning, cutting-edge field of world Christianity. Chapter 2 continues that discussion by asking a fundamental question, "What is Christianity anyway?" Readers will see the question is not as elementary as one might presume.

The second part dives into some of the most important theological issues in the history of Christianity, and how they have been impacted recently by the new global Christian paradigm shift. As Christianity has moved south, and as it has expanded exponentially, basic theological issues that seemed settled for centuries are being upended. In chapter 3, we question what exactly is "the church" anymore? Who is "in"? How do we determine what a "heresy" is?

Where is "pure" Christianity to be found? How large are its borders? How can Christians be unified in a context of such profound variety? In chapter 4 we turn our attention to Jesus. Who gets to define him? When the Maasai of East Africa speak of Jesus, they have something in mind that is very different from what a secularized German Christian might say about him. Similar questions arise with the Holy Spirit, the subject of chapter 5. Why has the Holy Ghost suddenly become the more prolific member of the Holy Trinity after having taken a back seat to the Father and the Son for so many centuries? And what is at stake? In chapter 6 we examine what some of Christianity's most important voices today are saying about afterlife. Certain thinkers in the West are asking whether there even *is* an afterlife. Others assert that the afterlife has been misunderstood for two millennia, and it is time to open up the conversation again. In the sixteenth century, Martin Luther cast serious doubt on the whole concept of purgatory—a place most Catholics assumed was real. Is there another paradigm shift happening in our understanding of the afterlife here in the early twenty-first century?

In part 3, "The Church and the World," I try to give readers a sense of what is happening in two worlds that are often disconnected: Roman Catholicism and Protestantism. For example, in chapter 7 I take a good look at Pope Francis and how he has impacted the world's largest denomination in such a short period of time. The chapter also gives readers a sense of the gargantuan scale of the Roman Catholic denomination; it is something Protestants have a hard time getting their heads around. The Protestant chapter (8), shows just how distinct and irreconcilable Christianity can become if each person is enabled to think about Christianity for him- or herself. It quickly becomes a tangled, ecclesiological mess! We discuss the powerful Iglesia Ni Cristo movement in the Philippines, and look at how the Protestant principle of questioning authority has impacted the continent of Africa. We conclude by asking the age-old question of purity or unity: Which one should be privileged within the Christian faith? Chapter 9 unpacks the volatile issue of secularization. There is a huge disagreement in the academy right now over whether a secularization process is even happening. Insights from the non-Western world seem to point toward a worldwide religious revival. In chapter 10 we discuss the new missionaries who are crisscrossing the globe, taking faith with them wherever they go: migrants. No longer are missions the world of a professional class of Westerners, trained in evangelical methods and having sophisticated linguistic prowess. No, today's missionary is more commonly a person who migrates to another country in search of a better life. And they bring faith with them, as their luggage.

Part 4 looks at three massive changes in Christianity that have taken place in recent decades: sexuality, the role of women in the church, and the radical transformation that has occurred in Christian music. Sexuality is pervasive in the twenty-first century. Rapid advances in media have taken a topic that was once rather taboo, and placed it right into the public square. And Christians simply do not agree on what to think about these changing attitudes about sex and marriage. There are liberals and there are conservatives, and they are poles apart on these issues. In chapter 12 we look at some of the pioneers who fought to give women an equal place in Christianity, particularly in the pulpit. And judging by a glance at mainline Protestant Christianity in Europe and North America we can see that they won. However, not everybody agrees with the changes, certainly not those in the Orthodox or Roman Catholic traditions. The final chapter (13) provides a glimpse of Christianity in its earliest years, as well as a survey of how Christians sing and praise today. We will take a look at Ethiopian Orthodox music as well as at John Lennon. How's that for strange bedfellows?

And, as stated, in the conclusion I will try to answer the book's title question: To whom does Christianity belong? Hopefully by then you will be on the edge of your seat, craving some resolution to the complex array of questions, issues, rituals, and beliefs that Christianity has become.

2

What is Christianity, Anyway?

John 1:14

The Word became flesh and made his dwelling among us. We have seen his glory, the glory of the one and only Son, who came from the Father, full of grace and truth.

How do we define Christianity? Is it the Apostles' Creed, the original Nicene Creed, or the Nicene-Constantinopolitan Creed? Is it the *gospel*, a word that simply means "good news"? If so, then what is the news that is considered by Christians to be so good? Theologians say the *kerygma*, or the "preaching" is the essence of Christianity. But which sermon? Should we focus on Jesus's teachings, say, in the Sermon on the Mount? Or perhaps Paul's postresurrection teachings are at the heart of what we mean when we say *Christianity*? Should we emphasize James, with his laser focus on behavior, or "works"? Or is Christian faith more of a grace-centered, I'm okay, you're okay, Jesus did the work on our behalf type of body of beliefs?

Who Gets to Define It?

Some scholars researching Christianity approach this question solely as an academic discipline. They study much like someone would study in the natural sciences, like a geologist would study tectonic plates. They try not to think about the material in a personal way. Their goal is to look at Christianity strictly as a human phenomenon. These scholars might even have very little emotional investment in Christian faith. While not necessarily antagonistic toward it, they simply have no claim to it. Regarding the central question of this book, "To whom does Christianity belong?," they would respond that it does not belong to them. They do not commit to it nor do they want to allow their beliefs to affect the outcome of their research. Are they successful in their endeavor to separate the two? That's debatable.

There is much more at stake, however, for those who study Christianity *and* commit to it personally. It is a tall order to ask someone to be dispassionate about something that is inherently full of passion. Inherited wisdom tells us there are two things we should not discuss in polite company: religion and politics. The person who coined this phrase must have understood the link between religion and passion.

Thus when religious scholars—myself included—write about religion, there is ambivalence involved. We are religious, but we are also trained to check our passions at the door. We try to be honest when we present our research. We understand the difference between a university lectern and a pulpit because there is a very big difference. However, it would be foolish to claim we are without bias. It would be foolish for *anyone* to make that claim. The *religious* scholar of religion has to reason through these issues, perhaps even more carefully. We have to be able to say, "Admittedly, I have an emotional investment in Christianity, but for this lecture (or essay or book) I am going to be as unbiased as possible. I will try to relay to you my knowledge without my beliefs—unless you ask."

Hopefully, some of the complexities and dilemmas in writing a book of this nature are now revealed. By asking the question, "To whom does Christianity belong?," we must deal with other questions: What is Christianity, anyway? Who gets to define it? The believer or the nonbeliever? The Christian scholar or the non-Christian scholar? There are pressures on both sides. One can argue that the Christian scholar is inherently biased because she is a Christian. However, are we to believe that non-Christians are somehow unbiased? Christianity is so much more than a collection of facts—it is, after all, a faith. Words like *objective* or *unbiased* or *dispassionate* seem hopelessly naive. So, does a non-Christian have the right to define Christianity? Does a non-Christian even understand Christianity? This is a potentially volatile question.

Case in point: Reza Aslan, professor of creative writing at the University of California, Riverside. Aslan caused a stir in 2013 when he released his bestselling book *Zealot: The Life of and Times of Jesus of Nazareth*. Fox News was lambasted when one of its reporters questioned whether Aslan, a Muslim-turned evangelical Christian-turned Muslim again, could write about Jesus with any degree of objectivity. Some charged that Aslan lacked the academic credibility. In reality, Aslan is highly trained in religious studies, with multiple degrees from excellent institutions. The real problem, however, was this: Who has the right to discuss a religion? Can a Muslim write fairly about Jesus? In his review of Aslan's book in the *New York Times*, Yale professor Dale B. Martin answered, "This should be no more controversial than a Christian scholar's writing a book about Islam or Muhammad. It happens all the time."[1]

I think the more fundamental issue at play in the Reza Aslan case is that some of his conclusions are already fixed. He does not believe Jesus is who Christians say he is. Aslan endorses the Muslim interpretation: Jesus is not the son of God. He was an amazing man and an important prophet, but he was not uniquely God in flesh. It would be like a Christian scholar commenting on whether the Qur'an is actually the precise words of God. Of course a Christian disagrees with that idea.

Indeed, those of us who choose to study Christianity *and* practice it are faced with dilemmas. We deeply respect this faith, yet as academics we are obliged to discuss its foibles. We raise our children in church, yet know well the church's fallibility. We abide by Christian teaching, yet participate in the struggles to define it. In short, Christianity is dear to us. And when something is dear to us it raises the stakes of its importance. Thus when we define it, we bear the burden of being personally invested in our outcomes.

This is the general predicament of those who study religion. Should a scholar of religion be religious or irreligious? Who gets to create the definitions? Who gets to tell the history? Who gets control of how the story is told? There is a very big difference between history and the past. The past is what actually happened. History is an interpretation of what happened. For each historian there is a set of assumptions that shapes the narrative. If a historian of Christianity is an atheist, he will tell the story in his own way. If he is a Protestant, he will tell the story a bit differently than a Roman Catholic would.

Who even *is* a Christian? The answer is not as obvious as one might think. All vested parties have different takes. Denominations do not always recognize each other. Once I listened to a Roman Catholic from Latin America argue vehemently that Catholics are not

1. Dale B. Martin, "Still a Firebrand, 2000 Years Later," *The New York Times*, August 5, 2013.

"Christians." What she actually meant was there is a big difference between a Catholic and a *Protestant*.

The point here is this: Christianity is defined by those who tell the story. And the story will vary, depending on the teller. Until recent times there were restrictions on who was allowed to tell Christianity's story; this was the domain of priests, pastors, and professors. In an age of radical freedom, however, the story is being told by many, and from very different angles: Protestants, Catholics, Orthodox, clergy, laity, rich, poor, influential, oppressed, and even those from other faiths, as we saw above. Thus, in the next section, we hear several voices from very different backgrounds trying to answer the chapter's key question, "What is Christianity, anyway?"

A Smorgasbord of Answers

To the apostle Paul, Christianity was the beginning of a new testament, a new agreement that God had made with humankind. Jews were his chosen people, but gentiles were now welcomed and encouraged to come in. No longer was God constrained to limits of ethnicity, tribe, or language. God was reaching out to all human beings in all directions. As Christians know, these were strange teachings to the early Christians. But Paul fought like no one else to guarantee that the new covenant with non-Jews remained. In the face of great resistance he preached what he believed was the "good news": that God was bringing together all tribes and races into one fellowship. "You are no longer foreigners and strangers, but fellow citizens with God's people and also members of his household" (Eph. 2:19).

To the African church father Saint Anthony (251–356), known as the father of all monks, Christianity's essence is found in the radical, sacrificial teachings of Jesus. Anthony withdrew to the desert to focus on prayer, to conquer lust and gluttony, and to separate from the materialistic attractions of this world. Anthony gets the credit for putting the entire monastic movement into motion. And in many ways Anthony was right: Christ calls us to withdraw. We must forsake our families, our comforts, and even our very lives in order to participate in the kingdom of God. The kingdom of God is within us, and the path to God is through focused contemplation.

In a similar vein, Saint Francis of Assisi (1181–1226) understood Christianity to be a renunciation of wealth and a willingness to condescend to the most vulnerable and despised people among us. God called true disciples to poverty, and to preaching to those on the margins. He gave up shoes and good clothes, adopted a beggar's outfit, and began working with lepers, a group so scorned throughout history that their mere presence was repulsive and illegal in the towns.

Saint Catherine of Siena (1347–1380) died a young woman, but during her short life she believed Christ called her to a life of political engagement. It was very rare for a woman to have such profound influence upon governance and politics in her day. In her twenties she carried on an extensive correspondence with Pope Gregory XI. At a time when the papacy had moved to Avignon, France, she was determined to put pressure on the church to get the papacy back to Rome, where she thought it belonged. She also believed she had been called to become mystically married to Jesus, and to fast in extreme ways, existing only on the bread and wine of the Eucharist for large periods of time. It is believed she may have fasted herself to death.

One of the more shocking interpretations of Christianity occurred in China during the 1840s, 1850s, and 1860s when Hong Xiuquan, son of a Han farming family in the south, came across a Chinese translation of the Bible. His reading of the text convinced him that he was the younger brother of Jesus Christ and would take the leading role in driving out the ruling Manchu people from the land. It was his aim to purify Chinese society using a highly literal—and extremely apocalyptic—interpretation of Christianity. He condemned other religions, forbade sex, declared males and females to be equal (as it was a very patriarchal society), and required government examinations to be centered on the Bible rather than on Confucius. Xiuquan issued the death penalty for those who gambled, consumed alcohol or tobacco, or committed certain sexual acts such as prostitution and polygamy. He swiftly acquired followers and conquered major portions of China. He declared himself the "heavenly king" of the Taiping Heavenly Kingdom with its capital at Nanjing. At his movement's apex he had thirty million people under his rule. It led to a catastrophic civil war. Estimates are that twenty million people died either in combat or in the famines that ravaged in the rebellion's aftermath.[2]

Another Chinese interpretation of Christianity is that of Liu Zhenying, known more popularly as Brother Yun. Born in 1958, Brother Yun is one of the best known leaders of the Chinese house church movement. Very few of the Chinese house church preachers are known in the Western world. But due to Yun's writings, especially his autobiography, as well as his dynamic preaching, he has become the face of underground Chinese Christianity for Westerners. He is also one of the prominent leaders of the Back to Jerusalem Movement—a highly ambitious campaign to evangelize that vast swath of land between the east coast of China and Jerusalem. Back to Jerusalem focuses on the old Silk Roads, since "the nations along the ancient Silk Road are the most unevangelized in the whole world."[3] With tremendous resolve, Brother Yun devotes his

2. See Jonathan Spence, *God's Chinese Son: The Taiping Heavenly Kingdom of Hong Xiuquan* (New York: W.W. Norton, 1996).

3. Brother Yun and Paul Hattaway, *The Heavenly Man* (Grand Rapids, MI: Monarch Books, 2002), 278.

indefatigable energy to preaching Christ among all Muslims, Buddhists, Hindus, and Jews in his path:

> Our aim is not merely to evangelize the city of Jerusalem, but the thousands of unreached people groups, towns and villages located between China and Jerusalem. The vision for Back to Jerusalem is now the primary goal of all the house church leaders in the Sinim Fellowship. This is not one project we have among many. This is the main thrust and focus of all our activities. We talk about it over breakfast, lunch and dinner. We pray unceasingly, asking God to raise up laborers and remove all obstacles. We dream about it in our sleep.[4]

Other Asians have joined with the movement, even giving their lives for the cause. In 2007, a group of twenty-three South Korean evangelists were held hostage in Afghanistan while attempting to bring Christ to the region. Two of the men were executed. It is believed that the Korean government negotiated a multimillion dollar ransom for their release. The events of the South Korean hostage crisis caused some to label the Back to Jerusalem Movement as reckless, putting people's lives at risk for the sake of evangelism.[5]

One of the most prominent interpretations of Christianity in recent memory comes from Gustavo Gutierrez, a Peruvian theologian who shook the foundations of Christian thought with his 1973 book *A Theology of Liberation*.[6] Urging a Marxist reading of the Gospels, Gutierrez's work is a broadside on the field of theology in his argument that we have neglected praxis in favor of theory. This leads to rampant and unchecked injustice, he argues. Christianity is supposed to be about "the transformation of this world and the action of man in history" rather than some collection of abstruse philosophy.[7] Jesus focused on the poor and dispossessed, and he

---

4. Ibid., 285.
5. See Jennifer Veale, "Korean Missionaries Under Fire," *Time Magazine*, July 27, 2007.
6. Gustavo Gutierrez, *A Theology of Liberation* (Maryknoll, NY: Orbis, 1973). It was published first in Spanish in 1971.

challenged his society's elites. Although an atheist, Karl Marx provided a way out of this problem that plagued the church for centuries. Marx handed us tools to see what really matters is bridging the chasm that separates humans by their income and possessions. What is needed is a theology that brings people together on account of their dignity as human beings, made in the image of God. Gutierrez's clarion call to the theologians of his era was that that they should operate by a "praxis of liberation."[8] Like Marx did, Gutierrez realizes that class struggle will be an inevitable consequence of defending the weak and poor. Oppressors must be exposed and combated as enemies of the good. Christ urged his followers to love their enemies, not to pretend they had no enemies. And in the context of Latin America, loving others will mean resistance, even subversion of the elites. "Universal love . . . becomes concrete and effective by becoming incarnate in the struggle for the liberation of the oppressed."[9]

A similar interpretation of Christianity comes out of India, known as "Dalit theology."[10] Dalits are the group of people—around 25 percent of India's population—known commonly as outcastes, pariahs, and untouchables. In India today, however, these people prefer the term *Dalit*, which basically means "crushed." It is etymologically connected to the word *dal*, which is dried lentils that have been ground into a powder and served as a soup in India. Thus, Dalits see themselves as having been "crushed" or "ground down into powder" by the dominant castes of India. There is today an assertive movement coming out of India's most rejected people, and

---

7. Ibid., 9.
8. Ibid., 14.
9. Ibid., 276.
10. See V. V. Thomas, *Dalit and Tribal Christians of India: Issues and Challenges* (Nilumbur Post, Kerala: Focus India Trust, 2014).

the Christian Dalits are borrowing from Christ's teachings in order to formulate their arguments.

In 2013 I interviewed a young Dalit theologian named Pearly Walter during a World Council of Churches gathering in Korea. Ms. Walter grew up with the social stigma of being considered a pariah, or, a Dalit. During her childhood, she observed no defiance by her family against the grave injustices of India's caste system. Her parents simply accepted their lot, saying "this is just the way it is." Through the years, her family assumed their own inferiority, and feared the protestations of Brahmins in everything, especially cooking and eating. Brahmins are typically vegetarian, and they often complained when they smelled Ms. Walter's family cooking meat. And because of the firm grip of the caste system, Ms. Walter's parents always complied with these protests. Dalits don't even have the freedom to eat like they want. The caste system allows upper caste people to freely and authoritatively critique the every move of lower caste people, keeping them in their place.

Further, Dalits are seen as inferior in the school systems, even to the point of sitting on the floor while dominant caste children get to sit in chairs. Dalits have very little money and even less hope that the cycle will break in a fiercely traditional society like India. Pearly told me that even Gandhi did not oppose the idea of untouchables, or, as he called them, "children of God" (harijans). Dalits see this as condescending. They are not children. They are people. They are human, and they deserve full human rights. And Christian Dalits—seen as outside the mainstream of India in so many ways—are some of the most oppressed of all since their "Western" religion makes them ineligible for many social benefits and welfare programs offered by the state.

Pearly Walter is one of those Dalits who are angry. There is anger at Gandhi for doing nothing about this when he had the opportunity to do so. There is anger at the government for looking the other way while oppression, even slavery, goes on right under their noses. For Christian Dalits, there is even anger at Christianity. Since Paul never condemned slavery, they are in a situation like American blacks were during slave times in the United States. Their culture, even their Christian culture, seems to tolerate these injustices. There is an implicit allowance for discrimination, oppression, even violence against the socially weak . . . even in the church! And Ms. Walter is not alone. This is a very common complaint in India: the church seems quite content to function by the same caste prejudices that go on in Hinduism.

Ms. Walter is currently pursuing a doctorate in biblical studies at the University of Hamburg. She is amazed at how humane a society Germany is. As I saw the sparkle in her eye when she spoke about Germany, I wondered to myself whether she would return to India. No doubt she will have to gear up for a fight if she chooses to return to the land of caste. As a Dalit woman, the odds are stacked against her. But her commitment to Christianity means she cannot simply remove herself from India. Her faith calls her to action, to fight the oppression.

At the other end of the spectrum, Christianity is often seen as a sign of God's favor. Joel Osteen, pastor of one of America's largest churches—Lakewood Church in Houston, Texas—urges millions of people all over the world that Christianity can propel you to heights unseen, both spiritually and materially. Osteen is a millionaire many times over due to his television contracts and bestselling books. He cites himself as a perfect example of the prosperity that awaits us all if we live obediently and trust God to increase us:

> God has already stored up businesses, contracts, buildings, increase, promotions, and ideas. They already have your name on them, and if you'll just keep being your best, blessing others, honoring God,

and dreaming big, then eventually they will find their way into your hands. . . . Increase is looking for you. Favor is looking for you. Promotion is looking for you. Contracts are looking for you. . . . It's an explosive blessing.[11]

Osteen cites himself as an example of God's generously bestowed favor on the committed disciple. The Houston Rockets arena—worth $400 million—is now his church building. He advises his audiences around the globe that the key to advance is to "increase your capacity to receive."[12] And by no means is Osteen alone. Some of the most influential pastors in America are saying the same thing: T. D. Jakes, Creflo Dollar, Benny Hinn, Joyce Meyer, and Paula White.

Many people denounce Joel Osteen and company as heretics, imposters, charlatans. However, this would be a highly subjective, emotive accusation. They are Christian pastors with a very common vision of the church: that it deserves to be large and influential. The church deserves our best, our first fruits. And in return God's blessings return to us. It is certainly not an unbiblical notion. Both the Old Testament and the New Testament teach people to give liberally to the institutions of their faith. In the Old Testament, Jews were to offer their best to God through sacrifice and, later, to the building of an extravagant temple. In the New Testament, Jesus promises something similar:

> Give, and it will be given to you. A good measure, pressed down, shaken together and running over, will be poured into your lap. For with the measure you use, it will measured to you. (Luke 6:38)

To whom should we give? For two thousand years Christians have interpreted this to mean we give to the properly sanctioned institutions of our faith. So what's the big deal?

---

11. Joel Osteen, *Break Out!* (New York: FaithWords, 2013), 43.
12. Ibid., 47.

Osteen's vision is not unlike the thousands of pastors all over the world who build Christian empires selling books and t-shirts, appear on television, obtain larger and ritzier properties for ministry, and shape cultural attitudes. This vision of the church is nothing new. It is much like the medieval Catholic, or the Constantinian one: wealth is a sign of God's favor. How did the Roman Catholic Church obtain the richest collection of art in the world? How does the Russian Orthodox Church support its ambitious building campaign—restoring the ostentation of older churches while erecting hundreds of new ones, including two hundred brand new churches in the city of Moscow alone?[13] Why are the churches of the world some of the most grandiose, ornamental, and powerful structures on the face of the earth? It is because throughout Christian civilizations there have been people, like Osteen, who believe it a worthwhile cause to build up the institutions of the church. Christianity is meant to be big, classy, grandiose, and important. It deserves our best. Some will criticize, asking why churches should be built at all when there are homeless people needing shelter. This back and forth is common, and it illustrates the competing visions of what Christianity is supposed to be.

After looking at these various perspectives we are still left with the question of the chapter: What is Christianity, anyway? As a church historian, part of my calling is to look at Christianity as an institution, and to understand the history of that institution. And without doubt the Christian church has ebbed and flowed throughout the centuries. However, overall, I would say the church has expanded gradually and globally in innovative, unpredictable ways. One thing is certain: Christianity is changing. Christian theology, long dominated by

---

13. Anna Vasilieva, "200 New Orthodox Churches in Moscow Causes Public Stir," in *Russian Beyond the Headlines*, March 26, 2013, located at http://rbth.com/society/2013/03/26/200_new_orthodox_churches_in_moscow_causes_public_stir_24285.html.

Europeans, is being augmented and even reinvented in the Global South. As leading African theologian John Mbiti put it, Africa now has its chance with Christianity, describing it as "an African opportunity to mess up Christianity in our own way. For the past two thousand years, other continents, countries, nations and generations have had their chances to do with Christianity as they wished. And we know that they have not been idle! Now Africa has got its chance at last."[14] Indeed the same could be said of China, the Pacific, Latin America, Korea, and the Philippines. According to Congolese prophet Simon Kimbangu, there is a passing of the baton from whites to blacks taking place.[15] And with that process, our understanding of "Christianity" must give way to "Christianities." The new narrators of Christianity may or may not speak English, and they probably will not give great concern to Euro-American issues. Christianity has become the world's largest religion, but in the process it has changed . . . probably forever. But such is the nature and dynamic of Christian faith. It is programmed for change. It is about as stagnant as the human spirit.

What Is Changing?

The most obvious change is that Christianity has become a global reality. And this affects how we think about it. Our mental maps of Christianity are being redrawn, demographics are being transformed, and immigration is making deep impacts on societies. Theologically, Christianity is in uncharted territory: the new ecumenism, the postmodern context, and the debunking of long-trusted paradigms. The globalization of Christian scholarship means that increasingly

---

14. John Mbiti, quoted in Noel Davies and Martin Conway, *World Christianity in the 20th Century* (London: SCM Press, 2008), 118.
15. Ogbu Kalu, ed., *African Christianity: An African Story* (Trenton, NJ: Africa World Press, 2007), 36.

scholars from outside the Western world will become the major voices for understanding Christianity in a context of profound interconnectedness.

Like Coca Cola, Harry Potter, Adidas, and iPhones, Christianity is found all over the globe now. Its importance in the world today can hardly be overstated, claiming well over a third of humanity. A good argument could be made that the Roman Catholic Church—which claims half of the world's Christians—is the largest and most global human institution of all time. What could possibly rival it? One out of every six or seven people on earth is Roman Catholic!

Christianity is a relatively new faith in many places. In sub-Saharan Africa, for example, Christianity was a small religion in 1900, scattered here and there across the continent. Today it is the largest faith in Africa, with half a billion members.[16] Similarly, in South Korea, Christianity's rise has been nearly as spectacular. While good statistics for China are lacking, it is clear that Christianity is growing there. Some estimate that China's Christian population may be as high as 10 percent. In a nation of over a billion souls, that's 100 million people.

Not only is Christianity crossing borders and expanding into new frontiers, it is changing from within as well, causing fundamental questions to be asked, such as the title of this chapter, What is Christianity? An institution? A relationship with Jesus? A good moral code for society? An intellectual system? A philosophy? What is it . . . and what is the point of it? One author put it this way: "The point of being a Christian is to save one's own soul and to get to heaven."[17] Is that it? If so, then how do we get there?

---

16. My statistics come from two main sources: Brill's World Christian Database (www.worldchristiandatabase.org/wcd/), and Pew Forum, notably its "Global Religious Landscape" study (http://www.pewforum.org/2012/12/18/global-religious-landscape-exec/).
17. Mary Eberstadt, *How the West Really Lost God* (West Conshohocken, PA: Templeton Press, 2013), 194.

What did Jesus, the namesake of this faith, have to say about Christianity? Obviously we do not know because "Christianity" took shape after his death. However, if we look at his teachings, we gain insight into what he wanted from people. For instance, in Matthew 25 Jesus seems to be talking about judgment day and how a person can attain eternal life. He provides a pretty straightforward list: feed the hungry, give drink to the thirsty, house the immigrant, clothe the destitute, tend to the sick, and visit those in prison. Those who fulfill these basic acts of dignity to others will be declared "righteous."

So what about all the theology and doctrines and creeds? Do they matter? It depends on who you talk to. Some scholars like American Baptist pastor Walter Rauschenbusch (1861–1918) wanted to focus on the teachings *of* Jesus rather than the doctrinal assertions *about* Jesus. As one of the key leaders of the Social Gospel movement, he did not think of Christ's life and death as effecting individual salvation, but rather as an ideal for social reform. Christ was not so much trying to get everyone into heaven as he was trying to bring the ideals of heaven to earth. Jesus was a social critic. His goal was to reach out to the marginalized. And Rauschenbusch put great energy in trying to do the same in his own society. These ideas caused a reaction, known to church historians as "fundamentalism."

The Fundamentals were a series of pamphlets produced by Lyman and Milton Stewart, two wealthy Christian brothers who made their fortunes in the oil business. They teamed up with a Baptist pastor named Rev. A. C. Dixon and engineered a project that would lay out what a Christian should be expected to believe. They recruited dozens of Protestant scholars and over the course of six years (1910–1915) published the now-famous twelve-volume collection of articles called *The Fundamentals: A Testimony to Truth*. Rauschenbusch and other liberals were denounced, and longstanding Christian doctrines such as the virgin birth, inerrancy of scripture, substitutionary atonement, and a physical resurrection were affirmed.

Much of this is old news, but what is new is that this longstanding debate within Christianity over what constitutes real and true religion has become a global conversation. Indeed, the central question of this book—*To Whom Does Christianity Belong?*—has gone global. It is a question not just for Euro-American elites anymore. It is a question for Nigerian Christians being slayed and kidnapped by Boko Haram. It is a question for Rwandan, Sudanese, and Congolese Christians in the aftermath of genocide. It is a question for Christian child soldiers in Liberia and the Central African Republic. To whom does Christianity belong? Who gets to set Christianity's agenda in the twenty-first century?

Like Rauschenbusch did, a new generation of Christian intellectuals is struggling to answer the questions, and it is offering radically different answers. Emerging church leaders in America like Brian McLaren are arguing against putting new wine into old wineskins. In his books *Everything Must Change* and *A New Kind of Christianity* he throws down the gauntlet:

> We are like lawyers trying to save an old contract, adding more and more fine print on page after page, until the provisos are weightier than the original contract. . . . At some point, though, more and more of us will finally decide that it would make more sense to go back and revise the contract from scratch. And that process has begun. It is nowhere complete, but the cat is out of the bag.[18]

African Christians urge us to take seriously the miracles of the Bible as phenomena that happen still today: healing, exorcism, deliverance from demons, the efficacy of prayer, even resurrection. Chinese and Eastern European Christians are emerging from the depths of

---

18. Brian McLaren, *A New Kind of Christianity: Ten Questions That Are Transforming the Faith* (New York: HarperOne, 2010), 142.

atheistic communism and in many cases rediscovering Christianity for the first time. Brazilian Pentecostals are experiencing the unleashing of the Holy Spirit in ways unthinkable just a few decades before; indeed Brazil—once firmly Catholic—now has the largest national Pentecostal population in the world. Christians in the Middle East are showing us what Christianity looks like when under extreme duress, perhaps even an irreversible decline. Thousands of Christians die for Christ each year, something Westerners cannot relate to. Indeed in parts of the Middle East the church has been utterly crushed.

New issues. New problems. New questions. While Americans debate homosexuality, Africans debate polygamy. While Europeans rediscover paganism, Christians in the Global South leave it behind. While Westerners shy away from the miraculous *within* the context of faith, Southern Christians proclaim from the rooftops that Christianity *without* miracles is incomprehensible.

Conclusion

So what *is* Christianity, anyway? The short answer, as one famous personality stated, "It depends upon what the meaning of the word *is* is."

The long answer: it's complicated. It depends on the beliefs of the person defining it.

PART II

Theological Loci

3

The New Church

Ephesians 2:19–22

You are no longer foreigners and strangers, but fellow citizens with God's people and also members of his household, built on the foundation of the apostles and prophets, with Christ Jesus himself as the chief cornerstone. In him the whole building is joined together and rises to become a holy temple in the Lord. And in him you too are being built together to become a dwelling in which God lives by his Spirit.

What is church? Is it simply "where two or three gather" in the name of Christ?[1] Is it an organized denomination, complete with officers, budgets, and creeds? Is it something that must be recognized by a government in order to be legitimate?

In the broad sweep of world Christianity, we can see that Christians come to very different conclusions about what church is. In this chapter we look at a few different ways that Christians globally interpret the meaning of church. In the American context, our understanding has always been profoundly impacted by our

---

1. Matt. 18:20.

nation's most prolific pastors. And in this chapter we look at two of the giants who have shaped, and continue to shape, our thinking: Billy Graham and Rick Warren. The chapter also presents a more global and inclusive understanding of church, as we highlight the work of the World Council of Churches—perhaps the most international and ecumenical forum for understanding global Christianity today. Finally, we take a case study of a relatively new church: the Kimbanguists of Africa. The Kimbanguist Church is an African movement that demonstrates how Christianity changes, indigenizes, and adapts itself into new contexts. It presents a pattern that continues globally today, paving the way for the new churches emerging worldwide. However, there are times when new churches challenge well-established norms of Christian orthodoxy. The case of the Kimbanguist Church aptly illustrates this tension.

Rick Warren—Successor to Billy Graham

Rick Warren's influence on American Christianity is incalculable. His vision has become the new archetype for how Americans do church in the twenty-first century. While he did not create the model by himself, he certainly blazed a trail, and thousands of pastors worldwide look to him as a guide and an inspiration. Already Christians in North America and beyond look to him with deep respect. Here is a unique personality, perhaps the only American pastor capable of receiving the baton from Billy Graham as the next leader of the powerful, collective voice of America's Christian millions.

Similarly, Billy Graham shaped twentieth-century Christianity in powerful and lasting ways.[2] He embraced the civil rights movement and joined forces with Martin Luther King Jr. He preached to

2. An excellent introduction to Billy Graham is David Aikman, *Billy Graham: His Life and Influence* (Nashville: Thomas Nelson, 2007).

audiences of thousands, drawing in crowds on a scale that only the most famous rock stars were capable. He was embraced by several US presidents, serving as advisor to them regardless of their political affiliation. He tapped the power of media in fresh, innovative ways through print, radio, television, film, and a significant Internet presence. Billy Graham understood the globalization of Christianity like few others before him, and he preached to live audiences in nearly every country of the world. With grace, class, and a unique appeal to reach the unchurched, he became a cultural icon, gracing the covers of important news magazines during his storied career. He even received a star on the Hollywood Walk of Fame, a rare feat for a preacher. People raised eyebrows when Graham allowed his name to be embossed on a street not known for religious conviction, yet he humbly replied, "We're all sinners. Everybody you meet all over the world is a sinner. . . . I couldn't condemn Hollywood Boulevard any more than any other place."[3]

Rick Warren's rise was less conspicuous. While Graham first came to national prominence during his landmark 1949 tent revival crusade in Los Angeles, attended by 350,000, Warren caused a mild sensation in evangelical circles with his 1995 book *The Purpose Driven Church*. It was read by America's pastors. However, it merely set the stage for his wildly successful follow-up book in 2002 that was directed not just to pastors, but to all: *The Purpose Driven Life*. No one seems to know how many copies have been sold, but estimates range from 30 to 60 million. Zondervan, the publisher, claims it has been translated into more than eighty-five different languages, making it "the bestselling hardback non-fiction book in history."[4]

3. Sheryl Stolberg, "Billy Graham Now a Hollywood Star," *Los Angeles Times*, Oct. 16, 1989, http://articles.latimes.com/1989-10-16/local/me-93_1_evangelist-billy-graham.
4. See Zondervan's website: http://www.zondervan.com/the-purpose-driven-life-2.html.

Both Billy Graham and Rick Warren are Baptist preachers. And both of them have an uncanny ability to reach out to people of all persuasions: left and right, Catholic and Protestant, prosperous and poor. Like Graham, Warren has been iconoclastic. Just when evangelicalism was being stereotyped as antiscience, insular, right wing, unconcerned with the poor, and overly concerned with the United States of America, Warren broke several molds. He backed the Evangelical Climate Initiative in 2006, brokered an unprecedented and exemplary partnership with the government of (mainly Catholic) Rwanda, and spoke of Barack Obama in very positive ways.[5] That's not quite what America might expect from the pastor of Saddleback Church, one of America's largest Southern Baptist Convention member churches, known for their conservative stances.

Warren is at the vanguard of a new church. It is global. It emphasizes social justice. It is ambitiously evangelistic, planting churches and offering humanitarian services all over the globe. And, importantly, the new church is very ecumenical. It shies away from endless doctrinal disputes, embracing all Christians on the ground that serving the poor—in the name of Jesus—is the priority at this moment in history. Warren seems to take seriously the words of Paul at the beginning of this chapter. He envisions the household of God as being very big. And he wants to build it bigger. In Pauline fashion, he wants to broaden the existing definition of what that word *church*

5. Signatories of the Evangelical Climate Initiative can be found here: http://www.aeseonline.org/aeseonline.org/Evangelical_Climate_Initiative.html. For the "friend" quotation as well as Warren's views on politics, see Naomi Schaefer Riley, "What Saddleback's Pastor Really Thinks about Politics," *The Wall Street Journal*, Aug. 23, 2008, http://online.wsj.com/article/SB121944811327665223.html. Warren's work in Rwanda is well known. See for example Nicola Menzie, "Saddleback Pastor Rick Warren Visits Rwanda to Advance PEACE Plan," Aug. 29, 2013, http://www.christianpost.com/news/saddleback-pastor-rick-warren-visits-rwanda-to-advance-peace-plan-103290/; and David Van Biema, "Warren of Rwanda," *TIME Magazine*, 15 August 2005, http://content.time.com /time /magazine /article /0,9171,1093746,00.html.

seems to encompass. For Warren and the new church, the ecclesia is a concept that we have unjustifiably limited to our own experience. Those borders, however, must be lifted. The question everyone is asking, however, is where those borders end. Is Christianity, perhaps, a religion without borders?

Ecclesia

Earlier we looked at how the first-century church had to deal with the issue of identity. Does Christianity belong to Judaism? Did Paul's unpredictable and sweeping success as a missionary to the gentiles change the essential nature of the church by switching it over to them? It is fascinating that many of those complex discussions of Christian identity are still happening today, yet for very different reasons.

Ephesians 2:19–22 is a description of the church that reads as fresh today as it did twenty centuries ago. It is a snapshot of Paul's thinking just as Christianity was transforming from a Jewish-majority religion to a gentile-majority one. Notice the metaphors he employs:

- These gentiles are no longer foreigners, on the margins. They are now "fellow citizens." Christianity now belongs to them, too.

- The church is God's house. The concrete floor is the collective voice of the prophets and the apostles. Jesus Christ is the cornerstone, the most important part of a foundation because all other stones will be set according to its positioning.

- The church—consisting of both Jews and gentiles—is a holy temple, a sacred space. gentiles are no longer profane. They are now holy, just like Jews. They can come in—not as pollutants, but as full-fledged "members."

- The church is constantly "being built together." It is not finished.

It is a dwelling place for God's Holy Spirit, even while under construction.

Paul's letter to the Ephesians proved too difficult for some Jews to accept. Others, however, found its brazen claims refreshing. If we could listen in, we would likely hear Jews asking major, fundamental questions about Paul's proposed changes: "Did God really open the door to gthentiles—the ones we have been taught to avoid? Have they been promoted or have we Jews been demoted? What's going on here? Who is this man who claims to speak for God?" Paul was doing something new. He was totally redefining what it meant to be a child of God. His teachings caused great offense for some, and provided spiritual liberation for others.

The New Testament uses many images to describe the church: architecture, family, body images (one body, many parts), a flock of sheep, a military unit, a married couple (Jesus is groom, people the bride), a school of students with Jesus as teacher, a kingdom. We could go on.

However, at the root of all of these metaphors is a Greek word that has been studied intensely for centuries: *ecclesia*—the word translated "church." Ecclesia has become a Christian word, but it was common in the Greek language before the New Testament era. In its most basic sense, it refers to a public assembly that has been called out by a herald, from the words *ek* (out) and *kalein* (to call). The word was used by the Greek translators of the Hebrew Bible to refer to Israel's gathering before the Lord (see Acts 7:38). New Testament scholar Geoffrey Bromiley noted the following insight about the concept of ecclesia: "It is of interest that behind the New Testament term stand both Greek democracy and Hebrew theocracy, the two being brought together in a theocratic democracy or democratic theocracy."[6] He goes on to point out that Jesus had little to say, explicitly, about ecclesia. He only mentioned it in two places: 1) Matt. 16:18, when Jesus says to Peter: "On this rock I will build my church"; and 2) Matt. 18:17, when Jesus discusses how to confront sin in the community: "Tell it to the church." This meager use of the term has caused some scholars to wonder whether Jesus even intended to establish a following.

However, if we interpret Jesus to mean "the church" when he speaks of "the kingdom," then we have tremendous evidence to indicate he indeed meant to establish a movement. In the New Testament, "the kingdom" is a chief concern for Jesus. Is the kingdom the same thing as the church? Bromiley says we do not know for sure. Whatever Jesus meant, it is quite clear that the apostles used the word liberally when referencing the various communities that gathered in Christ's memory. Acts and the epistles refer to the ecclesia often, and there seems to be a shared understanding among the New Testament communities what the word signified for them.

While imagery for understanding ecclesia is rich, Bromiley presents four traditional characteristics of the church that are assumed in the epistles: 1.) it is holy, 2.) universal, 3.) apostolic, and 4.) it is one.

1. The epistle that best emphasizes the church's holiness is 1 Peter, where Christ followers are referred to as "a holy nation" (2:9). Christians have been called out (2:9) and must be holy because God is holy (1:16).

2. The universality of the church—often called its catholicity—is emphasized in repeated claims throughout that "there are no external qualifications of age, sex, generation, descent, or status.

---

6. G. W. Bromiley, "Church," in *The International Standard Bible Encyclopedia*, rev. ed. (Grand Rapids, MI: Eerdmans, 1979), 693.

In Him [Christ] these distinctions have no reality" (Col. 3:11 and Gal. 3:28).[7]

3. The church's apostolicity means it was founded on the testimony of the apostles (Acts 1:8 and Eph. 2:20) and has been preserved faithfully for two millennia.

4. Finally, the church is one. Jesus prayed that all those who believe in him might ". . . be one, Father, just as you are in me and I am in you. May they also be in us so that the world may believe that you have sent me" (John 17:21). Likewise Paul urged Christians to "Make every effort to keep the unity" since there is only "one Lord, one faith, one baptism" (Eph. 4:3, 5).

This last point merits elaboration.

An Ecumenical Age—The World Council of Churches

The word *ecumenical*, from the Greek word *oikoumene* (to inhabit), refers to a range of movements trying to unite a divided Christianity. It has been defined variously, but when used today it refers to *a quality or attitude*. An ecumenical person longs to see the church unite. Christ prayed intensely for unity, so how can Christians allow the deep fractures in Christianity to continue? It seems patently immoral to perpetuate division within the body of Christ when the teachings of Jesus and the apostles so clearly advocate unity.

The Christian church today is prospering, globalizing, and transforming much like it did in New Testament times. It is also uniting like never before. It is entering an ecumenical age.

The modern ecumenical movement became prominent in the twentieth century, but its historical roots run deep, as far back as the sixteenth century. As the Protestant Reformation created new

7. See ibid., 694.

denominations seemingly every year, it became clear to many that a divided church ran against Jesus's famous prayer for unity in John 17. The ecumenical voice was rather inconsequential until the nineteenth century, when missionaries in the field—from diverse denominational backgrounds—began to see they had much in common with each other. In the Western world, churches quarreled over whether Jesus was *really* present in the Eucharist or *symbolically* present. Should baptism be administered through immersion, sprinkling, or pouring? Should the church baptize babies or adults? Are people saved by good works or by God's grace? Which Christian creed or confession is correct? How closely connected should the church be to the government?

These issues were raw, painful, and provocative in Europe and North America. In the mission field, however, it was often very different. A Methodist missionary in China might begin to see that there is little difference between himself and the Presbyterian working a few miles away. They began to have fellowship. They began to help each other. They began to cooperate in order to witness more effectively for Christ. Their families interacted. And the denominational walls they had built up in their minds began to crumble. Esteemed historian of missions Kenneth Scott Latourette stated it thusly:

> The compelling motive in all the co-operation . . . has been evangelism. The missionary enterprise arises from the divine commission to bear witness to the Gospel throughout the world and to win all men to discipleship to Christ. From this came the ecumenical movement, and the growth of that movement was due primarily to it. Unity was sought not as an end in itself but as a means to evangelism. . . . Christians found that in them the apparently impossible was being realized; underneath the barriers which had long divided them they were finding an inclusive unity in Christ.[8]

8. See p. 402 in Kenneth Scott Latourette, "Ecumenical Bearings of the Missionary Movement

Indeed it was the missionary movement that first began to heal a divided Christendom.

Eventually, many missionaries began to view the entire system of Christian denominationalism as destructive. In the mission field, the evils of competition were obvious. Missionary gatherings became increasingly interdenominational. They needed one another, and they were willing to face criticism from their sponsoring churches in the Western world in order to preserve the unity they were experiencing in Asia and Africa. Missionaries developed a reputation for being theologically suspect, too eager to jettison time-tested doctrine for the sake of unity.

In 1910 an important missionary conference took place in Edinburgh, Scotland, that sparked a new epoch in world Christianity.[9] At that conference—known as "Edinburgh 1910"—ecumenism became a reality that no longer could be ignored. The movement gained traction during the interwar years and at the end of the Second World War, an international organization was established called the World Council of Churches (WCC), based in Geneva, Switzerland.

The WCC is the most important institutional expression of the ecumenical movement. It was officially launched at a conference in Amsterdam in 1948. Initially, it was a merger of two important organizations: "Life and Work" and "Faith and Order." The first was focused on service to humankind; the second was concerned with doctrine. In 1961, a third institution joined: the International Missionary Council, further strengthening the institutional importance of the WCC. The fourth and final major institution to join the WCC was the World Council of Christian Education, in

and the International Missionary Council," ch. 8 in *A History of the Ecumenical Movement 1517–1948*, ed. Ruth Rouse and Stephen Neill (Philadelphia: The Westminster Press, 1967).

9. The best resource for understanding "Edinburgh 1910" is Brian Stanley, *The World Missionary Conference, Edinburgh 1910* (Grand Rapids, MI: Eerdmans, 2009).

1971; its roots were in the Sunday school movement. After beginning in England in the 1780s, Sunday schools have become an indispensable feature of global Christianity.

Today, the WCC includes around 350 denominations comprising nearly 600 million Christians from the Orthodox and Protestant church families. The Roman Catholic Church—which represents about half the world's Christians—participates enthusiastically in the WCC, but does not allow its members to vote for the various resolutions brought up at general assemblies. Like the rest of Christianity, the WCC's center of gravity is now in the Global South, although the current general secretary is Olav Fykse Tveit, a pastor from Norway. A new crop of WCC presidents were elected in 2013 at the Tenth Assembly in Korea, coming from South Africa, South Korea, Sweden, Colombia, Canada, Tonga, Syria, and Armenia.

When the WCC gathers for its general assembly every eight years or so, it is probably the most diverse gathering of Christians on earth. The general assemblies are important events, setting a tone for much of the Christian world by passing resolutions and bringing critical issues to the forefront of the global church. These meetings bring together some of the brightest minds and most active leaders in the churches today, with the goal of addressing issues faced by the global church. Here is a list of where and when each of the general assemblies took place, with a brief word about their major concerns:

1. Amsterdam, Netherlands, 1948: founding of the WCC.
2. Evanston, United States, 1954: racism and colonialism were strongly critiqued.
3. New Delhi, India, 1961: Soviet Union's Orthodox churches begin to join the WCC, signaling a Christian fellowship that transcended the Cold War.
4. Uppsala, Sweden, 1968: Martin Luther King Jr. was to be the

opening speaker but was assassinated shortly beforehand. Racism and the Vietnam War dominated discussions. Roman Catholics, emerging from the Second Vatican Council, were present and were warmly welcomed.

5. Nairobi, Kenya, 1975: women's issues came to the fore; nuclear arms were condemned; half of all delegates were from the Global South, signaling the changing face of the world church.

6. Vancouver, Canada, 1983: known as the "worshiping assembly" because of its vibrant and joyful aura; celebration of the famous Lima Document: *Baptism, Eucharist, and Ministry*, which broke new ecumenical ground.

7. Canberra, Australia, 1991: end of the Cold War was celebrated; the Gulf War was condemned; finances of the WCC were diminishing.

8. Harare, Zimbabwe, 1998: AIDS in Africa; homosexuality; globalization concerns; President Robert Mugabe's participation was contested.

9. Porto Alegre, Brazil, 2006: held at a Catholic university; disappointment expressed by the youth that they are not given a proportionate voice; struggling WCC finances; consensus decision-making style was adopted; WCC critiqued for being overcommitted, it needs a sharper focus.

10. Busan, South Korea, 2013: it was becoming clearer than ever that Christianity's heartland is in the Global South. Social justice and ecological concerns took center stage. A conservative-progressive divide was evident at the assembly. Orthodox Christians caused controversy by their call for traditional values while Korean Evangelicals (non-WCC members) protested outside the venue.

These ten assemblies have impacted the ethos and the direction of the world church greatly. However, they speak less for the Catholic, Orthodox, Evangelical, and Pentecostal forms of Christianity than they do for the historic Protestant denominations. Nevertheless, they are an apt reflection of what matters to Christians at a definite moment in time.

For decades, the Roman Catholic Church (RCC) took no official part in the activities of the WCC. The 1928 encyclical *Mortalium Animos* declared the only way the unity of Christians could be achieved would be "by promoting the return to the one true Church of Christ of those who are separated from it."[10] Schismatics (i.e., Protestants) were outside the church in most cases unless the titles of *separated brethren* or *baptized by desire* applied to them, which is difficult to ascertain.

There were a few Catholics through the years who promoted ecumenism, but formally, the church resisted. Pius XII (1939–1958) had no interest in the ecumenical movement. He denied Catholic participation in it and promulgated certain teachings—such as the assumption of Mary, in 1950—which damaged Protestant-Catholic relations even more. Catholics were prohibited by Pope Pius XII to attend the Amsterdam assembly in 1948. This would all change, however, when Angelo Roncalli, John XXIII, came to power in 1958. Pope John XXIII was elected mainly to be a caretaker pope. He was elderly and wise; he would be a stable force during turbulent times. Early in 1959, however, he surprised everybody by calling a Second Vatican Council. It would prove to be monumental. His colleagues were astonished; some were aghast. An outspoken Italian cardinal labeled the new pope "rash and impulsive," asking, "How dare he summon a council . . . only three months after his election?"[11]

10. *Mortalium Animos*, article 10, 6 January 1928, located at http://www.vatican.va/holy_father/pius_xi/encyclicals/documents/hf_p-xi_enc_19280106_mortalium-animos_en.html.

In 1960, John XXIII established the Secretariat for Promoting Christian Unity. He named five official observers to attend the third WCC Assembly in New Delhi, in 1961. He also invited Protestant and Orthodox observers to Vatican II. He died in 1963 with the ecumenical ball rolling.

Paul VI (1963–1978) succeeded "good Pope John." He too was an ecumenical man. In 1964, Paul VI met with the Orthodox patriarch Athenagoras I of Constantinople. That meeting led to official declarations of regret from both sides for damages done through the years. The infamous mutual excommunication of 1054—which split Catholics and Orthodox Christians—was removed. Pope Paul VI established a Joint Working Group to facilitate Catholic-WCC dialogue and promulgated one of the most important Roman Catholic decrees in recent history: *On Ecumenism*.[12] Rome was firmly positioned inside the modern ecumenical movement.

While John Paul II and Benedict XVI were not nearly as ecumenical as their immediate predecessors, Pope Francis took ecumenism to another level. He reached out to homosexuals with the well-reported words, "Who am I to judge?" and extended an olive branch to atheists in his now-famous sermon in May 2013:

> The Lord has redeemed all of us, all of us, with the Blood of Christ: all of us, not just Catholics. Everyone! "Father, the atheists?" Even the atheists. Everyone! . . . We are created children in the likeness of God and the Blood of Christ has redeemed us all! If we, each doing our own part, if we do good to others, if we meet there, doing good, and we go slowly, gently, little by little, we will make that culture of encounter: we need that so much. We must meet one another doing good. "But I don't believe, Father. I am an atheist!" But do good. We will meet one another there.[13]

---

11. Thomas Cahill, *Pope John XXIII* (New York: Viking, 2002), 179.
12. Officially, the decree "On Ecumenism" is called *Unitatis Redintegratio* (Restoration of Unity). See http://www.vatican.va/archive /hist_councils /ii_vatican_council/documents /vat-ii_decree_19641121_unitatis-redintegratio_en.html.

Taken at face value, Pope Francis's ecumenicity is very generous indeed. Catholic commentators have been quick to point out that his statements are entirely in keeping with Catholic tradition. They claim the media, however, sensationalized his message.[14]

A New Church: Case Study of the Kimbanguists

While Catholics and Protestants discuss unity, a new phenomenon has emerged in the Global South: independent churches that have little connection to the West. According to sociological paradigms such as Max Weber's, these churches look more like sects. Weber argued that *churches* are more formalized. They are older, having established hierarchies and settled theological stances. *Sects*, however, are religious movements that have broken away from the main, and are inventing and reinventing themselves on the fly. They are able to innovate more because of this relative lack of stability. They are more prophetic and charismatic, leaving room for new interpretations, new signs and wonders. Often it is the case that individuals splinter off from churches and establish sects. Sects—if they survive for long—will typically settle, thus creating new churches and established denominational structures. Something of a cycle occurs. Denominations breed new sects and sectarian movements tend to

13. For the transcript of the "Even atheists" sermon, see http://en.radiovaticana.va/news/2013/05/22/pope_at_mass:_culture_of_encounter_is_the_foundation_of_peace/en1-694445.   Francis's comments were actually in keeping with his first encyclical—*Lumen Fidei*—which he coauthored with his predecessor Benedict XVI. For the text of that document, see http://www.vatican.va/holy_father/francesco/encyclicals/documents/papa-francesco_20130629_enciclica-lumen-fidei_en.html. For the "Who am I to judge?" comment, see Rachel Donadio, "On Gay Priests, Pope Francis Asks, 'Who Am I to Judge?,'" *New York Times*, July 29, 2013, located at http://www.nytimes.com/2013/07/30/world/europe/pope-francis-gay-priests.html?pagewanted=all&_r=0.

14. See David Gibson, "Pope Francis' Outreach to Atheists Not as Controversial as It Seems," *National Catholic Reporter*, September 13, 2013, located at http://ncronline.org/blogs/francis-chronicles/pope-francis-outreach-atheists-not-controversial-it-seems.

slowly morph into institutions. These patterns are alive and well in areas where Christianity is relatively new.[15]

The Kimbanguist Church, officially known as the Church of Jesus Christ on Earth through His Special Envoy Simon Kimbangu, is one of the most prominent African Initiated Churches—churches rooted in indigenous African culture. It was founded by Simon Kimbangu (1887–1951) in what is today the Democratic Republic of the Congo. Its membership is estimated to be over five million.[16]

As a young man Kimbangu came under the influence of Baptist missionaries; he and his wife Marie Muilu were baptized in 1915. The turning point in his life was in March 1921, when he began to perform miracles and establish a ministry of his own in Nkamba, the village of his birth, which he named the New Jerusalem. His reputation as a powerful healer and miracle worker spread quickly and he became known as a *Ngunza*, translated into English as "prophet" or even "messiah."[17] In his teaching he promoted a purified form of Christianity: no dancing, no polygamy, no drinking alcohol, and no dishonest gain. He invoked the ancestors and urged Africans to see themselves as full partakers in the kingdom of God rather than second-class citizens to whites. He was not overtly anticolonial in his preaching, however.

15. On the church-sect typology see Max Weber, *The Protestant Ethic and the Spirit of Capitalism* (New York: Charles Scribner's Sons, 1958; originally published in German in 1904), Ernst Troeltsch, *The Social Teachings of the Christian Churches*, vol. 1 (London: George Allen and Unwin, 1931), Rodney Stark and William Bainbridge, *Religion, Deviance, and Social Control* (New York: Routledge, 1997), and Lorne Dawson, *Comprehending Cults: The Sociology of New Religious Movements* (Oxford: Oxford University Press, 1998). George Chryssides is one leading thinker in the study of New Religious Movements who has called into question the use of terms and definitions in the classification of religion. See Chryssides, "New Religious Movements—Some Problems of Definition," published online at http://basr.ac.uk/diskus_old/diskus1-6/CHRYSSI2_2.TXT.

16. Heinrich Balz, "Kimbanguism Going Astray," *Exchange* 38 (2009): 355. For good introductions to Kimbanguism within its African context, see Lamin Sanneh, *West African Christianity: The Religious Impact* (Maryknoll, NY: Orbis, 1983), and Elizabeth Isichei, *A History of Christianity in Africa* (Grand Rapids, MI: Eerdmans, 1995).

17. Sanneh, *West African Christianity*, 206.

Belgian authorities were threatened by the rapid expansion of the sect, and in September 1921 they condemned Kimbangu to death, although the sentence was commuted to life imprisonment due to the intervention of Baptist missionaries. He and some of his followers received 120 strokes of the whip. Kimbangu's conduct during the trial was that of a persecuted martyr. During his thirty-year imprisonment he became a potent symbol for European injustice, stirring the fires of African independence. It is remarkable that his ministry lasted only six months and was entirely peaceful, yet proved so provocative and threatening to Belgium. The colonial government granted legal recognition to the church in 1959, shortly before Congolese independence in 1960.

Kimbangu's reputation grew and his followers multiplied exponentially in spite of harsh persecution. His wife emerged as the main leader, although numerous other prophetic personalities claimed to be successors, fragmenting the movement. In 1957 Kimbangu's youngest son, Joseph Diangienda Kuntima (1918–1992), took the reins of leadership with the support of his two older brothers. Upon Diangienda's death in 1992, the second eldest of the brothers—Salomon Dialungana Kiangani—became the spiritual leader; he died in 2001. After Salomon, the mantle of leadership was passed to his own son Simon Kimbangu Kiangani.[18]

Kimbanguism evolved significantly from what it had been in the early years, especially in the remarkable identification of Kimbangu as the promised Holy Spirit, according to John 14:15–17. One Kimbanguist Church confession describes Kimbangu as "not God . . . but the envoy of Christ," and claims their prophet "died, rose again, and is with us in spirit."[19] There is also a complex belief among some

---

18. See Leon Nguapitshi Kayongo, "Kimbanguism: Its Present Christian Doctrine and the Problems Raised by It," *Exchange* 34, no. 3 (2005): 135–36. For the theological controversy, I consulted Kayongo's article as well as Balz's "Kimbanguism Going Astray."

that Simon of Cyrene—the African who carried Jesus's cross—was the same spirit as Simon Kimbangu, signaling that "God was changing the baton from whites to blacks."[20]

In 1969 the church was accepted for membership into the World Council of Churches, the first African Independent Church to gain admission. Its relationship with the WCC has been stormy due to the Kimbanguist belief that their prophet and his successors are divine. Several churches have canceled their ecumenical cooperation with the Kimbanguists as their doctrine continues to evolve well beyond the preaching of Simon Kimbangu.[21]

In recent years, controversy has surrounded Kimbanguist thinking on the Trinity. The turning point was in 1987, at the centenary celebration of Kimbangu's birth, when leader Joseph Diangienda Kuntima proclaimed that Simon Kimbangu was, and is, God the Holy Spirit. Kimbanguists now associate Kimbangu and his three sons with the incarnate ("earthly") Holy Trinity using John 14 and the traditional rendering of 1 John 5:7–8: "There are three that testify in heaven . . . And there are three that testify on earth." Additionally, some Kimbanguist theologians interpret Matt. 1:18–20 (Mary impregnated through the Holy Spirit) as conveying the idea that Kimbangu—the Holy Spirit—is a cofather to Jesus Christ.

Drawing from 1 Corinthians 15, the church holds that Kimbangu was resurrected and appears to his followers on a regular basis—a phenomenon known as a "Kimbanguphany."[22] He is believed to possess the gift of ubiquity and can therefore make earthly

19. See Norbert C. Brockman, "Diangienda, Joseph," *Dictionary of African Christian Biography*, located online at http://www.dacb.org/stories/demrepcongo/diangienda_joseph.html.
20. For the "whites to blacks" quotation see Ogbu Kalu, ed., *African Christianity: An African Story* (Trenton, NJ: Africa World Press, 2007), 36. For the Kimbangu-Simon of Cyrene connection, see Andre Droogers, "Kimbanguism at the Grass Roots: Beliefs in a Local Kimbanguist Church," *Journal of Religion in Africa* 11, no. 3 (1980): 198.
21. Kayongo, "Kimbanguism," 136.
22. Ibid. 146.

apparitions. There is also a belief that Kimbangu was reincarnated in his youngest son Joseph Diangienda as well as his grandson Simon Kimbangu Kiangani. Most Kimbanguists, therefore, believe that God the Holy Spirit is incarnate in their leader. The Kimbanguist Faculty of Theology in Lutendele (near Kinshasa) has divided over these matters, and bitter debates among their theologians continue.

Another controversy involves one of the Kimbanguist Church's holy days. The most important dates in the Kimbanguist calendar are April 6—when Kimbangu's ministry began; October 12—his death; and May 25—the "real" date of Christ's birth. However, the "real" date of Christ's birth was changed by Kimbanguists only in 1999. This is significant because May 25, 1916, was the birthday of Kimbangu's second son, Salomon. Both Christ and Salomon are celebrated during the Christmas festivities since it is believed Christ reincarnated in Salomon.

The Kimbanguist Church is one of many African Initiated Churches that fits very well Weber's description of a sect. A similar process goes on in churches all over the world. The United States is home to many innovative forms of Christianity, including the Mormon Church, certainly one of the most significant sect-to-church examples in history.[23] Latin America is home to several innovating churches, for example the Universal Church of the Kingdom of God. If China eventually loosens up its tightly controlled system of registered churches, many of the "underground" movements will evince similar trends.[24] Indeed they already have, such as in the millenarian Taiping Heavenly Kingdom revolt we

---

23. Many scholars label the Mormon Church a New Religious Movement, or even a cult. Although nomenclature is debated, Joseph Smith's movement was definitely an attempt to create a purified form of Christianity.

24. Three important works provide rich introductions to the underground churches of China: Lian Xi, *Redeemed by Fire: The Rise of Popular Christianity in Modern China* (New Haven: Yale University Press, 2010); David Aikman, *Jesus in Beijing* (Washington, DC: Regnery Publishing, 2003); and Liao Yiwu, *God Is Red*, trans. Wenguang Huang (New York: HarperOne, 2011).

looked at earlier. Its founder, Hong Xiuquan, claimed to be Jesus's brother. His cause was finally crushed after a bitter civil war that claimed the lives of perhaps twenty million people. Both Sun Yat-sen and Mao Zedong held this perplexing, Christian movement in high regard. The Chinese government has good reason to be suspicious of indigenous Christian movements. They can spin out of control. For hundreds of years, the Roman Catholic Church had similar misgivings. And these fears are routinely justified when bizarre sects emerge, claiming to be legitimate churches, yet resulting in catastrophic and even deadly consequences.

Conclusion

To whom does Christianity belong? The Taiping Heavenly Kingdom or the Kimbanguists? The megachurches of North America or the Vatican's inner circle in Rome? Does Christianity belong to the state? Constantine's landmark shift—from Christianity being an illegal sect to being crowned as the religion of empire—has various manifestations throughout history. The Byzantine Church, medieval Europe's Holy Roman Empire, Calvin's Geneva, Peter the Great's Holy Synod, and Vatican City are all examples of churches enmeshed within the state to an indistinguishable extent. Today this model is dying in the Western world. Eastern Europe, however, is an example where it seems to be coming back into vogue after the brutal treatment of the church in Soviet times.

Rather than allowing the state to determine "to whom Christianity belongs," most Christians today would probably measure orthodoxy by how Jesus is understood by their own clergy. It is a wonder how this one man could spawn so many depictions. The first few centuries of Christianity witnessed mighty theological battles over Jesus, battles that continue. And that leads us to the next chapter.

4

Jesus

John 18:37–38a

"You are a king, then!" said Pilate. Jesus answered, "You say that I am a king. In fact, the reason I was born and came into the world is to testify to the truth. Everyone on the side of truth listens to me." "What is truth?" retorted Pilate.

Early Christianity was far from decided about what to make of Jesus of Nazareth. As witnessed in the New Testament documents, one of the most important discussions about Jesus was whether his followers had to be Jewish, or at least observe Jewish laws. As we saw earlier, the Council of Jerusalem in Acts 15 was devoted to this problem.

Several Jewish-Christian sects emerged in early Christianity that leaned in the direction of observing Jewish law, such as the Ebionites, Nazareans, and Elkesaites. Several so-called gnostic (Greek for "knowledge") groups emerged in the early centuries of the faith, emphasizing different ideas and following different gurus such as Simon Magus, Menander, Saturninus, Basilides, and, most importantly, Valentinus, who exerted tremendous authority in the second century in Alexandria and Rome.[1] Christianity was also torn from within by Montanism—a group that emphasized prophecy and the gifts of the spirit. Another important movement that split the church was the Marcionites; they rejected the Jewishness of Christianity and exaggerated Paul's emphasis on grace.

While Emperor Constantine's attempt to unite Christianity at the Council of Nicea in A.D. 325 had some success, the impulse to innovate and deviate from the majority never quite died out. That impulse to innovate was labeled *heresy*. Heresy is tricky to define. It is based on the notion that history is told by the victors. Losers don't really get their say . . . unless of course we dig up what they said after the fact, which is precisely what happened with the *Gospel of Thomas* and the *Gospel of Judas* and so many more. The extent to which we take "heretical" documents seriously, however, varies considerably.

Will the Real Jesus Please Stand Up?

The great British scholar Bishop Stephen Neill once made the following observation about our sources for understanding Jesus:

> It is not surprising that, when that major force called Jesus of Nazareth struck human life, the fragments flew off in every direction. No single mind could encompass the whole, no single hand could draw the definitive portrait of him. Each took what he was able to grasp and recorded it in this way or in that. . . . A great deal of what was remembered, reported, and recorded is now irrecoverably lost to us. Some of the fragments were so far out to left or right that the church decided that they were more misleading than revealing. . . . What we have in the New Testament is a collection of those fragments of memory and interpretation that seemed to the church to reflect Jesus as he was, and to carry with them the authentic echo of his voice. We may regret that we have no more; we may feel that at certain points the judgment of

---

1. See Everett Ferguson, *Church History: From Christ to the Pre-Reformation* (Grand Rapids, MI: Zondervan, 2013). For Jewish Christian movements, see 45–48. For gnostic movements, see 88–96.

the church was at fault, both in what it retained and in what it rejected. *But this is the material with which we have to work, and we must make the best of it.*[2]

We must make the best of it, but what if we find more material? And what if new insights into Jesus are made? Are we allowed to reenvision Jesus for a completely different age, or are we stuck with the old Jesus—the one passed to us from those who came before?

One of my favorite exercises in teaching history of Christianity classes is to read from the rejected gospels. I try to get students to identify whether a particular saying is canonical or not. Sometimes I read from the *Gospel of Thomas*, which shares many of the sayings of Jesus. Students are shocked to discover that while the book itself is not canonical, much of its contents are, due to their being replicated by the Synoptics in several places: the parable of the Sower, the mustard seed analogy, seeing the speck in your brother's eye when you do not see the beam in your own eye, and "A prophet is not acceptable in his own town."[3] There are many more examples.

Similarly, I read from *The Infancy Gospel of Thomas*, one of several early Christian writings describing Jesus' childhood. Students laugh aloud when I read the story of Jesus taking mud, shaping it into twelve sparrows, and then making them come alive, much to the annoyance of his father Joseph who did not appreciate his son working on the Sabbath.[4] Jesus' explosive temperament makes for entertaining reading, such as when his buddy drains some water he collected. Jesus responds, "Damn you, you irreverent fool!" Then Jesus curses the boy, making him dry up and wither away. The horrified parents shout to Joseph, "It's your fault—your boy did all

2. Stephen Neill, *Jesus through Many Eyes* (Philadelphia: Fortress Press, 1976), 4. Italics are mine.
3. See Marvin Meyer, trans., *The Gospel of Thomas: The Hidden Sayings of Jesus* (New York: HarperSanFrancisco, 1992). See the following passages: Thomas 9, 20, 26, and 31.
4. See "The Infancy Gospel of Thomas," in Robert J. Miller, ed., *The Complete Gospels* (New York: HarperSanFrancisco, 1994), 371.

this."[5] After another similar situation, the distraught parents blame Joseph: "Because you have such a boy, you can't live with us in the village. . . . He's killing our children!" Joseph grabs Jesus by the ear, causing Jesus to unload on him: "Don't you know that I don't really belong to you? Don't make me upset." Presumably Joseph backed off.[6]

Some students get a little uncomfortable when I read the story of the twelve-year-old Jesus who gets left in the temple in Jerusalem, impressing the scholars with his knowledge. The *Infancy Gospel of Thomas* chapter 19 sounds eerily similar to Luke chapter 2 in this case. How could a text so bizarre contain a canonical story like that? It is a difficult question to answer, but it shows the complexity of the New Testament documents, as well as the complexity of the canonization process. At some point, we have to resign ourselves to what John had to say at the end of his Gospel: "Jesus did many other things as well. If every one of them were written down, I suppose that even the whole world would not have room for the books that would be written."[7]

The Jesus of History

The quest for the historical Jesus has had at least two major phases. First, there was the era of the seven ecumenical councils, from Constantine's Council of Nicea in 325 to the last one, also held in Nicea, in 787. These seven councils made the decisions that defined the Christian faith. The conclusions of the councils are considered orthodox by most Christians living today. One of the most important conclusions of those councils was the true nature of Jesus Christ. Was he man, God, or a mix of both? Even now, our understanding of the

---

5. Ibid. 372.
6. See ibid.. These stories occur in the first five chapters.
7. John 21:25.

Trinity is essentially the same as the decisions those clergymen—the church fathers—made.

The second quest for the historical Jesus began in the modern European Enlightenment, when virtually nothing was too sacred for scientific scrutiny. It continues today, and is in fact a successful genre in the publishing field. Led by scholars such as Hermann Reimarus (eighteenth century), David Friedrich Strauss (nineteenth century), and Albert Schweitzer (twentieth century), they tried to demythologize Jesus with the assumption that the miracles were magical byproducts of a premodern age. Their task was to extract the Jesus of history from the Christ of faith. We moderns know angels don't appear to people, gods don't come to earth, and virgins don't give birth. Here the *Jefferson Bible* comes to mind, an attempt by the great American politician to take a razor to the miraculous in the Gospels, leaving an emaciated text glued together and bereft of anything supernatural. We are left with what Jefferson thought the "real" Jesus said and did. Jefferson's Jesus was a morally rigorous sage, perfectly matching Jeffersonian theology, deism: there probably is a god, but Jesus was not it.

The search for the historical Jesus continues unabated, and is a publishing boon for authors such as N. T. Wright, John Dominic Crossan, Bart Ehrman, and Craig Evans. Reza Aslan, the Muslim-American professor mentioned earlier, weighed in on the topic in 2013 and made headlines more because of his own life story than his book. Here was a Muslim immigrant from Iran who had a born-again experience and converted to evangelical Christianity, even "traveling around the United States spreading the gospel."[8] In college he converted back to Islam. His book was a massive bestseller due

8. This quote comes from "Amazon.com Review Q&A with Reza Aslan" on the Amazon web page for his book *Zealot: The Life and Times of Jesus of Nazareth* (New York: Random House, 2013), located at http://www.amazon.com/Zealot-Life-Times-Jesus-Nazareth/dp/140006922X.

partly to the wide coverage it received in the press. The quest for the historical Jesus was back in the limelight . . . again.

Who is the real Jesus? Is he a firebrand preacher? Did he raise dead people and walk on water? Did he rise from the dead and appear to his followers? Is he really encountered in bread and wine? Are Christians to pay more attention to the meaning of his death and resurrection or to his teachings? Historically, Christians emphasized the former, with a heavy emphasis on concepts like transubstantiation and the ingesting of Christ's body and blood in order to effect salvation in the communicant. More recently, particularly in the Western world, there has been a renewed emphasis on the content of Jesus's teachings—such as in Tony Campolo's "Red Letter Christians" movement, inspired by Bibles that print the words of Jesus in red.[9] The stakes are high for the two-plus billion people who believe Jesus to be the Son of God, and part of God—as testified in the doctrine of the Holy Trinity. However, the historical Jesus conversation is generally kept in the seminaries and universities; the masses trust the biblical record as it stands. Let us investigate what that record says.

Eric Meyers and Mark Chancey write, "Although scholarly debate surrounds most aspects of the life of Jesus, the basic geographical parameters . . . are generally accepted."[10] Galilee was his hub, but he went out to preach in the countryside villages and rural areas. It is likely that the only city he entered was Jerusalem. Jesus taught in synagogues, in homes, and in natural settings such as hillsides. His message was complex, but revolved around the kingdom of God. He challenged many traditional assumptions of Jewish teachers and

9. See Tony Campolo, *Red Letter Christians: A Citizen's Guide to Faith and Politics* (Ventura, CA: Regal Books, 2008), and *Red Letter Revolution: What If Jesus Really Meant What He Said?* (Nashville: Thomas Nelson, 2012), coauthored with Shane Claiborne. See also the Red Letter Christians website: http://www.redletterchristians.org/.
10. Eric Meyers and Mark Chancey, *Alexander to Constantine: Archaeology of the Land of the Bible* (New Haven: Yale University Press, 2012), 177.

conflicted with them often. He performed signs and wonders such as healings, exorcisms, and even resurrections. He was crucified under Roman prefect Pontius Pilate, ostensibly for his peculiar teachings as well as one action in particular that provoked the ire of many: the "cleansing of the temple" by overturning tables and chastising the moneychangers.[11] Events after his death shocked his disciples and they went out proclaiming his resurrection.

The earliest Christian movement remained predominantly Jewish until Peter and especially Paul began to argue that Jesus's life and teachings—and especially his death and resurrection—signaled a new era: God was reaching out to *all* people, much like he had reached out to the Jews throughout history. gentiles could become "grafted in" to this Jewish story if they place faith and hope in this Jesus.[12] By the end of the New Testament, in the book of Revelation, the pacifist prince of peace has become an intrepid soldier in a cosmic battle, the Christ Pantocrator ("all-powerful")—an image vital to the Eastern Orthodox Churches. Elaine Pagels writes, "When the battle reaches its climax, Jesus appears as a divine warrior, mounted on a white horse as he rides forth from heaven to lead armies of angels into war. From his mouth comes a sharp sword with which to strike down the nations, and he will rule them with a rod of iron. . . . Then Jesus judges the whole world."[13] For two thousand years, various depictions of Christ have captured the imagination of his disciples: the baby in swaddling clothes, the prophet confronting the rich, the compassionate healer giving someone a new start in life, the suffering servant on the cross—an image so treasured for the world's billion Roman Catholics.

11. All four Gospel writers mention the incident: Mark 11, Matthew 21, Luke 19-20, and John 2.
12. See Romans 11.
13. Elaine Pagels, *Revelations: Visions, Prophecy, and Politics in the Book of Revelation* (New York: Penguin, 2012), 6–7.

These icons are etched in the Christian mind, and they are a resource during times of need. They are reminders of Jesus' promise in John chapter 12: "Where I am, my servant also will be" (v. 26). Rowan Williams, the former Archbishop of Canterbury, questions,

> How do you learn to be with Christ at the Diocesan Board of Finance? How do you learn to be with Christ when you are dealing with a clerical marriage in difficulties? How do you learn to be with Christ when you are counting to twenty over an irritating letter of angry complaint that you have just received about something you have no particular responsibility for? You have to be with Christ there, because Christ is with you there. To open that moment to God just by letting myself be drawn into the present moment—that's my cure.[14]

The Christian tradition is rife with images of Jesus Christ, and the point of having them has little to do with historical veracity; rather, the point is to edify and inspire the believer.

Perhaps the one image of Jesus that manages to stoke the fires of imagination while at the same time tempting the rational mind is the Shroud of Turin—the burial cloth of Jesus. Yet again, however, the magic of the shroud—perhaps the most important Christian relic on earth today—is what it does to the believer who stands in the room and stares at it. In 2010 I traveled to see the shroud. As I stood in the church and stared at what many believe is a virtual photograph of the crucified body of Christ, I was flooded with emotion. I looked around at the mothers and young men and grandfathers and children all around me and realized the power this man Jesus still plays in the lives of others—even in a supposedly "secular" Italy.

---

14. Rowan Williams, *Where God Happens: Discovering Christ in One Another* (Boston: New Seeds Books, 2005), 97–98.

A German Jesus

Italians and their Western European counterparts have dramatically changed in their churchgoing ways. What has surprised religion scholars is how sudden the changes occurred. France, England, Scandinavia, Germany, Holland . . . all of them are known today as being mainly secular countries. What is so shocking is that only a century ago Western Europe was an extremely Christian place. I am fascinated by these changes: from religious to irreligious, from Christian to post-Christian. Most scholars call it a secularization process, although that idea is hotly debated. Why did these changes happen? Were they a reaction to something? Has this former stronghold of Christianity decided to divorce itself from Jesus Christ? Why did that relationship turn sour? Is there any chance Western Europeans will return to Christ one day, or is the separation final?

In 2013 I attended the Tenth Assembly of the World Council of Churches in Busan, South Korea. While there, I conducted some qualitative interviews with Western Europeans in attendance with hopes they might help me to understand this phenomenon better—a phenomenon so misunderstood in the relatively religious United States. I also wanted to explore how Western European pastors are dealing with these shifts. How do they function in a context where so few are apt to proclaim Jesus the King of Kings and Lord of Lords anymore?

One of my interviewees was a highly educated, articulate German pastor and theologian named Rev. Dr. Jutta Koslowski.[15] I asked her why Germany is secularizing. She clarified, "It is not a matter of 'is secularizing.' It *is* a very secular country. People just don't involve themselves in church anymore." Jutta said that Germany has reached

---

15. Interview with Jutta Koslowski, Nov. 6, 2013, at HanWha Resort, Busan, South Korea. Pastor Jutta is part of an ecumenical community that is committed to living counterculturally: www.kloster-gnadenthal.de.

that secular point that scholars have been pointing toward for years. But she continues to preach Christ anyway, focusing on his teachings rather than on his deity. She believes that while the deity of Christ is no longer compelling, the core of the gospel is still very relevant to Germans.

Curious, I asked her what she means by "the gospel." She said the gospel message has changed in Western Europe, and it should change. She said we need to discover new aspects of our theology such as creation care, social justice, and adapting the gospel message to an age of science and medicine. There is a big shift happening, and the church must be ready. The Christian message must change, or risk becoming irrelevant. But right now, the German people "are interested in environmentalism; this is when Germans start to listen to the message." These new concerns are eclipsing the old ones. She went on,

> Trinity, two natures within Christ, these ideas are put aside. Not necessarily wrong. I've put it aside. Historically, Christians focused on the Trinity. But we should change this. Trinity and divinity of Christ; these two doctrines are actually incomprehensible. These teachings have always been incomprehensible. The church fathers said, "It is a mystery." How do we know? Revelation? This does not convince people anymore.

Jutta is struggling with questions unimaginable for most American Christians, where orthodox Christology is unshakable: Jesus was both human and divine, just as the Bible says.

Jutta then described how she was trying to introduce her own children to Jesus in post-Christian Germany. It is very difficult, she admitted. "My son is twelve. He is not a Christian. He does not like church and spirituality." I asked her about her own parents. Her parents are "militant atheists," which is problematic for her on several levels. There is tension when the grandparents want to babysit the grandkids. Her parents never introduced her to Jesus, and her society offered little help:

> I was raised with atheism. From a city near Frankfurt. At the age of fourteen I would not have known if Jesus was a woman or even when he lived. I just knew the church was a failure. I knew about witch burnings, crusades, inquisitions, but not about Jesus. . . . My parents threatened that they would send me to a boarding school if I was baptized. They were not tolerant at all. No Bible was allowed in the home. . . . My parents are still atheist. They want to look after our four kids [aged two–twelve] but . . . my kids come back asking, "Why do we pray before meals? There's no need."

At the end of our conversation I told Jutta that Americans are very different from Germans when it comes to these topics. She disagreed. She said she has traveled extensively in the United States and really did not see much of a difference. In her view, Americans may have more "orthodox" understandings of Jesus, but many of their national policies are "very unchristian":

> They are materialistic people in the USA. Americans seem not to have problems with owning guns on a large scale. This seems unchristian. Americans are not very environmentally conscious. This does not seem very Christian. American active participation in Christianity has not really accomplished a Christianized society. Europeans are not going to church, but they are much more "Christian" in the sense that they are more environmentally conscious, they are more cautious about guns, and they are not as materialistic.

Jutta closed the interview with a rhetorical question: "What good has Christianity done for the American people if it does not make them more Christian in their attitudes?"

My interview with Jutta takes us to the core of Christian faith. What is at that core? Is it that we should emulate Jesus of Nazareth, repeat what he said, believe the way he believed? Or is it that we should accept his *acts*—his atonement and sacrifice—realizing his teachings were directed more at Jews than at his gentile followers two thousand years later, and on different continents?

The Maasai Jesus

With the world Christianity revolution happening today, we are witnesses to a proliferation of Jesus images. Depictions of Jesus, his life, and his teachings are always enmeshed in the culture trying to assimilate him, and much of what the culture values most gets superimposed onto him. Jesus in India gets depicted as a guru, Jesus in China is likened to a Confucian priest, Jesus in Africa is depicted as a black man. Missionaries who took the gospel to foreign shores were often shocked or disappointed by the fruits of their labor. Jesus goes into one culture looking like, say, a white European, but once he gets into the heart and mind of another, the interpretation must change. Receiving cultures are empowered by Christ's teachings as they make them their own; indeed, they become shareholders of Christ's message. As Leonardo Boff has written, "Christianity is a syncretism par excellence."[16]

Several years ago Lamin Sanneh introduced me to the writings of Father Vincent Donovan, a Roman Catholic missionary who worked among the Maasai people of East Africa from 1955 to 1973. Sanneh had contributed a response to the twenty-fifth anniversary edition of Father Donovan's important 1978 book *Christianity Rediscovered*, a riveting account of his years evangelizing the Maasai.[17] During his

---

16. Leonardo Boff, *Church, Charism and Power: Liberation Theology and the Institutional Church* (London: SCM, 1985), 92ff. Cited in John S. Pobee and Gabriel Ositelu II, *African Initiatives in Christianity: The Growth, Gifts, and Diversities of Indigenous African Churches* (Geneva: WCC Publications, 1998), xi.

17. Vincent Donovan, *Christianity Rediscovered* (Maryknoll, NY: Orbis, 1978). I have used the twenty-fifth anniversary edition (published 2003) which includes the African Creed and insights on the book by Lamin Sanneh, Eugene Hillman, and Nora Koren, Donovan's sister. I am particularly indebted to Lamin Sanneh's insightful comments on Donovan's book at the end of the book, 151–59.

years of service, Father Donovan realized his missionary training was wholly inadequate. The good news of Jesus Christ would have to be shorn of its Western packaging if it was to make any sense to the Maasai. There were implications in doing this, however. Donovan would have to "rediscover" the faith he thought he was familiar with. He had to "jettison the Western hardware, and begin from the ground up." The typical missionary model was to bring Enlightenment, meaning "material advancement: . . . schools and literacy, planned development, hospitals and clinics, sanitation, organized nation-states, [and] individual fulfillment."[18] Donovan wanted nothing less than for the Maasai to discover Jesus Christ in their own culture, in their own methods, and in their own history. And they did, eventually. But they did it on their own terms.

When the Maasai were able to be their own missionaries, and when Father Donovan was able to point out that God had been with them all along and they simply needed to understand God in light of Christ, a conversion process began. The Maasai took control of how Jesus should be interpreted and how the gospel should work in their own worldview. Father Donovan watched this reappropriation unfold while his own understanding of Jesus became deeply challenged. The Maasai came to recognize Jesus as Lord, even penning their own "African Creed":

We believe in the one High God, who out of love created the beautiful world and everything good in it. He created man and wanted man to be happy in the world. God loves the world and every nation and tribe on the earth. We have known this High God in the darkness, and now we know him in the light. God promised in the book of his word, the Bible, that he would save the world and all the nations and tribes.

We believe that God made good his promise by sending his son, Jesus Christ, a man in the flesh, a Jew by tribe, born poor in a little village,

18. Sanneh, "Vincent Donovan's Discovery of Post-Western Christianity," in Donovan, *Christianity Rediscovered*, 156.

who left his home and was always on safari doing good, curing people by the power of God, teaching about God and man, showing that the meaning of religion is love. He was rejected by his people, tortured and nailed hands and feet to a cross, and died. He lay buried in the grave, but the hyenas did not touch him, and on the third day, he rose from the grave. He ascended to the skies. He is the Lord.

We believe that all our sins are forgiven through him. All who have faith in him must be sorry for their sins, be baptized in the Holy Spirit of God, live the rules of love and share the bread together in love, to announce the good news to others until Jesus comes again. We are waiting for him. He is alive. He lives. This we believe. Amen.[19]

It is a very different creed than the one assembled at Nicea in 325, or at Constantinople in 381. Sanneh considers the African Creed to be "majestic."[20]

By the end of his work in Africa, Father Donovan's understanding of Jesus Christ had changed significantly. He had *rediscovered* Jesus, he had *rediscovered* what it means to follow Christ, and he was his own first convert. He was a foreigner to his own culture's understanding of Christ when he returned to the United States. His own sister—who nursed him to his death in 2000—wrote the following:

He worked in Africa from 1955 to 1973, and the experience changed him forever. His struggle to honestly present the Christian gospel to people of a different culture caused him to wrestle with his own faith and everything that he had taken for granted about creation, the incarnation, Jesus Christ, the church, priesthood, the sacraments, the Holy Spirit. That struggle never ended.[21]

It is unnerving to think of having to rediscover Jesus Christ in order to communicate his message effectively to others. However, Lamin writes, "It is an eminently logical outcome if you think at the deeper

---

19. Donovan, *Christianity Rediscovered*, 148.
20. Sanneh, "Vincent Donovan's Discovery of Post-Western Christianity," 158.
21. See Nora Koren's essay, "A Sister Remembers Her Brother," in Donovan, *Christianity Rediscovered*, 167.

level of the *missio dei* that lies in the fact of God having preceded missionaries in the mission field."[22]

The Jesus of Islam

Lamin Sanneh's voice is a unique and important one when it comes to discussing how Jesus gets translated into the world's cultures. His pioneering study *Translating the Message: The Missionary Impact on Culture* has impacted the academic discipline of world Christianity like few others, largely because Sanneh understands the issues like few others.[23] His autobiography—a devout, Muslim boy from a poor, polygamous family in the British colony of Gambia ends up a renowned professor at Aberdeen, Harvard, and Yale—is a captivating story.[24] Along the way, Sanneh converted to Christianity, but his primary expertise has always been in Islamic studies, causing intrigue by scholars around him.

Sanneh has compared Christianity and Islam extensively in his writings. One of his most important points is that Islam is a religion centered on the Arabic language. The "word of God" is literally a text that comes word for word from God—in Arabic. Muslims do not revere the Qur'an in English, or any other language; only in Arabic is it truly considered scripture.

Christianity's "word of God," however, is a man—Jesus. Texts and languages are useful insofar that they point toward Jesus—the Word. And scripture is no substitute. The earliest Christians did not even have a New Testament. They had Jesus, and after his death they had stories about him. Many Christians continue to miss this point by referring to the Bible as the "word of God," instead of

22. Sanneh, "Vincent Donovan's Discovery of Post-Western Christianity," 157–58.
23. Lamin Sanneh, *Translating the Message: The Missionary Impact on Culture*, 2dn ed. (Maryknoll, NY: Orbis, 2009).
24. See Lamin Sanneh, *Summoned from the Margin: Homecoming of an African* (Grand Rapids, MI: Eerdmans, 2012).

acknowledging that the Bible should always play second fiddle to the Word made flesh, the one who walked among us. The Greek New Testament is not the "original." It is already a translation, since most of the initial events involving the life of Jesus played out in the language of Aramaic. Nevertheless, the Greek texts—which were one step away from the original events—do not become diluted in the eyes of Christians because the words have always served a higher purpose: they point Christians to Jesus—the Word incarnate. This is why Christians can read the New Testament in their own vernacular without feeling that they must have knowledge of Aramaic. The translation suffices, since the critical point has little to do with language anyway. Language is only a metaphor that gets us to the man Jesus.

At the core of Islam is a text. At Christianity's core is a man. The two religions are radically different at the very base. These issues are more than just scholarship for Sanneh. For him, the stakes are very high. He realized that he had to make a decision about which religion was right. And that decision cut him off from participating in the Islam of his youth.

Islam's understanding of the Judeo-Christian scriptures is that they were corrupted due to careless copying, poor theology, and half-truths that had been passed down haphazardly. In the Qur'an, Jesus is not the son of God; he did not even die on the cross. The crucifixion of Jesus is an invented story. Jesus was protected from such a brutal, heinous act—far below the dignity of a prophet—and was assumed into heaven directly. Surah 4:155–159 reads,

> No! God has sealed them in their disbelief, so they believe only a little—and because they disbelieved and uttered a terrible slander against Mary, and said, "We have killed the Messiah, Jesus, son of Mary, the Messenger of God." (They did not kill him, nor did they crucify him, though it was made to appear like that to them; those that disagreed about him are full of doubt, with no knowledge to follow, only

supposition: they certainly did not kill him—God raised him up to Himself. God is almighty and wise. There is not one of the People of the Book who will not believe in [Jesus] before his death, and on the Day of Resurrection he will be a witness against them.)[25]

The gnostic *Gospel of Basilides* (early second century) argues ideas strikingly similar to the Qur'an on this topic, although it was dismissed by mainstream Christianity as being heretical. Gnostic theories similar to these have been categorized under "the semblance theory," arguing that while Jesus may have appeared to have been crucified, it was probably someone else such as Simon of Cyrene or Judas. There is little doubt that Basilides—or someone with a very similar understanding of Jesus' death—influenced how early Muslims understood the crucifixion.[26] Nevertheless, Jesus is revered in Islam. He is the Messiah, was born of the Virgin Mary, and will come to earth again for the Judgment.

Gandhi's Jesus

Likewise, Jesus is also revered in India. Hindus hold him in very high regard, believing he was probably an avatar. Gandhi's attitude towards Jesus is a case in point. When the famous American missionary E. Stanley Jones (1884–1973) befriended the Mahatma ("great soul") and tried to persuade him to believe in Jesus, Gandhi responded with the following:

First, I would suggest that all of you Christians, missionaries and all, must begin to live more like Jesus Christ. Second, practice your religion without adulterating it or toning it down. Third, emphasize love and make it your working force, for love is central in Christianity. Fourth,

25. M. A. S. Abdel Haleem, *The Quran* (Oxford: Oxford University Press, 2005), surah 4:155–159.
26. J. P. Arendzen, "Basilides," in *The Catholic Encyclopedia*, vol. 2 (New York: The Encyclopedia Press, 1913). Basilides was the teacher of one of the most famous gnostics in the second century: Valentinus (100–175). See Nicola Denzey Lewis, *Introduction to "Gnosticism": Ancient Voices, Christian Worlds* (Oxford: Oxford University Press, 2013), 63.

study the non-Christian religions more sympathetically to find the good that is within them, in order to have a more sympathetic approach to the people.[27]

Jones ruminated on Gandhi's response a few days before admitting,

> [Gandhi] put his finger unerringly on the four weak spots in our individual and collective lives. . . . We were worshiping Christ more than following him. Jesus said, "If any man serve me, let him follow me." It is possible to serve Christ and not follow him—not follow him in Christlike living. . . .
>
> The greatest Hindu leader says, Your faith doesn't need to be changed; it doesn't need to be added to or subtracted from; it needs to be lived *as it is.* . . .
>
> The Mahatma need not have said anything more.[28]

Jones recounted how a fiery Indian nationalist once said, "I never understood the meaning of Christianity until I saw it in Gandhi."[29]

Time and time again in India, Jones encountered Indians who thought of Gandhi as the "modern Christ." Others believed him to be, literally, Christ reincarnated. Jones reports one incident in North India where an Indian man exclaimed, "Why do you preach on the second coming of Christ? He has already come—he is here—Gandhi." Jones admitted, "Gandhi is their ideal, and they are identifying that ideal with Jesus." Indians quite naturally compared the suffering of Jesus with the suffering Gandhi endured as the peacemaking liberator of India.[30]

The Maasai of East Africa, Lamin Sanneh of West Africa, and the Mahatma of India. They all encountered Jesus, and they reached different conclusions about him. But the underlying unity to their

---

27. E. Stanley Jones, *Gandhi: Portrayal of a Friend* (Nashville: Abingdon, 1948), 51–52.
28. Ibid. 52, italics in the original.
29. E. Stanley Jones, *The Christ of the Indian Road* (London: Hodder and Stoughton, 1925), 101.
30. Ibid., 76–77.

responses is this: Jesus cannot be dismissed. Indeed, Jesus has probably made a greater impact on the human race than any person in history.

Conclusion

A few years ago I held a series of gatherings of college students at my house on the topic "Christ who lives in me," from Gal. 2:20. When asked to describe "Christ," one student said Christ is in the ocean when he surfs with his dad. Another said Christ is a homeless man in the food line down at the shelter. Another thought of Christ as the great judge by whose standards we are measured. Clearly Christ means different things to people, and always has.[31]

Which version of Jesus is the truth? This chapter opened with Pilate's famous question to Jesus during his trial: What is truth? Our answer determines how we respond to this Galilean Jew whose life so deeply impacted—and continues to impact—our world and our reality. As Andrew Walls has written, since the earliest days of the Christian movement, "It was not Christianity that saves, but Christ."[32]

---

31. There are several works dealing with how Jesus is interpreted globally. See Priscilla Pope-Levison and John Levison, *Jesus in Global Contexts* (Louisville: Westminster/John Knox, 1992); Gregory Barker and Stephen Gregg, eds., *Jesus beyond Christianity: The Classic Texts* (Oxford: Oxford University Press, 2010); Volker Küster, *The Many Faces of Jesus Christ* (Maryknoll, NY: Orbis, 1999); and Kwame Bediako, *Jesus and the Gospel in Africa* (Maryknoll, NY: Orbis, 2004).
32. Andrew Walls, *The Missionary Movement in Christian History* (Maryknoll, NY: Orbis, 1996), 66.

5

The Holy Ghost

John 14:12, 14

Very truly I tell you, whoever believes in me will do the works I have
been doing, and they will do even greater things than these, because I
am going to the Father. . . . You may ask me for anything in my name,
and I will do it.

My students were shocked. I was lecturing on the pervasive,
enduring belief in miracles among the world's Christians when I gave
an offhanded reference to a resurrection that had occurred a few days
earlier in Ohio. The students had no problem understanding miracles
in Nigeria, apparitions in Mexico, or healings in India. But when
I referred to a resurrection in Ohio in August 2013, they scoffed.
"What? Where's the evidence?" I could only refer them to the story
as it broke in the media on ABC News.[1]

---

1. Sydney Lupkin, "Ohio Man Declared Dead Comes Back to Life," *ABC News*, August 22,
2013, located at http://abcnews.go.com/Health /ohio-man-declared-dead-back-life
/story?id=20027401.

What happened was this: a thirty-seven-year-old mechanic named Tony Yahle went into cardiac arrest during the night. His wife, a nurse, performed CPR but could not help him. First responders arrived and shocked him to the point that they found a faint pulse. They got him to the hospital but his heart stopped again. For an additional forty-five minutes doctors worked on him to no avail. But then a seventeen-year-old charismatic pastor who is a relative of the family laid his hands on the family and "the Lord spoke through him." Immediately the so ran down the hall to his dead father and shouted, "Dad, you're not going to die." The pastor then "spoke against the spirit of death." Suddenly a heartbeat returned.[2] The cardiologist involved, Dr. Raja Nazir, was as astonished as anyone else: "In the last 20 years, I've never seen anybody who we have pronounced dead . . . and then for him to come back, I've never seen it. Actually I've never heard of it." Later, at his church in Bellbrook, the revived mechanic had an explanation for his Christian community: he believes a miracle happened that day, and God extended his life.[3]

Miracles

Pentecostal Christians all around the world would be encouraged by this story, but they would not be shocked by it. They would say that you will find these stories occurring regularly if you just look around, and remain open to the Spirit of God working on the earth. Jesus promised his disciples that they would do "greater things than these" once he went back to the Father.

2. Charlene Aaron, "Back from the Dead: Man's Faith 'Stronger Than Ever,'" *CBN News*, August 30, 2013, located at http://www.cbn.com/cbnnews/us/2013/August/Back-from-the-Dead-Mans-Faith-Stronger-Than-Ever/.
3. Associated Press, "Dead Ohio Man Tony Yahle Comes Back to Life after 45 minutes with No Heartbeat, Stumping Doctors," *CBS News*, August 23, 2013, located at http://www.cbsnews.com/news/dead-ohio-man-tony-yahle-comes-back-to-life-after-45-minutes-with-no-heartbeat-stumping-doctors/.

Indeed, in the book of Acts, after Jesus' ascension back into heaven, the apostles began doing "greater things." It all began on the Jewish festival of Pentecost when the apostles were gathered at Jerusalem. Suddenly a violent wind came, accompanied by fire, and they all claimed to be "filled with the Holy Spirit." Peter stood up from among them to address the phenomenal scene to the international crowd of onlookers who were "amazed and perplexed." He quoted the Hebrew prophet Joel:

> In the last days, God says, I will pour out my Spirit on all people. Your sons and daughters will prophesy, your young men will see visions, your old men will dream dreams. . . . I will show wonders in the heavens above and signs on the earth below.[4]

It was a wild scene. Luke, the writer of the book of Acts, an educated disciple of Jesus, noted that many people refused to take the whole scene seriously, arguing instead that the Christians were drunk: "Some, however, made fun of them and said, 'They have had too much wine'" (v. Acts 2:13). Peter explained to them that they were not drunk—it was only 9:00 a.m.! Rather, this was the Holy Spirit at work. And if his listeners would "repent and be baptized" then they too would "receive the gift of the Holy Spirit" (v. 38) About three thousand people became Christians that day.

Under the Influence

Christians today are witnesses of an important theological development in world Christianity: the Holy Spirit has made a major comeback. Shortly after reaching a high point in the lives of the earliest Christians, it became mired in controversy, particularly when adopted by Montanus, one of the better known "heretics" of the second century. The Holy Spirit has since struggled to regain its

4. Acts 2:17–19. This paragraph mentions several events and quotations from Acts chapter two.

rightful place as God. The Nicene Creed of 325, for example, after devoting several lines to explaining the nature of Christ, gives a very meager line to the Spirit: "And [we believe] in the Holy Ghost." Protestant theologian Daniel Migliore wrote, "The doctrine of the Holy Spirit has seldom received the attention given to other doctrines of the faith such as Christology and the authority of scripture."[5]

All this has changed, however. Probably not since the *filioque* controversies of medieval times has pneumatology been at the forefront of developments in global Christianity. This is due largely to global Pentecostalism's rapid growth in several key places. If the Azusa Street revival of 1906 is accepted as the dawn of modern Pentecostalism, then this movement is mesmerizing in its rapidity of growth. Perhaps as many as 500 million people in the world today are under the influence of Pentecostalism. If we were to ask a Pentecostal theologian what caused this dazzling growth rate, it is likely the answer would revolve around a discussion of pneumatology, the study of the Holy Spirit.

Around the year 2000, Pentecostalism surpassed the Eastern Orthodox family of churches as the second largest grouping in all of Christianity, second only to the Roman Catholic tradition. Pentecostalism could reach majority status if trends continue. Perhaps this development is not as evident in the West, but Global South churches have caught the winds of God—and they are on fire.

World Christianity doyens Philip Jenkins and Harvey Cox brought this somewhat unexpected reality to a larger public audience. Jenkins's widely celebrated *The Next Christendom* raised eyebrows among those following global Christian trends: "By most accounts, membership in Pentecostal and independent Churches already runs

5. Daniel Migliore, *Faith Seeking Understanding* (Grand Rapids, MI: Eerdmans, 1991), 166. Migliore acknowledged a "resurgence of interest in the Holy Spirit" in more recent times, citing the Canberra 1990 General Assembly of the World Council of Churches' theme "Come, Holy Spirit—Renew the Whole Creation."

into the hundreds of millions, and congregations are located in precisely the regions of fastest population growth. Within a few decades, such denominations will represent a far larger segment of global Christianity, and just conceivably a majority."[6] Ironically, it was Harvey Cox—famous for his writings on secularization—who clued in to this revolution in Christian demographics in 1995 with his *Fire From Heaven: The Rise of Pentecostal Spirituality and the Reshaping of Religion in the Twenty-First Century*. In the 1960s Cox was warning that the world was becoming increasingly secular, but after observing Christianity in Asia, Africa, and Latin America, he realized trends in the Western world were not at all mirrored in the Global South, known more for its poverty than its faith.

> The Pentecostal movement . . . erupted from among society's disenfranchised, and it envisioned a human community restored by the power of the Spirit, a Jerusalem rejoicing where Parthians, Medes, and Elamites all came together, and where weeping, injustice, and death are abolished. . . . The Pentecostal movement is thriving. For millions of people it offers a vital hope and an alternative vision of what the world should be; and its powerful attractiveness to the disinherited of our own time constitutes an ongoing reproach to the status-quo.[7]

Jenkins reiterates that sentiment: "Christianity is flourishing wonderfully among the poor and persecuted, while it atrophies among the rich and secure."[8]

While modern Pentecostalism began as a movement among poor people, it would be inaccurate to assume that Pentecostalism is a religion embraced exclusively by poor people today. Pew Forum's impressive 2006 study of Pentecostalism found that in South Korea,

6. Philip Jenkins, *The Next Christendom: The Coming of Global Christianity* (Oxford: University Press, 2002), 7–8.
7. Harvey Cox, *Fire from Heaven: The Rise of Pentecostal Spirituality and the Reshaping of Religion in the Twenty-First Century* (Cambridge, MA: Da Capo Press, 1995), 24–25.
8. Jenkins, *The Next Christendom*, 220.

India, and South Africa the members of Pentecostal churches tend to have higher incomes. In the United States, the majority of Pentecostal Christians are in the lower income brackets, but this is not the case globally.[9] And while early Pentecostals in the early twentieth century may have been poor, the movement has matured, and now we are seeing large, wealthy, and even opulent Pentecostal churches. And they are often supported by affluent church members, some of whom might purchase a private jet for their pastor. This is precisely what happened to Nigerian pastor Ayo Oritsejafor.[10] While some Pentecostals would say this lavishness is simply God's decision to bestow "prosperity," other Pentecostals condemn this entire "prosperity gospel" way of thinking—something we will look at later in the chapter.

Backgrounds

Ecstatic utterances, miraculous healings, exorcisms, baptism in the Spirit, speaking in tongues, holy laughter, slaying in the Spirit . . . these are some of the manifestations routinely associated with Pentecostalism. And while they appear bizarre to those unacquainted with the movement, they figure prominently in world Christianity, particularly in the Global South. It is also important to point out that manifestations such as these have always been part of Christianity. Christian history is replete with claims of miracles, ecstatic visions, and God's activity in the mundane realm. And still today, there are detractors such as those overheard at the first Christian Pentecost, when the disciples were accused of having had "too much wine."

9. "Spirit and Power: A 10-Country Survey of Pentecostals," PewResearch, October 5, 2006, located at http://www.pewforum.org/2006/10/05/spirit-and-power-a-10-country-survey-of-pentecostals5/.
10. See Nick Street, *Moved by the Spirit: Pentecostalism and Charismatic Christianity in the Global South*, (Los Angeles: Center for Religion and Civic Culture, University of Southern California, 2013), 29. Pastor Oritsejafor was publicly chastised by fellow Nigerian pastor Tony Rapu for accepting the jet.

Los Angeles, California is crucial to the history of the rise of modern Pentecostalism, as that is where the Azusa Street Revival began in 1906. But there is much more to the story than that. There were other revivals around that time that were remarkably similar, such as in Wales, India, and Chile. Indeed, revivals have been a part of American church history for centuries, such as in the so-called Great Awakenings. For example, the Cane Ridge Revival in Kentucky in the summer of 1801 had all the hallmarks of an American Pentecost: people falling during worship, "the jerks," dancing, spiritual "barking," holy laughter, and running to the point of collapse during church services.[11] Church historians are fully aware that there was a much larger context for the epochal events that happened on Azusa Street in 1906. Three of the most significant precursors of Azusa are Wesley's Methodist movement, Edward Irving's emphasis on tongue speaking, and the global influence of the Keswick "higher life" conventions.

First, there was the Methodist movement of John Wesley (1703–1791). Wesley was an Anglican priest who became known for his intense piety while at Oxford University. He was once listening to a reading of Martin Luther's *Epistle to the Romans* and he felt his heart "strangely warmed." He became convinced that Christians could receive a "second blessing" from God, a concept that profoundly impacted the world of evangelical Christianity during and after his day, particularly the "born again" experience that so many Christians relate to today. Jesus taught, "No one can enter the kingdom of God unless they are born of water and the Spirit."[12] Very few Christians, if any, have explored the concept of the Holy Ghost as fully as John Wesley. It is at the core of his thinking and voluminous writings. In a

---

11. Vinson Synan, *The Century of the Holy Spirit: 100 Years of Pentecostal and Charismatic Renewal* (Nashville: Thomas Nelson, 2001), 33.
12. John 3:5.

letter to a Roman Catholic friend he summarized his teaching on the Spirit thus:

> What sort of work is the Spirit doing? Every step along the way the Spirit is:
> enlightening our understandings,
> rectifying our wills and affections,
> renewing our natures,
> uniting our persons to Christ,
> assuring us of our adoption as sons and daughters,
> leading us in our actions, purifying and sanctifying our souls and bodies
>   to a full and eternal enjoyment of God.[13]

Wesley's ideas expanded globally, wherever the British had a presence. The most fertile soil for Wesley was the United States, where a "holiness" style of Christianity became the direct ancestor to the Pentecostal outbreak of 1906. Wesley was not alone, but he was the root. His close colleague John Fletcher spoke often of a "baptism in the Holy Ghost." Before long others were asserting that a new and miraculous era in Christianity had dawned.

A second important figure in the rise of modern Pentecostalism was Edward Irving (1792–1834). Irving was a powerful Presbyterian pastor in London who emphasized glossolalia—speaking in tongues—after hearing that a young Scottish housewife named Mary Campbell had spoken in a foreign language unknown to her. After visiting her and witnessing the incident, he became convinced that tongue speaking was the "standing sign" of having been baptized in the Holy Ghost. He believed it was the "root and stem from which all the other gifts flow." One of Irving's church members in London, Henry Drummond—a member of Parliament—also showed signs of "receiving the Holy Ghost." As more of his parishioners began to speak in tongues and experience other manifestations, Irving became

---

13. Thomas C. Oden, *John Wesley's Teachings*, vol. 2: *Christ and Salvation* (Grand Rapids, MI: Zondervan, 2012), 106.

convinced that a new Holy Ghost era had begun, much like that experienced on Pentecost Sunday in the book of Acts. For the authorities, it was too much, too soon, and Irving was removed from his church and accused of "losing mental balance." In response he started his own congregation, The Catholic Apostolic Church.[14]

A third precursor to the modern Pentecostal movement was a series of revivals known as Keswick conventions that have flourished in England and British territories since their beginning in 1875. Keswick is the town in northwest England that hosted the first of these meetings, but related gatherings were exported all over the British world during the heyday of its empire. Aimed at deepening Christian faith, Keswick conferences still happen around the world. During British colonialism the Keswick "higher life" conventions served as a convenient infrastructure for renewalist Christians to network and exchange ideas on a global level. Since the sun never set on the British Empire, new ideas could travel quickly within the evangelical community, and many of them connected through Keswick revivals. Keswick participants often spoke of these conventions providing them with a "second blessing," a kind of fresh beginning in the life of a believer wherein a person felt empowered by the Holy Spirit to live a life nearly, or even fully, devoid of sin. Sometimes this process of eradicating sin was labeled *entire sanctification.* Some of the greatest evangelicals in late nineteenth and twentieth century Christianity were leaders in, or were touched by, the Keswick movement, such as

- Hannah Whitall Smith (1832–1911), a women's rights activist, temperance movement leader, and bestselling author.

- Dwight L. Moody (1837–1899), one of the great preachers of his

14. Vinson Synan, *The Holiness-Pentecostal Tradition: Charismatic Movements in the Twentieth Century* (Grand Rapids, MI: Eerdmans, 1997), 87.

era and founder of Moody Bible Institute. He claimed that when he was baptized with the Holy Spirit he "dropped to the floor and lay bathing his soul in the divine," while his room was "ablaze with God."[15]

- Hudson Taylor (1832–1905), founder of the China Inland Mission.

- Amy Carmichael (1867–1951), author and missionary to India.

- A. B. Simpson (1843–1919), founder of the Christian and Missionary Alliance denomination.

- R. A. Torrey (1856–1928), educator, global evangelical pastor, and author.

- John Stott (1921–2011), Anglican evangelical and one of the most prolific church leaders of the late twentieth century.

Perhaps the most famous Christian to be influenced by the Keswick movement was Billy Graham (born 1918). In 1975, Graham spoke at the hundred-year Keswick anniversary. In his lecture he outlined the six ways that Keswick had, rightly, emphasized the following:

1. Any Christian can live a life of victory in Christ.
2. The life of a Christian is a "Spirit-filled life," indeed, "it is a great sin not to be filled with the Spirit."
3. The Christian should practice "full surrender" to Jesus.
4. Keswick Christianity practices "biblical unity," uniting Christians of "peculiar distinctives."
5. The central role of prayer in the life of a Christian.
6. "Scriptural holiness," based on the Bible's understanding of morality.

15. Synan, Century of the Holy Spirit, 30.

At the end of his speech Graham concluded, "The world is experiencing a crisis of the Spirit." He asked his audience, "Will Keswick lift its eyes to behold the rising tide of unbelief? The disarray of nations? The decline of great cultures? The threat of anti-Christian ideologies and a rampant denial of Christian values? . . . The tide seems to be going out, the sun seems to be setting. The night seems to be falling." Graham then exhorted his listeners, "We are bound, every one of us who names the name of Christ, to be holy, to be separated from evil, to walk by the Spirit."[16]

Azusa

Charles Fox Parham (1873–1929) was a sickly child but believed God had healed him. He started studying to be a Methodist pastor but then went into medicine. That did not work out so he decided to be an independent itinerant evangelist and faith healer. Parham established Bible schools in Topeka, Kansas and Houston, Texas. It was in Topeka on the night of December 31, 1900—the turn of the century—that one of Parham's students, Agnes Ozman, spoke in Chinese after he laid hands on her and prayed. She had never taken Chinese language classes. Other students began to speak in Swedish, Russian, Bulgarian, Japanese, Italian, and more.[17] These claims would be disputed for years to come, but they are seen by modern Pentecostals as a point of departure for the amazing events that followed, including Azusa—quite possibly the greatest revival in all of Christian history.

In 1906 an African-American preacher named William Joseph Seymour (1870–1922) made history when the Azusa Street revival

---

16. Billy Graham's 1975 sermon at the hundred-year anniversary of the Keswick conventions can be heard at the website for the Billy Graham Evangelistic Association, located at http://billygraham.org/audio/keswicks-one-hundredth-birthday/.
17. Synan, *Century of the Holy Spirit*, 44.

broke out during his ministry in Los Angeles. Seymour was from Louisiana and was the son of slaves. He had worked as a porter for the railroad and waited tables before contracting smallpox, blinding his left eye. Seymour had been trained by Parham (who was white) in 1905–1906 when they were both in Houston. These were segregation days so most of Seymour's education came by listening through a crack in the door instead of sitting as a full participant in the classroom. Seymour learned much, however, and in 1906 received an invitation from a female Baptist pastor in Los Angeles, Sister Julia Hutchins, to come and preach. Parham bestowed ministry credentials onto Seymour and pledged financial support for him, and Seymour was off to Los Angeles.

Things did not begin well for Seymour when he arrived to California. Sister Hutchins was appalled by his teaching that the evidence for baptism in the Holy Spirit was actually tongue speaking. She and her members thought they had already received baptism in the Holy Spirit. They had not spoken in tongues, however. Hutchins locked Seymour out of the church and he began ministering to a small group in a friend's house.

On April 9, 1906, Seymour was praying with an Irish American man named Owen Lee at the home of Richard and Ruth Asberry, located on 214 North Bonnie Brae Street. Suddenly Mr. Lee started speaking in tongues. Oddly, Seymour himself had never experienced glossolalia, but upon witnessing the event, he and seven others "fell to the floor in a religious ecstasy, speaking with other tongues."[18] People started coming from the neighborhood, praising God and speaking in tongues. Jennie Moore, the woman who became William Seymour's wife, began playing the piano and singing in Hebrew. She had never played the piano and had never studied Hebrew. According to reports, miraculous occurrences were plentiful. They met twenty-

18. Ibid., 49.

four hours a day for three days straight. So many people crowded into the four-room house that the foundation collapsed, although nobody was injured. The Azusa Street Revival had begun.

Those involved with these historic events went looking for a safer place to hold their revival. They found an abandoned two-story building on Azusa Street that was once used by the Stevens African Methodist Episcopal (AME) Church. Prior to attracting Seymour's interest, it had been used as a lumberyard, stockyard, and tombstone shop. It was located "in the old downtown industrial district, which was a part of the original African-American ghetto area."[19] Seymour and several others slept upstairs and they used the bottom floor for the church services that ran from 10:00 a.m. until midnight every day. They named their new church the Apostolic Faith Mission.

Word about the revival spread like wildfire. Reporters from the *Los Angeles Daily Times* wrote articles that were harshly critical. The paper's headline on April 18, 1906 brought widespread attention to the revival:

> Weird Babel of Tongues; New Sect of Fanatics Is Breaking Loose; Wild Scene Last Night on Azusa Street; Gurgle of Wordless Talk by a Sister.[20]

The reporter was aghast by what he saw:

> Meetings are held in a tumble-down shack . . . the most fanatical rites . . . [they] work themselves into a state of mad excitement in their peculiar zeal. Colored people and a sprinkling of whites . . . night is made hideous in the neighborhood by the howlings of the worshippers, who spend hours swaying forth and back. . . . They claim to have the "gift of tongues" and to be able to understand the babel.[21]

19. Ibid., 50.
20. *Los Angeles Daily Times*, April 18, 1906.
21. Synan, *Century of the Holy Spirit*, 52.

The very next day, the famous San Francisco earthquake hit, killing three thousand people and virtually destroying the city. The participants believed the earthquake and the unleashing of the Holy Spirit was evidence of the end times. After all, Jesus had said the signs of the end of the age would include earthquake and famine and persecution.[22]

Reporters were not the only ones to have grave misgivings about the revival. The fire department came out on several occasions. The Child Welfare Agency spoke out against the revival due to children running around without parental supervision. The Health Department protested the unsanitary conditions. Local churches became resentful, largely because they were losing members to Seymour. Some even denounced the revival as being from the devil. One preacher called it "the last vomit of Satan."[23] A damning book was published called *Demons and Tongues*.[24]

The Azusa Street Revival was ahead of its time in many ways. Seymour was a public relations genius: he distributed a paper entitled *Apostolic Faith* free of charge to some fifty thousand subscribers. Like it does in today's social media, word spread far and wide, causing a sensation in the Wesleyan and Holiness churches across America and the world. People came to Azusa as pilgrims, wanting to catch the fire and return to their home congregations rejuvenated. Many missionaries resulted from the revival, taking the Pentecostal message to Brazil, South Africa, and cities all across the Western world. Azusa Street in Los Angeles became a missions hub, serving as a base for global Pentecostalism in its early days.

---

22. See Mark 13.
23. Synan, *Century of the Holy Spirit*, 54.
24. Alma White, *Demons and Tongues* (Bound Brook, NJ: The Pentecostal Union, 1910). White was a well-known racist and was heavily involved with the Ku Klux Klan. This would explain her outright opposition to the revival, which was largely African-American.

The Azusa Street Revival also featured a high degree of female leadership, evinced by pictures showing women leaders.[25] The major role played by women pastors in the early Pentecostal movement is clear. For instance Jennie, William Seymour's wife, took over pastoral responsibilities whenever he would go on long preaching tours, and she took charge after he died. The greatest Pentecostal preacher of the first half of the twentieth century was Aimee Semple McPherson, founder of the Foursquare denomination that spans the globe with its sixty-six thousand churches.[26] She too was based in Los Angeles, taking the Pentecostal movement to new heights through her extremely popular radio ministry. The enormous, magnificent church built for her, Angelus Temple, is a lasting tribute to McPherson's life and work.[27]

Another key area where the revival was ahead of its time was in its racial mixing, something considered taboo in America in 1906. An *L.A. Times* article shows that months after the revival began, local reporters were still ranting against it, describing what they thought to be "disgusting scenes":

> Muttering a jargon of unintelligible sounds which no man can interpret, the worshipers in the barn-like negro church on Azusa street worked themselves into paroxysms of religious fervor last night. . . . Men and women embraced each other in an apparent agony of emotion. Whites and negroes clasped hands and sang together. The surprise is that any respectable white person would attend such meetings as are being conducted on Azusa street.[28]

One observer to the revival wrote, "The color line was washed away in the blood."[29]

25. Synan, *Century of the Holy Spirit*, 54.
26. For statistics on the Foursquare Church see their website: http://www.foursquare.org/about/history.
27. See Matthew Avery Sutton, *Aimee Semple McPherson and the Resurrection of Christian America* (Cambridge, MA: Harvard University Press, 2007).
28. Street, *Moved By the Spirit*, 11. The article is from September 3, 1906.

What is so ironic about the opposition to the Azusa Street Revival is that it is precisely what made that first Christian Pentecost in the book of Acts so unforgettable. Not only were Jews welcomed into the kingdom of God, it was for all people: Parthians, Medes, Asians, Egyptians, Libyans, visitors from Rome, Cretans and Arabs, and so on. This was the "good news" that the early Christians had to offer. God was reaching out to *all* tribes and nations, regardless of race. But it is a message that seems difficult for people in all epochs to digest. Even the apostles themselves struggled to make sense of it. Alas, the early Pentecostal movement also succumbed to racial distrust, and the American Pentecostal movement effectively split along racial lines: the largely black Church of God in Christ, and the largely white Assemblies of God.

For those who came to Azusa in those early years, however, race was irrelevant. The miracles, power, and love was palpable and at times overwhelming. There was no hymn book or order of worship. It was all spontaneous: a cappella singing, personal testimonies, confessions of sin, and recommitments to Christ. Seymour sat behind a pulpit made of two shoeboxes and prayed quietly most of the time. When he did preach it was not spectacular; rather, he focused on Jesus, healing, the Holy Spirit, and righteous living.

What made the revival so powerful was what happened to people once inside. Skeptics turned into believers when they experienced the Holy Ghost power radiating out of that little church on Azusa Street. One foreign-born reporter was sent to write an article that mocked the "circuslike" atmosphere of the revival. However, after witnessing an untrained woman speak in his native language, "the reporter renounced his sins and accepted Jesus as his personal Savior. After this, the young man returned to his newspaper and told them he

---

29. Synan, *Century of the Holy Spirit*, 54.

could not write the false, ridiculing piece they sent him to produce. The reporter then offered to write a truthful story of what had happened to him at the mission. His employers fired him on the spot."[30]

Holy Ghost Goes Global

Who could have predicted that a small group of domestic servants and washers, led by a half-blind, rejected preacher in the black ghetto of Los Angeles would alter the course of world Christianity? But it happened. People came from far and wide to catch the Azusa fire, and they carried it to Asia, Africa, Latin America, Eastern Europe, Western Europe, Scandinavia, the Pacific, and to the ends of the earth. Some of these missionaries met great success, such as John Graham Lake, who took the message to South Africa, encountering very fertile soil. Several denominations were influenced by Lake's work, including the important Zion Christian Church—famous for holding what may be the largest annual Christian gathering in the world. Each Easter millions of their members gather at Zion City Moria, in South Africa. Ogbu Kalu writes of the "direct links between Azusa Street and Zionism through the Apostolic Faith Mission," a ministry Lake helped to establish in 1908.[31]

William Durham was another Azusa pilgrim who played a major role in the expansion of Pentecostal teaching. After his Azusa experience he returned to Chicago and ignited a missionary movement that resulted in numerous church plants in various parts of the world, especially in Latin America. Two Chicago-based Swedes—Daniel Berg and Adolf Gunnar Vingren—took the Pentecostal message to Brazil and established the Brazilian Assemblies of God, the largest Protestant movement in that nation. Historian

---

30. Ibid., 61.
31. Ogbu Kalu, *African Pentecostalism: An Introduction* (Oxford: Oxford University Press, 2008), 75.

Gary McGee writes, "By far the most spectacular growth of Pentecostalism anywhere in the world has been in Brazil."[32]

Other Azusa-inspired missionaries "returned home heartbroken" when they realized they had not trained properly and were unable to speak the language miraculously, as they had expected.[33] Nevertheless, it is truly amazing what has happened since the outbreak of modern Pentecostalism. From humble origins in a small African-American church in downtown Los Angeles in 1906, the Pentecostal movement is now mainstream.[34] Holy Spirit movements have been unleashed all over the world, and Pentecostal Christians are at the vanguard of the changes in world Christianity. Some of these changes have perplexed Christians in the Western world, such as the number of missionaries now working in North America and Europe. For example, the Nigerian-based Redeemed Christian Church of God has been covered by National Public Radio and the *New York Times* for their eight hundred church plants in the United States alone![35]

32. Gary McGee, "To the Regions Beyond: The Global Expansion of Pentecostalism," chapter 4 in Synan, *Century of the Holy Spirit*, 93.

33. See McGee, "To the Regions Beyond," 81.

34. I should make note of Allan Anderson's important thesis that the modern Pentecostal movement is best understood as having "polynucleated origins." See Anderson, "The Emergence of a Multidimensional Global Missionary Movement: Trends, Patterns, and Expressions," in *Spirit and Power: The Growth and Global Impact of Pentecostalism*, ed. Donald Miller, Kimon Sargeant, and Richard Flory (Oxford: Oxford University Press, 2013), 25. Anderson argues that historians have overemphasized Azusa Street and its consequences. While I agree with his polycentric thesis in principle, it is rather difficult to overstate the importance of the Azusa Street Revival's impact on modern, global Pentecostal movements. Anderson critiques the common assumption that Pentecostalism is a "made-in-the-USA product that has been exported to the rest of the world" (38). He wants historians to emphasize a "history from below" (37), a historiographical move that is well justified. However, it seems the William Seymour-led Azusa Street Revival is precisely what he is calling for—history "from below."

35. See John Burnett, "Nigerian Church Spreads African-Style Zeal across North America," *NPR*, May 18, 2014, located at http://www.npr.org/2014/05/18/313612376/nigerian-church-spreads-african-style-zeal-across-north-america?ft=1&f=1001. See also Andrew Rice, "Mission From Africa," *New York Times*, April 8, 2009, located at http://www.nytimes.com/2009/04/12/magazine/12churches-t.html?pagewanted=all&_r=0.

I have witnessed this religious fervor myself. For several months in 2005 I worshiped at a Pentecostal church in Pune, India, and learned how Dalit (outcaste) Christians are empowered when the Holy Spirit's leveling work is taken seriously.[36] All people—even the most rejected and crushed—become equals in the eyes of a God who honors neither Jew nor Greek, slave nor free, male nor female. One's baptism promises dignity, freedom, and equality. It is baptism that puts a person into covenant with other church members. The Pentecostal message contrasts acutely with the hierarchical caste system that has plagued the Indian subcontinent for millennia. While there are still many problems to be overcome regarding casteism in India, even among Christians, there is certainly hope as more and more people realize the implications of that first Christian Pentecost in the second chapter of Acts.

In Brazil in 2006 I entered a Universal Church of the Kingdom of God on a Tuesday night and witnessed hundreds of people worshiping the Lord midweek, with great passion and exuberance. This highly influential denomination has been around only since 1977 and it already has millions of members. It became a powerful political force in Brazil in the 1990s through its radio and television stations. "By the 2000s it had hundreds of foreign missionaries, including dozens in the United States," although their most successful mission work has been in Portugal and sub-Saharan Africa. Paul Freston writes, "It is possible that no Christian denomination founded in the Third World has ever been exported so successfully and so rapidly." Today, about a quarter of Brazilians are Protestant, and most of the nation's Protestants are Pentecostal. Brazil is now being called "a new center of Christianity."[37]

36. A member of that church is Indian historian V. V. Thomas. See his book *Dalit Pentecostalism: Spirituality of the Empowered Poor* (Bangalore: Asian Trading Corporation, 2008).
37. Todd Hartch, *The Rebirth of Latin American Christianity* (Oxford: Oxford University Press, 2014), 103 and 189–90. The Freston quotation is on 190. See also "Brazil's Changing Religious

In 2012 I witnessed an unforgettable worship service led by Claudio Freidzon in Buenos Aires, Argentina, at his impressive Rey de Reyes (King of Kings) church.[38] He is one of the most charismatic and powerful preachers I have ever witnessed. He walks down the aisles of his church, an entourage of men behind him, laying his hands on people as their knees buckle. His men are there to catch them when they get overwhelmed and fall. As he preaches, the people get more and more excited. The music builds up to a climax, people cry out "Hallelujah," and Freidzon excitedly points to a section of the congregation and they all fall back as one—as if he literally has power in his fingertips. Shouting into the microphone he commands evil spirits to depart from the teenagers who have lined up for healing.

In recent years I have hosted a family in my home while they visit friends in southern California, where I live. They are international missionaries, having served for years in South Korea and currently in Indonesia. They are also Pentecostal. One night we were visiting with them on the living room couch when my wife mentioned a health problem. They immediately stopped the conversation and asked, "Can we pray for that health problem right now because we believe God will heal you." We were not used to this. But we complied, bowed our heads, and listened attentively as they rebuked the illness and the evil powers associated with it, and then gave thanks for the healing that was being granted due to prayer. Whether or not healing immediately occurred, it was encouraging to have someone show such concern for my wife's welfare. It was also impressive to see

Landscape," PewResearch, 18 July 2013, located at http://www.pewforum.org/2013/07/18/brazils-changing-religious-landscape/.

38. For a good discussion on Freidzon, see Matthew Marostica, "Learning from the Master: Carlos Annacondia and the Standardization of Pentecostal Practices in and beyond Argentina," chapter 10 in *Global Pentecostal and Charismatic Healing*, ed. Candy Gunther Brown (Oxford: Oxford University Press, 2011).

such conviction. They were quite sure that healing was happening, and that she would notice her health improve in the very near future.

And the examples could continue. Benny Hinn, Reinhard Bonnke, Yonggi Cho, Sunday Adelaja, Joel Osteen, T. D. Jakes, and Joyce Meyer are among the most prolific of the charismatic/Pentecostal pastors living today, as they fly around the world holding revivals in huge stadiums, preaching a message that is often demonized as "health and wealth" or "prosperity gospel." For better or for worse, they are making a huge impact on the world of Christianity. They write books that are devoured by millions, they pack arenas in a way only rock stars can accomplish today, and they offer the promises of God to those who will trust in Christ. Some of the churches are huge.

- Pastor Yonggi Cho's church in Seoul, South Korea, is the largest in the world, with somewhere around a million members. When I visited in 2013 I was astounded at the operation: many languages and translators, orchestra, choir, and an extremely savvy public relations department that answered all of our questions.

- Joel Osteen's Lakewood Church in Houston has been called the largest congregation in the United States. Osteen fills professional sports venues when he goes on speaking tours, and his congregation bought the former arena of the Houston Rockets for their church services.

- T. D. Jakes inspires Christians to come out of poverty through the power of Jesus. His Potter's House in Dallas has a dazzling array of ministries that reach out to unwed mothers, those with substance abuse problems, people with AIDS, the abused, the homeless, and those recently released from prison. For all of the criticism of prosperity preachers, it certainly appears that they are offering solutions to people, equipping them to succeed in the world and, yes, have a little prosperity rather than a life of despair and defeat.[39]

- German evangelist Reinhard Bonnke is perhaps the preacher with the largest audiences in the world today, and that is because he focuses on the Global South, where Christianity is vibrant and wildly popular. Virtually unknown in the United States, his sights are set on the continent of Africa, where his nearly six decades of crusades have resulted in 72 million people converting to Christianity. One of his meetings was attended by 1.6 million people. Historian Vinson Synan regards Bonnke as "the greatest evangelist of all time, even greater than Billy Graham as far as numbers of converts."[40] Bonnke's ministry, Christ for All Nations, operates from an explicitly Pentecostal worldview. He has been associated with several resurrections, one in Nigeria which attracted great interest in the Western world due to its being so well documented. The man had been dead for three days in the mortuary when his wife took the body to a Bonnke event, thinking he could be revived. A film was made about the resurrection and has, according to Bonnke, led thousands of people to Christ.[41]

- One notable aspect of Pentecostal Christianity is how women are empowered to preach and lead. Since the early days of Pentecostalism, women played an important role, as in the cases of Jennie Seymour and Aimee Semple McPherson. That trend continues today, probably most visibly in the global television

39. See the various ministries of Potter's House at http://www.thepottershouse.org/Local/Local-Ministries.aspx.
40. John Kennedy, "The Crusader," Christianity Today, October 22, 2013, at http://www.christianitytoday.com/ct/2013/november/crusader.html.
41. See "Reinhard Bonnke Tells of Nigerian Man Raised from the Dead," interview with Pat Robertson, on The 700 Club, http://www.cbn.com/700club/features/bonnke_raisedpastor.aspx.

and publishing ministry of Joyce Meyer. It is also striking how many Pentecostal pastors serve in tandem with their wives. It is a concept rather unique in Christianity. The wives are given an authority equal to their famous husbands, typically as "first ladies" of the church. As Christianity expands globally, it is striking how many Pentecostal women are enabled to thrive. For example, two important Korean Pentecostal women are Jashil Choi and Seen-Ok Ahn. Choi worked shoulder to shoulder with Yonggi Cho, her son-in-law, to expand the ministries at the above-mentioned Yoido church. Ahn pioneered Korea's largest Foursquare church and established a school in Daejon City that serves over eight thousand students.[42]

Conclusion: Why Pentecostalism?

Pentecostal Christianity's influence is large, growing, and will continue to expand in all likelihood. Even in the Western world, where Christianity is declining, Pentecostalism is faring better than most other religious movements. How do we explain the phenomenal growth? Why are people turning to Pentecostalism?

Many scholars are investigating this question. Donald Miller and his colleagues at the Center for Religion and Civic Culture at the University of Southern California have offered informed, rich responses. At the core of their analysis is this: Pentecostals are meeting needs. They are socially engaged. They see Jesus in the eyes of the street vendor. They establish nursery schools for abandoned children. They see dignity where others might see race and class. Many of them understand what it means to be hooked on heroin or caught in the web of prostitution because they have lived that life. To put it

---

42. See Julie Ma, "Asian Women and Pentecostal Ministry," in *Asian and Pentecostal: The Charismatic Face of Christianity in Asia*, ed. Allan Anderson and Edmond Tang (Oxford: Regnum, 2005), 137–39.

theologically, they see the *imago Dei*—the image of God—in others. They believe God speaks to people today through his Holy Spirit. They believe God can turn people around, saving them from the wages of their sins.[43]

Another reason Pentecostalism grows is because it understands the modern, existential crisis that today's youth go through. It has a unique ability to connect with them. Statistician David Barrett claimed Pentecostalism has more children under the age of eighteen than it has adults.[44] Pew Research found that Brazilian Pentecostals tend to be younger and more urbanized.[45]

In Harvey Cox's excellent analysis of Pentecostalism, he speculated that it has been so successful because it meets the needs of people with its raw, primal spirituality. It emphasizes *experience* whereas many religions emphasize the cerebral. Historically, humans have been religious, and Pentecostalism connects us with our seemingly built-in need for the supernatural. Religion is something deep within us, a primal impulse. Speaking in ecstatic tongues, healing, exorcising evil spirits, having visions and prophecy, fervent belief in miracles . . . Pentecostalism embraces these things. Religious experience is taken extremely seriously, rather than being dismissed or relegated.[46]

Another straightforward reason Pentecostalism seems to grow is because it is where the people are: in cities. Globally, people deal with rapid urbanization and swiftly changing economic realities. They cling to religion to help them cope with the sudden jolt of moving from the countryside to the city. Abandoning traditional village life, they look for work in metropolitan areas. Pentecostalism has proven extremely deft at assisting these people along their journey, bringing

---

43. See Donald Miller and Tetsunao Yamamori, *Global Pentecostalism: The New Face of Christian Social Engagement* (Berkeley: University of California Press, 2007), 223.
44. David Barrett, "The Worldwide Holy Spirit Renewal," in Synan, *Century of the Holy Spirit*, 383.
45. PewResearch, "Brazil's Changing Religious Landscape."
46. Cox, *Fire from Heaven*, 81.

them into a new family, helping them to make the transition. He writes, "The Pentecostal movement worldwide is principally an urban phenomenon, and not a rustic or 'hillbilly religion,' as some people still believe. It is proliferating most rapidly today in the gigantic megacities of the third world such as São Paolo, Seoul, and Lusaka."[47] This tactic was used by the early church when the faith was catching on in several urban centers such as Corinth, Ephesus, Antioch, and Rome.

A final question is this: Why are people so fascinated by Pentecostalism? In 2007 I did an interview with CNN on the topic of Pentecostalism. It was in the news because Sarah Palin was discovered to have a Pentecostal background. My interviewer, Randi Kaye, was surprised to learn that Pentecostalism is so mainstream now. She was very curious about this religious "sect" that Palin was involved with, but during the interview I repeatedly tried to stress that Pentecostalism is not a sect anymore. The largest church in America is Pentecostal, and many of the largest churches in the world are Pentecostal.

The Pentecostal movement is impacting even the Roman Catholic Church in profound ways. John Allen Jr. writes,

Catholicism's version of the Pentecostal explosion is the Catholic Charismatic Renewal, the roots of which in North American date to a 1967 retreat at Duquesne University in Pittsburgh, when a group of Catholic professors and students say they experienced baptism in the Spirit. Like Pentecostalism, the Catholic Charismatic movement has become especially pervasive in the global South.[48]

Pentecostalism is impacting world Christianity, world religion, societies, and politics. Scores of public figures were at one time, or still are, associated with it such as John Ashcroft, Denzel Washington,

---

47. Ibid. 15.
48. John Allen Jr., *The Future Church* (New York: Doubleday, 2009), 384.

the Jonas Brothers, Elvis Presley, Jerry Lee Lewis, Katy Perry, and many others. This is not a little sect hidden somewhere. This is a movement that is larger than people realize. And as Christianity continues its move to the Global South, we will see Pentecostalism receive even more attention in the future.

To whom does Christianity belong? It certainly belongs to Pentecostals, particularly if we ask, "To whom does the *future* of Christianity belong?" And for those Christians who might still be cautious of the perceived extreme and zealous reputation of the movement, the words of Jesus in Mark chapter 9 are fitting: "Whoever is not against us is for us." Indeed, in that passage, Jesus was speaking to the apostle John about an exorcist who was driving out demons in the name of Jesus. While many Christians have all but ceased doing exorcisms, Pentecostal Christians believe strongly in this New Testament practice and in its continuing relevance in the twenty-first century. Indeed, Pentecostalism challenges us to envision Christianity's future by re-discovering its ancient past.

6

Afterlife

1 Thessalonians 4:16–17

For the Lord himself will come down from heaven, with a loud command, with the voice of the archangel and with the trumpet call of God, and the dead in Christ will rise first. After that, we who are still alive and are left will be caught up together with them in the clouds to meet the Lord in the air. And so we will be with the Lord forever.

John Lennon's megahit "Imagine" is truly one of the most iconic songs today. The Beatles superstar's 1971 utopian ballad topped charts all over the Western world and continues to impact new generations today. For several years running, "Imagine" has been played—almost like a religious ritual—when the New Year's Eve ball drops on Times Square in the Big Apple, further cementing its status as one of America's most important hymns. As the previous year ends and as a new one begins, we are softly and eloquently reminded to imagine a world without religion, without heaven, without hell. The song's evangelistic fervor is subdued by the piano as it gently beckons us all to join in so that the world will finally become one. *Rolling Stone* magazine lists it as the third greatest song of all time, behind only "I Can't Get No Satisfaction" by the Rolling Stones and "Like a Rolling Stone" by Bob Dylan.[1]

After visiting around 125 nations of the world, former US president Jimmy Carter made the following observation during an interview with National Public Radio: "You hear John Lennon's song 'Imagine' used almost equally with national anthems. So John Lennon has had a major impact on some of the countries that are developing in the world."[2] President Carter, well-known for his deep-seated Christianity, must have an ambivalent reaction to the song. On the one hand, he is a deeply pious Baptist, describing himself a "born again evangelical Christian."[3] Thus I wonder if he might squirm a bit when he sees millions of people, hands raised, spurning religion, singing about a godless existence devoid of afterlife. On the other hand, President Carter's career shows a man deeply committed to Lennon's vision of a world without hunger, without killing, a world where people are at peace with one another. For many years Carter has steered his decidedly Christian worldview toward initiatives such as Habitat for Humanity, racial reconciliation, free and fair elections, and global disease prevention. He received the 2002 Nobel Peace Prize for these works. Thus it is something of an oddity that while Lennon linked religion with violence, and peace with irreligion, Carter has spent much of his career utilizing religion to quell violence, to bring peace, to heal, and to feed the hungry.

---

1. See Rolling Stone, "500 Greatest Songs of All Time," located at http://www.rollingstone.com/music/lists/the-500-greatest-songs-of-all-time-20110407/john-lennon-imagine-20110516.
2. Debbie Elliott, "Carter Helps Monitor Nicaragua Presidential Election," *NPR*, November 5, 2006, located at http://www.npr.org/templates/story/story.php?storyId=6439233.
3. Jimmy Carter, *Our Endangered Values: America's Moral Crisis* (New York: Simon & Schuster, 2005), 6.

Imagining Afterlife

Perhaps no other concept has stirred the Christian imagination for two thousand years than the afterlife. Still today pop culture is saturated with imaginings of what happens after we die. Dan Brown's book *Inferno*—the bestselling book of 2013—hooked many readers with its focus on Botticelli's "Map of Hell" and Dante's vision of the hereafter for the less fortunate.[4] The *Left Behind* series, rooted in a dispensationalist understanding of the end times, dominated the publishing world from 1995 to 2007 and spawned movies and countless other products. Its publisher, Tyndale House, claims to have sold 63 million copies.[5] The series takes 1 Thess. 4:17—the verse atop this chapter—extremely seriously. This Bible passage undergirds a concept known to many Christians as "the Rapture," when some people leave earth to "meet the Lord in the air" while others get "left behind." A list of songs, movies, and books that deal with heaven or hell would be a long list indeed. The book *Heaven Is for Real* was a runaway bestseller and a smash hit in movie theaters. It is one of many books detailing what happened to individuals who died and were revived.[6] *Flight to Heaven, Embraced by the Light, My Journey to Heaven, Saved by the Light: The True Story of a Man Who Died Twice, To Heaven and Back, Proof of Heaven: A Neurosurgeon's Journey into the Afterlife* are but a few in this genre.

---

4. See Bob Minzesheimer and Christopher Schnaars, "Dan Brown's 'Inferno' Tops All Book Sales in 2013," *USA Today*, January 16, 2014, located at http://www.usatoday.com/story/life/books/2014/01/15/usa-today-best-selling-books-of-2013/4451561/.
5. The series is now available in twelve languages, "with another 16 languages either newly released or in preparation." See Tyndale House's *Left Behind* website: http://www.leftbehind.com/05_news/viewNews.asp?pageid=542&channelID=17. The authors of the book series are Tim LaHaye and Jerry Jenkins.
6. Medical doctor Raymond Moody played a key role in the rise of the "near-death experience" with his widely read book *Life after Life* (New York: Bantam, 1975), which examined numerous cases of people who were revived and shared their experiences.

Whether these so-called near-death experiences are ornate imaginings or good faith descriptions of what happened after a temporary death probably depends more upon the reader's decision to believe than anything else. However, these popular accounts tap into a deep reservoir of faith, prompting people to offer them a fair hearing. Obviously, Christians have believed in life after death since the very beginning of the faith, when Jesus died and rose again. It was a fundamental conviction of early Christians, though evidently not without a few detractors. The apostle Paul captured the mainstream Christian view succinctly in 1 Corinthians 15:

> For if the dead are not raised, then Christ has not been raised either. And if Christ has not been raised, your faith is futile . . . If only for this life we have hope in Christ, we are of all people most to be pitied. (vs. 16–17, 19)

It is clear that Paul's argument is directed toward Christians who may have doubted the idea of a future resurrection. Thus, while church tradition upholds a belief in the afterlife, there have always been—then as now—Christians who doubt.

It is no surprise that the afterlife is one of the most unsettled areas of Christian theology today. There are many questions, especially in light of modern science. For example, what happens to those who were born and died outside of the Judeo-Christian narrative? Can they inherit salvation? What about our human prototypical ancestors? Will Cro-Magnons and Neanderthals and other earlier human-like creatures share in our salvific inheritance? And what about their ancestors? How far back in the evolutionary tree shall we go? Or is it possible that "salvation" is a much broader concept that applies to many species, perhaps even all organisms? Will the entire created order get redeemed by God at the end of time?

If we assume only humans inherit salvation, then other, perhaps even more vexing questions arise such as, What is a human? Is a zygote human? At what stage does an embryo become human? These questions are hotly debated today in conjunction with the abortion issue. It is intriguing to contemplate whether these early organisms inherit some form of afterlife; and it certainly impacts how one ponders the implications of terminated pregnancies, whether natural—as in a miscarriage—or humanly induced. Christian families that experience miscarriage cannot help but to wonder whether they will see their child in the hereafter. They can only imagine.

I should mention another famous song from recent years that encourages us to imagine. However, this one was written by the Christian band MercyMe when the lead singer, Bart Millard, lost his father to cancer. *I Can Only Imagine* is one of the most popular songs ever recorded in contemporary Christian music, and the first to go platinum in the digital era.[7] The song continues to resonate powerfully with Christians as it paints a picture of the afterlife: being in God's presence, surrounded by his majesty, dancing in front of Jesus, and singing "Hallelujah." Or perhaps, the song questions, we will be so overcome with God's glory that we simply fall to our knees, becoming speechless and still. We can only imagine what it will be like.

What Do Christians Think?

Bottom line, what do Christians believe about afterlife? This is an extremely complicated question to answer. This chapter will show

7. David Jenison, "A Severe Mercy," *Todays Christian Music*, 31 October 31, 2011, located at http://www.webcitation.org/62r6E7i5y. See also "Mercyme Makes History as I Can Only Imagine Surpasses 1 Million Downloads," *Christianity Today*, April 21, 2010, located at http://www.christiantoday.com/article/
mercyme.makes.history.as.i.can.only.imagine.surpasses.1.million.downloads/25752.htm (accessed 26 March 2015).

the breadth and complexity of Christian views, even within the three major forms of Christian faith today: Orthodox, Roman Catholic, and Protestant.

The world's major religions basically offer two umbrella responses to the question, "What happens after death?" South Asian traditions such as Hinduism, Buddhism, Jainism, and Sikhism offer various forms of reincarnation, while Abrahamic traditions (Judaism, Christianity, Islam) tend to believe humans get one chance to live in the flesh before the afterlife. While reincarnation (also known as metempsychosis, or transmigration of the soul) is not typically embraced by Christians, some do entertain the idea. For example in 2009 Pew Research found that 22 percent of American Christians believe in reincarnation.[8]

Many societies in antiquity held to some form of reincarnation: the Egyptians, Greeks, Indians, Manicheans, and even some Jews:

> The notion of soul-wandering is familiar to the Jewish Rabbis. They distinguish two kinds of transmigrations, (1) *Gilgul Neshameth*, in which the soul was tied down to a life-tenancy of a single body; (2) *Ibbur*, in which souls may inhabit bodies by temporary possession without passing through birth and death. Josephus tells us that transmigration was a doctrine of the Pharisees, who taught that the righteous should be allowed to return to life, while the wicked were to be doomed to eternal imprisonment. . . . On the other hand some of the Talmudists invoke endless transmigration as a penalty for crime.[9]

One important church father, Origen (lived 185–251), speculated about the preexistence and transmigration of the soul:[10]

---

8. See "Many Americans Mix Multiple Faiths," *Pew Research Religion & Public Life Project*, December 9, 2009, located at http://www.pewforum.org/2009/12/09/many-americans-mix-multiple-faiths/.

9. Michael Maher, "Metempsychosis," in *The Catholic Encyclopedia*, vol. 10 (New York: The Encyclopedia Press, 1913), 235–36.

10. See Robert J. Daly, "Origen," in *Encyclopedia of Early Christianity*, second ed. (New York: Routledge, 1999), 836.

St. Jerome tells us that metempsychosis was a secret doctrine of certain sectaries in his day, but it was too evidently opposed to the Catholic doctrine of Redemption ever to obtain a settled footing. It was held, however, in a Platonic form by the Gnostics, and was so taught by Origen in his great work *Peri archon*. Bodily existence, according to Origen, is a penal and unnatural condition, a punishment for sin committed in a previous state of bliss. . . . He does not seem to have considered it necessary to extend his theory to include lower forms of life. Punishment for sin done in the body is not vindictive or eternal, but temporary and remedial.[11]

Further, Origen speculated that God might in the end save all, a theory known as universal salvation. He based this idea on passages such as 1 Cor. 15:28, where Paul writes that in the end God will be "all in all." Origen reasoned that God's goodness and Christ's mediation on our behalf would eventually restore all people to salvation. However, he became angry when accused of extending salvation to the devil. Origen's complex thinking about the afterlife has confused many both during his life and since. One scholar writes that with Origen "we encounter an unfortunate amalgam of philosophy and theology. The system that results is not coherent."[12]

Early Christians were impacted to a large extent by what the Hebrews thought about afterlife. However, as we have seen, Jewish beliefs about afterlife could range widely during the time of Jesus. In Acts 23:8, Luke writes, rather frankly, "The Sadducees say that there is no resurrection, and that there are neither angels nor spirits, but the Pharisees believe all these things." Jesus clearly sided with the Pharisees here, and he would have been familiar with texts such as Isa. 26:19: "But your dead will live, Lord; their bodies will rise—let

11. Maher, "Metempsychosis," 236.
12. Ferdinand Prat, "Origen and Origenism," in *The Catholic Encyclopedia*, vol. 11 (New York: The Encyclopedia Press, 1913), 309. Prat writes that most of Origen's "dangerous" ideas are contained in the book *On First Principles* (*De principiis*). Prat writes that Origen's convictions are not readily apparent since he often discusses various positions "as an intellectual exercise or amusement" and not necessarily out of "real opinion." See 310.

those who dwell in the dust wake up and shout for joy . . . the earth will give birth to her dead." Dan. 12:2 would also have been known among Jewish teachers: "Multitudes who sleep in the dust of the earth will awake: some to everlasting life, others to shame and everlasting contempt." Ezekiel's dramatic "valley of dry bones" incident in 37:13–14 would have been familiar as well, as God gathers together the bones of the departed and wraps them with flesh, breathing life into them, saying, "Then you, my people, will know that I am the Lord, when I open your graves and bring you up from them. I will put my Spirit in you and you will live." Intertestamental Jewish texts such as the book of Enoch also teach a future resurrection:

> And in those days shall the earth also give back that which has been entrusted to it. And Sheol also shall give back that which it has received. And hell shall give back that which it owes. For in those days the Elect One shall rise. And he shall choose the righteous and holy from among them. For the day has drawn nigh that they should be saved. . . . And the earth shall rejoice. And the righteous shall dwell upon it. And the elect shall walk thereon.[13]

The writings of Paul exert tremendous influence on how Christians understand the afterlife today. He recognized that some doubted the resurrection and, like Jesus, he thought it important to correct this fallacy. Paul pointed out to his Corinthian readers that Jesus' resurrection was well attested. Many people saw the risen Lord, including "more than five hundred of the brothers and sisters at the same time, most of whom are still living" (1 Cor. 15:6). In a speech in Acts 22 Paul claimed that Jesus even appeared to him; the event changed Paul from an enemy of Christianity to a disciple.

---

13. See the book of Enoch chapter 51. I have used the edition translated by H.R. Charles (Oxford: Clarendon Press, 1917), located at http://www.sacred-texts.com/bib/boe/boe054.htm. It should be noted that the book of Enoch is canonical in the Ethiopian Orthodox and Eritrean Orthodox churches.

Paul teaches in 1 Corinthians 15 that those who "sleep" in Christ will inherit "imperishable" bodies when "the last trumpet" is sounded—ostensibly signifying a grand resurrection. Paul's statements are tantalizingly universalist, especially his idea that "For as in Adam all die, so in Christ all will be made alive" (v. 22). Christian philosopher Terence Penelhum writes that universalism "has never been more than a minority view, since it seems inconsistent with the fundamental thrust of Christian theology that each person is presented with a *choice* to accept or reject the route to salvation."[14]

Christians generally assume there will be a judgment day that will accompany the resurrection. The most explicit New Testament teaching here is by Jesus himself in Matthew 25, although it is not clear whether Jesus was describing a reality yet to come or was simply teaching about the kingdom of God by using this parable:

> When the Son of Man comes in his glory, and all the angels with him, he will sit on his glorious throne. All the nations will be gathered before him, and he will separate the people one from another as a shepherd separates the sheep from the goats, . . . Then the King will say to those on his right, "Come, you who are blessed by my Father; take your inheritance, the kingdom prepared for you since the creation of the world. For I was hungry and you gave me something to eat. . . ." Then he will say to those on his left, "Depart from me, you who are cursed, into the eternal fire prepared for the devil and his angels. For I was hungry and you gave me nothing to eat. . . . Then they will go away to eternal punishment, but the righteous to eternal life. (Matt 25:31–32, 34–35, 41–42, 46 niv-uk)

Jesus frequently spoke through word pictures, yet when it comes to specifics on "the end of the age," he argues that he is not privy to this information; only God knows: "But about that day or hour no one knows, not even the angels in heaven, nor the Son, but only the

---

14. Terence Penelhum, "Christianity," in *Life after Death in World Religions*, ed. Harold Coward (Maryknoll, NY: Orbis, 1997), 39. Italics his.

Father" (Matt. 24:36). Nonetheless, he provides lasting images of the end times that have made their way into the collective consciousness of Christians, particularly in the arts. Medieval Christians went to great lengths (and heights!) to depict the scene in all of its drama, perhaps most notably Michelangelo's "The Last Judgment" fresco in the Sistine Chapel. Christian art powerfully shapes the way Christians understand the end times, the judgment, and the resurrection. It is as if pictures can do more than words in capturing the essence of something so hallowed and vital, yet so elusive.

The New Testament provides rich images for the afterlife, but they can appear disconnected. We have no systematic treatment, rather, only scattered parables, ideas from Greek or Hebraic thinking, or even imagery borrowed from geography. For example, Jesus uses the word *Gehenna* several times in the Synoptic Gospels to refer to a place where sinners will go to be punished for their sins.[15] In English Bibles that word is typically translated into "hell." Gehenna was a place just outside Jerusalem. In Old Testament times it was associated with child sacrifice. In the intertestamental period it "came to represent the eschatological place of judgment or hell itself."[16] However, by New Testament times "it was the rubbish heap outside the southwest corner of the old city of Jerusalem. There is to this day a valley at that point that bears the name Ge Hinnom."[17]

Case Study: Orthodoxy and Afterlife

Several basic questions arise here about the Christian understanding of the afterlife:[18]

---

15. Matt. 5:22–30; Matt. 23:15, 33; Mark 9:43–47; Luke 12:5.
16. Gary Lee, "Gehenna," in *International Standard Bible Encyclopedia*, revised ed. (Grand Rapids, MI: Eerdmans, 1982), 423.
17. N. T. Wright, *Surprised by Hope* (New York: HarperOne, 2008), 175.
18. For these questions I have used Farnaz Masumian, *Life after Death* (Oxford: Oneworld, 1995), chapter 5, "Christianity."

- Are heaven and hell physical or celestial places?

- What will resurrect? The body, the soul, or both? If both, then do they arise at the same time or at different times?

- Are the descriptions of heaven and hell literal or symbolic? Is hell on fire or does the fire simply point to discomfort or destruction?

- Should Christians expect one judgment or two? Are people judged when they die—an individual judgment? Or are they judged with everyone else at a future time—a universal judgment? Or perhaps both? Presumably, an initial individual judgment would relegate the second judgment to a formality unless one could impact one's eternal destiny in the interim.[19] In other words, is there a state after death wherein one may improve his or her chances for the universal judgment?

These questions are answered variously in the Christian traditions. Let us take a look at what the oldest Christian theological tradition, Eastern Orthodoxy, has to say about afterlife.

Orthodox Christians believe in "but two ultimate alternatives, heaven and hell."[20] However, when it comes to more specific issues—such as prayers for the dead and the state of the soul between death and resurrection—"Orthodox teaching is not entirely clear, and has varied somewhat at different times."[21] For example, the issue of purgatory has been both embraced and rejected by Orthodox Christians throughout history. "Today most if not all Orthodox theologians reject the idea of Purgatory."[22] However, in the fifteenth century, when the Byzantines were being pummeled by the

---

19. Penelhum, "Christianity," 40.
20. In this paragraph I draw from Timothy Ware, *The Orthodox Church* (London: Penguin, 1997), 261.
21. Ibid., 255.
22. Ibid.

Ottoman Turks, they showed themselves willing to capitulate on finer points of theology in order to preserve their civilization. "The only hope of defeating the Turks lay in help from the West."[23] Thus, at the Council of Florence in 1439, the seven hundred Orthodox delegates agreed in principle to the Roman Catholic teaching about purgatory.[24] However, their decision was rejected by the majority of people they represented. Indeed, "Many of those who signed at Florence revoked their signatures when they reached home."[25] Military aid from the West was anemic. As a result, just fourteen years later in 1453—the bitterest year for the Orthodox—the Byzantine Empire was no more. Mehmed II conquered Constantinople and the world's greatest church, the Hagia Sophia, was converted into a mosque.

A cornerstone of Orthodox teaching about afterlife is the *apocatastasis*, or "the redemption and the glorification of matter."[26] It is said the righteous will rise up and be united to a transfigured, spiritual body. All things will be made new. God will create a new earth, and "the whole material order will be transformed."[27]

Orthodox Christians have not reached a consensus about hell. They do believe we have free will, but we will not be reconciled to God until we choose him. God will not force us to love him. However—and this is where it gets complicated—some Orthodox Christians uphold that there will be *in the end* a final, universal salvation. Eventually, all humans will choose to reconcile with God. All will come to their senses and believe in God and choose to be with God. Noted Orthodox theologian Kallistos Ware writes that

---

23. Ibid., 70.
24. The Council of Florence has a complicated history since it lasted from 1431 to 1449 and was held in three cities: Basel, Ferrara, and Florence.
25. Ware, *The Orthodox Church*, 71.
26. Ibid., 261.
27. Ibid.

this is one reason Orthodox Christians pray for the dead. A person who reflects Christ's love, a person full of mercy and compassion, yearns for the entire created order to be redeemed. Indeed, he writes, "Gregory of Nyssa said that Christians may legitimately hope even for the redemption of the devil."[28]

One motif that occurs regularly in Orthodox thinking about the afterlife is Christ's descent into Hades for the purpose of conquering it. It is an idea stemming from 1 Pet. 3:19–20, "After being made alive, he went and made proclamation to the imprisoned spirits—to those who were disobedient long ago when God waited patiently in the days of Noah while the ark was being built." Protestants tend to reject the doctrine of the "harrowing of Hell," as it is known, on grounds it is unscriptural. However, Roman Catholics argue that while it did indeed happen, it was to save the righteous ones who lived during the Old Testament era.

Some Orthodox theologians undergird their notions of universal salvation precisely at this point. In his impressive work on this topic, Orthodox Archbishop Hilarion Alfeyev writes, "Having descended into Hades, Christ opened the way to salvation for all people, not only for the Old Testament righteous. The descent of Christ into Hades is perceived as an event of cosmic significance involving all people without exception. . . . After Christ's descent into Hades there was no one left there except for the devil and demons."[29] Hilarion argues that Christ's descending into hell is alluded to in several New Testament texts that routinely go overlooked: Jesus's parallel to Jonah being inside the whale for three days (Matt. 12:40), Peter's speech in Acts 2 where he states that God did not abandon Jesus to Hades, and Paul's notion that Jesus descended to the lower, earthly regions

28. Ibid., 262.
29. Archbishop Hilarion Alfeyev, *Christ the Conqueror of Hell: The Descent into Hades from an Orthodox Perspective* (Crestwood, NY: St. Vladimir's Seminary Press, 2009), 10.

(Eph. 4:9).[30] There are several other key biblical texts that support the idea, and many noncanonical Christian texts from the early church fathers to the present. The Apostles' Creed includes Christ's descent into Hades as an essential tenet of Christian orthodoxy.

Archbishop Hilarion concludes that while Christ's descent into Hades is not questioned by the tradition of the church, the interpretation is. Hilarion himself believes the descent into Hades is crucial for the Christian faith, "significant not only for human destiny but also for the destiny of all creation."[31] He aligns himself with John of Damascus (lived c. 675 to 749) who taught that those condemned to hell can in fact come to faith while in hell because

> existence after death has its own dynamics. According to the teaching of the Orthodox Church, the fate of a person after death can be changed through the prayer of the church. . . . After death the development of the human person does not cease, for existence after death is not a transfer from a dynamic into a static being, but rather a continuation on a new level of that road which a person followed in his or her lifetime.[32]

Perhaps Paul's concept of "baptism for the dead" in 1 Cor. 15:29 makes more sense if the development of the person continues after death. The Orthodox refer to this ongoing process as *theosis* or *deification*—the goal of human life and afterlife is to continually progress toward unity with God.

A final issue regarding Orthodox notions of afterlife has to do with the mysterious notion of the tollhouses, an extremely lively and debated topic in Orthodox theology today. While many Orthodox Christians subscribe to the idea, Protestants know virtually nothing about it. I must admit I knew almost nothing of the idea prior to working on this book. However, when I had discussions with

---

30. See Hilarion's fuller discussion in ibid., 17–20.
31. Ibid., 212.
32. Ibid., 215, 217.

Orthodox friends regarding the afterlife, this topic came up repeatedly. The two Orthodox thinkers I was advised to read were St. John the Wonderworker and Father Seraphim Rose. Both were from the Russian Orthodox Church Outside of Russia. St. John the Wonderworker lived from 1896 to 1966 and eventually became Archbishop of San Francisco.[33] Seraphim Rose lived from 1934 to 1982 and spent his life in California. Both were known to be men of great holiness.

The tollhouse theory is that as a person dies, he or she begins to see things that are unseen to physical eyes. Once the soul leaves the body it is wanders freely for two days. On the third day it begins to face wicked spirits who are located at a series of twenty stations. These are the tollhouses. Each station represents a particular sin. The soul has to pass through each tollhouse while being confronted by demons throughout. The journey lasts for thirty-seven days. Those living should pray for the deceased to help them make it through successfully. On the fortieth day, the soul is assigned a waiting place that can be joyful or fearful, depending on its progression in life and in the afterlife period of wandering. There it waits until bodily resurrection. Humans remaining on earth can change the outcome of that person's resting place through prayers, giving of alms,

---

33. For a biographical sketch of St. John the Wonderworker, see http://orthodox.cn/saints/ johnmaximovitch_en.htm. For a biography of Seraphim Rose, see Hieromonk Damascene, *Father Seraphim Rose: His Life and Works*, third ed. (Platina, CA: St. Herman Press, 2010). My main source of information on tollhouses comes from Father Josiah Trenham, pastor of St. Andrew Orthodox Church in Riverside, California. He sent me a sermon from St. John of San Francisco entitled "I Believe in the Resurrection of the Dead" (no bibliographical data was included) that was helpful indeed. I also referred to "Life after Death: A Homily by St. John the Wonderworker, with Comments by Fr. John Mack," located at http://orthodoxinfo.com/death/ lifeafterdeath.aspx. It contains virtually the same information sent to me from Father Josiah, but with extensive comment. See a vigorous rebuttal from Fr. Michael Azkoul, "The Toll-House Myth: The Neo-Gnosticism of Fr. Seraphim Rose," located at http://www.scribd.com/ doc/252583959/Fr-Michael-Azkoul-The-Toll-House-Myth-The-Neo-Gnosicism-of-Fr-Seraphim-Rose#scribd. See also Fr. Seraphim Rose, *The Soul after Death* (Platina, CA: St. Herman Press, 2009).

celebration of liturgies, and good deeds done in the name of the deceased.

Protestant Perspectives: N. T. Wright and Rob Bell

Conversations about the afterlife are very lively in Western Christianity right now due to several important publications. The two that stand out are N. T. Wright's *Surprised by Hope* and Rob Bell's *Love Wins*. N. T. Wright is a bishop in the Church of England and one of the most outstanding Protestant biblical scholars today. His writings are read by Christians all over the theological spectrum. His book on the afterlife caused a stir when he declared that Western Christians have gotten the afterlife all wrong, or, they never really understood it in the first place: "So far as I can tell, *most people simply don't know what orthodox Christian belief is*. . . . In particular, most people have little or no idea what the word *resurrection* actually means or why Christians say they believe it."[34] Wright dispels the notion that the early Christians were "locked into thinking of a three-decker universe with heaven up in the sky and hell down beneath their feet."[35] Rather, he argues that early Christians would have known that heaven and earth are not even two different places. They understood earth to be the eternal abode of Christians. Heaven is on earth. It is "God's space." It is closely related to our space, not some place far off into the sky. And when the Bible speaks of Jesus coming back, it means there is a time coming "when heaven and earth are joined together in the new way God has promised." We will then know God as he is, and we will know ourselves as we really are, in "our true identity."[36] Wright roots his interpretation in 1 John 2:28 and 3:2:

---

34. Wright, *Surprised by Hope*, 12, italics his.
35. Ibid., 115.
36. Ibid., 134–35.

Now, children, abide in him; so that, when he appears, we may have confidence and not be shrink from him in shame at his presence [*parousia*]. . . . Beloved, we are now God's children; and it has not yet appeared what we shall be; but we know that when he appears, we shall be like him, because we shall see him just as he is.[37]

Wright has a catchy expression for his view: "Life *after* life after death."[38] He claims that Christians are mistaken and misled when they think of resurrection as a synonym for life after death. Resurrection, rather, is what happens when Jesus reappears. People will literally resurrect, like Jesus did after being in the tomb for three days. What happens right at the moment of death is a completely different state. The resurrection comes later. It is the "life *after* life after death." Wright's conclusion is passionate:

There is almost nothing about "going to heaven when you die" in the whole New Testament. Being "citizens of heaven" doesn't mean you're supposed to end up there. . . . Jesus is risen, therefore God's new world has begun. Jesus is risen, therefore Israel and the world have been redeemed. Jesus is risen, therefore his followers have a new job to do. And what is that new job? To bring the life of heaven to birth in actual, physical, earthly reality. . . . Jesus's resurrection is the beginning of God's new project not to snatch people away from earth to heaven but to colonize earth with the life of heaven. That, after all, is what the Lord's Prayer is about.[39]

We are left with the question, "What does Bishop Wright think happens when we die?" First of all, like a good Protestant, he rejects purgatory.

Purgatory is basically a Roman Catholic doctrine. It is not held as such in the Eastern Orthodox Church, and it was decisively rejected . . . at the Reformation. The main statements on purgatory come from Aquinas in the thirteenth century and Dante in the early fourteenth, but the notion

37. Ibid., 135.
38. Ibid., 151, italics his. The discussion begins on 148.
39. Ibid., 293.

became woven deeply into the entire psyche of the whole period. Huge energy was expended . . . developing the picture of purgatory. . . . I do not believe in purgatory as a place, a time, or a state. It was in any case a late Western innovation, without biblical support.[40]

And in his strongest rejection of purgatory in the book, he writes,

The last great paragraph of Romans 8, so often and so appropriately read at funerals, leaves no room for purgatory in any form. . . . "Who shall separate us from the love of Christ? Neither death nor life nor anything in all creation. . . ." And if you still want to say that Paul really meant "though of course you'll probably have to go through purgatory first," I think with great respect that you ought to see not a theologian but a therapist.[41]

Wright then points out the concept of purgatory has been questioned in Roman Catholic circles in recent years, most notably by theologian Karl Rahner (1904–1984) and former Pope Benedict XVI, Joseph Ratzinger. Indeed, for Wright, "The revival of a quasi purgatory in our own day . . . is a strange return to mythology.[42]

So if there is no purgatory, then what happens during the period between our death and our bodily resurrection? Wright's answer is fairly simple: "All the Christian departed are in substantially the same state, that of restful happiness. . . . Though this is sometimes described as sleep, we shouldn't take this to mean that it is a state of unconsciousness. . . . There is no reason why this state should not be called heaven."[43] Wright speculates that in this "sleep" state the departed Christians will be with Christ until the bodily resurrection. They will also share in the "communion of saints."

Wright argues it is perfectly reasonable to pray for the dead, not in order to hasten some abstract purgatorial experience, but simply

40. Ibid., 166, 170.
41. Ibid., 170.
42. Ibid., 171.
43. Ibid., 171–72.

because Christians—who are all saints in the Protestant understanding—should pray for each other at all times, and for all manner of reasons. Wright rejects the notion that the faithful departed pray for us, the living. He also rejects the idea that the dead somehow intercede on the behalf of the living,

> We should be very suspicious of the medieval idea that the saints can function as friends at court. . . . The practice seems to me to call into question, and even actually to deny by implication, the immediacy of access to God through Jesus Christ and in the Spirit, which is promised again and again in the New Testament. In the New Testament it is clear: because of Christ and the Spirit, every single Christian is welcome at any time to come before the Father himself.[44]

Wright sees our open access to God as really the crucial blessing of being a follower of Christ. There is no reason to ask someone else to intercede for us. Christ's death opens up our access to the throne room. No need to wait around in the lobby!

When the issue of hell comes up, Wright is guarded. He claims neither Jesus nor the writers of the epistles say much about it, and Acts is completely silent about it. The book of Revelation is simply too difficult to interpret with any certainty. Thus, we must be very careful not to dogmatize these issues. Both universalists and traditionalists have been guilty of claiming more than scripture allows here.[45] In reality this topic is "one of the darkest theological mysteries."[46] Wright humbly admits, "The last thing I want is for anyone to suppose that I (or anyone else) know very much about all this. Nor do I want anyone to suppose I enjoy speculating in this manner."[47] Nevertheless, Wright caused a minor outrage in the blogosphere when he speculated that Americans are unique in their

44. Ibid., 173.
45. Ibid., 177.
46. Ibid., 183.
47. Ibid.

fixation on hell: "Perhaps I should say this. I wonder why American culture is so fixated on this. This is the most rich, well-off, powerful, elite culture the world has ever seen. Why is it that so many people in this culture which—this isn't so in my culture—really want there to be a hell?"[48] Wright argues that when humans dehumanize themselves by worshiping sex, power, or money, they cease to be human. They become like the things they worship. They enter an "ex-human state, no longer reflecting their maker in any meaningful sense."[49] The bishop realizes his view of hell is not traditional, but he insists that this "great mystery" is not what Christians should be fixating on.[50] Rather, he writes,

> The whole point of my argument so far is that the question of what happens to me after death is *not* the major, central, framing question that centuries of theological tradition have supposed. . . . The question ought to be, *How will God's new creation come?* And then, *How will we humans contribute to that renewal of creation and to the fresh projects that the creator God will launch in his new world?*[51]

Humans are thus faced with a choice: get involved in God's work on earth, or allow themselves to become depraved, sinking to the point of, literally, dehumanization.

The other book that caused a sensation in the West on the topic of afterlife was evangelical pastor Rob Bell's bestseller *Love Wins: A Book about Heaven, Hell, and the Fate of Every Person Who Ever Lived.* Bell's book was not so shocking in its content—it basically argues for universalism—but the fact that he was an evangelical is

---

48. See the interview with Wright at Calvin College entitled "Rethinking Life after Death (NT Wright)," published April 26, 2012, located at http://www.youtube.com/watch?v=rZC6tbgpsl4. His comments on hell begin around the nineteen-minute point in the interview. The quotation is around 20:30.
49. Wright, *Surprised by Hope*, 182–183.
50. "Rethinking Life after Death (NT Wright)." Wright acknowledges his view is not traditional at 20:12 in the interview.
51. Wright, *Surprised by Hope*, 185.

what made headlines. Historically, evangelicals argued the road to heaven is narrow. The liberals were the ones who opened up the gates for all, including people from other faiths. Rob Bell seemed to switch sides, however, from evangelical to liberal, when he went after this sacred cow. On page 1 of his book he provocatively questioned the evangelical view that those who are presented the gospel and do not accept it are condemned to hell. When someone at his church asserted that Gandhi was in hell, he took issue: "Really? Gandhi's in hell? He is? We have confirmation of this?"[52] And striking right to the core of evangelical theology, he made some assertions that many found offensive: "As obvious as it is, then, Jesus is bigger than any one religion. He didn't come to start a new religion, and he continually disrupted whatever conventions or systems or establishments that existed in his day. He will always transcend whatever cages and labels are created to contain and name him, especially the one called 'Christianity.'"[53] In a poetic mix of scripture and personal stories that tug at the heart strings, Bell argues that God is love, and hell is what some people experience in this life, not in the hereafter.

At the time Rob Bell wrote *Love Wins*, he was pastor of Mars Hill Bible Church, a megachurch he founded in Michigan in 1999. Shortly after publication of the book, he resigned in controversy over his orthodoxy.[54] The hullabaloo surrounding these incidents snowballed when important evangelical writers and pastors such as Francis Chan, Mark Galli, and John Piper began to speak out (and

---

52. Rob Bell, *Love Wins* (New York: HarperOne, 2011), 1.
53. Bell, *Love Wins*, 150.
54. Bell's departure has been covered extensively in Christian media. See, for example, Nicola Menzie, "Rob Bell's 'Love Wins' Nudged 1000 People to Leave Mars Hill Bible Church, Says Michigan Megachurch Successor," *The Christian Post*, November 19, 2013, located at http://www.christianpost.com/news/rob-bells-love-wins-nudged-1000-people-to-leave-mars-hill-bible-church-says-michigan-megachurch-successor-109074/. See also Kelefa Sanneh's insightful article on Bell, "The Hell-Raiser," *The New Yorker*, November 26, 2012, located at http://www.newyorker.com/reporting/2012/11/26/121126fa_fact_sanneh.

publish) against Bell's claims. Martin Beshir attracted great interest for Bell's book when he interviewed the "rock star" pastor.[55] Academicians even got in on the action. James Wellman wrote a book attempting to figure out why Rob Bell touched such a nerve in American Christianity. His assessment hit the nail on the head:

> Bell's ideas are both controversial and appealing in the minds and hearts of many listeners and readers. To progressives, it reaffirms what they already believe. For evangelicals, there's a mixed reaction: to the younger evangelical generation it's part temptation, part seduction; to older evangelicals, particularly self-identified conservative Christians, it's heresy. Tearing down walls and questioning older forms is Bell's *forte*, done with a smile and a kind of cooing delight that tantalizes, and draws people in.[56]

Bell shattered the evangelical stereotype. Here was a Wheaton College graduate, raised in "a staunch conservative and Reagan Republican household," making statements that sounded like universalism. One of the deans of American evangelicalism, John Piper, tweeted, curtly, "Farewell Rob Bell."[57]

Conclusion: Cultural Responses to Afterlife

Rob Bell is a case study in the changing culture happening within American evangelicalism. A divide is emerging, and the all-important issue of hell shines a spot lamp on the fissure. N. T. Wright seems to represents the "middle way" of Anglicanism, striking a balance between Catholicism and Protestantism. Eastern Orthodoxy has generally allowed for a measure of vagueness when it comes

---

55. See the Bashir-Bell interview here: http://www.youtube.com/watch?v=Vg-qgmJ7nzA. For "rock star," see James Wellman, *Rob Bell and a New American Christianity* (Nashville: Abingdon, 2012), 4.
56. Wellman, *Rob Bell and a New American Christianity*, 13.
57. See the tweet at https://twitter.com/JohnPiper/status/41590656421863424.

to afterlife. The tollhouse theory is yet another vivid, contextual response to afterlife by committed Christians.

As Christianity expands, unique configurations of the afterlife continue to proliferate. For example, ritualized reverence for ancestors is preserved all across Asia, Africa, and Latin America. In Mexico, Christians enthusiastically celebrate the departed between October 31 and November 2, known as *Dia de los Muertos*. Private altars are built to honor those who have passed into the afterlife. The deceased are presented offerings of beer, tequila, sweets, and flowers.

In Africa, where Christianity has found extremely fertile soil over the last century, beliefs about the afterlife are rich and complex. As Africans continue to assimilate Christian faith into their own cultures, they will no doubt create new, appropriately African ways of thinking about afterlife. For example, the notion of ancestor veneration is common in Christian Africa. Jesus gets portrayed as a "Supreme Ancestor."[58] Many African Christians see profound continuity from the realm of the living to the realm of the ancestors:

> Such continuity, however, does not undermine the appropriation of some indigenous religiosity within Christianity too. The indigenous attitudes to sacrifices continue to be reflected in the emphasis often placed on thanksgiving, prayer and the search for explanations. . . . Furthermore there appears to be continuity in the understanding of the two identifiable real worlds; the world of people, which is made up of all created beings and things, and the spirit world, the abode of the creator, deities and ancestral spirits. These worlds are understood as inseparable; they make one whole and constantly interact with each other.[59]

The realm of the ancestors and the realm of the living are interdependent. Relationships continue beyond the grave. It is an

---

58. Kwame Bediako, *Christianity in Africa: The Renewal of a Non-Western Religion* (Edinburgh: Edinburgh University Press, 1995), 217.
59. Elijah Obinna, "Ritual and Symbol: Funeral and Naming Rituals in an African Indigenous Community," in *Critical Reflections on Indigenous Religions*, ed. James Cox (Farnham, UK: Ashgate, 2013), 168.

"unbroken bond of obligations" and a "seamless web of community."[60] It is not altogether different from Christian notions of communion of saints, the "cloud of witnesses" (Heb. 12), and prayers for the dead. The dead are with us, and one day the veil separating us from them will be lifted.

To whom does Christianity belong? To those who uphold the tollhouse theory? To those who might hold to the old Roman Catholic teaching *extra Ecclesiam nulla salus* ("outside the Church, no salvation")? To those who pray to Mary and the ancestors? To those who believe in eternal torment for the wicked? Who gets to claim their view as the Christian view? I suppose the answer would circle us back to the beginning of the chapter: we can only imagine.

---

60. Ibid. 170.

PART III

The Church and the World

7

Rome

Acts 23:11

The following night the Lord stood near Paul and said, "Take courage! As you have testified about me in Jerusalem, so you must also testify in Rome."

The Roman Catholic Church plays a huge role in the world today. It is the largest organized religious body on earth with well over a billion baptized members. Catholics are widely distributed across the nations of the world and organized into more than two thousand dioceses.[1] According to the respected *International Bulletin of Missionary Research*, there are fifteen countries in the world that have a Catholic population of over 20 million:[2]

---

1. Joanne O'Brien and Martin Palmer, *The Atlas of Religion* (Los Angeles: University of California Press, 2007), 36 and 109.
2. Catholic statistics come from "Roman Catholic Statistical Updates," *International Bulletin of Missionary Research* 38, no. 1 (January 2014): 41–42.

Brazil: 165 million
Mexico: 100 million
Philippines: 79 million
United States: 71 million
Italy: 58 million
France: 48 million
Spain: 43 million
Colombia: 43 million
DR Congo: 39 million
Argentina: 38 million
Poland: 37 million
Peru: 27 million
Venezuela: 26 million
Germany: 25 million
Nigeria: 25 million

To put these numbers into larger perspective, around 17 percent of humanity is Roman Catholic. About 70 percent of the Catholic Church is located in the Global South where birth rates are higher. Between 2006 and 2011 the Catholic Church grew 7.3 percent worldwide. The largest growth was in Africa, at 22 percent. Next was Asia, at 11.6 percent. But both Latin America's and North America's Catholic communities grew during the last five years, by around 5–6 percent. In other words, the future of the Roman Catholic Church is well-endowed.

The word *catholic* comes from a Greek word meaning "complete" or "entire." When speaking of the Roman Catholic Church we have to keep three concepts in mind: 1. a church; 2. a leader—the bishop of Rome; 3. a global membership. The word *catholic* is an adjective, indicating something very expansive. However, in the English language, it has come to be used almost exclusively for referencing Roman-based Christianity.

The Roman Catholic Church is diverse to a degree that Protestants and Orthodox Christians struggle to comprehend. Some statistics illustrate its scale and geographical diversity:[3]

- The largest Catholic bloc in the world is in Latin America, home to the two largest Catholic countries: Brazil and Mexico. These two countries have a combined total of 265 million Catholics.[4] The region of Latin America and the Caribbean is home to 40 percent of the world's Catholics (450 million).

- The second largest Catholic bloc in the world is in Europe, where around 25 percent of the world's Catholics live (300 million).

- Africa is home to the third largest continental bloc of Catholics, encompassing around 16 percent of the global Catholic population (180 million). The Catholic Church, like many churches, is growing fast on the continent of Africa because of high fertility rates.

- Asia is home to around 12 percent of the global Catholic Church (130 million), due largely to the Philippines, which contains the world's third largest national Catholic population (75 million).

- The United States is home to the world's fourth largest Catholic community; North America as a continental bloc contains around 8 percent of the world's Catholics (90 million).

- Oceania is a sparsely populated region of the world, but it is

---

3. The statistics in this section are based on the report "The Global Catholic Population," *PewResearch*, February 13, 2013, located at http://www.pewforum.org/2013/02/13/the-global-catholic-population/. I have also used O'Brien and Palmer, *The Atlas of Religion*, 36–37, 108–9, and catholic-hierarchy.org.

4. For Brazil and Mexico statistics, see "Roman Catholic Statistical Updates," 41–42.

strongly Christian, and about a third of those Christians are Roman Catholic.

- There are many small Catholic communities scattered throughout the Islamic world. In some cases their history goes back many centuries.

Perhaps no word is more fitting to describe this situation than *catholic*.

The Catholic Church is in a unique position of influence in the world today. A recent study of faith-based nongovernmental organizations (NGOs) shows the profound influence that Christians, especially Catholics, have on the United Nations. The study concluded that Christian NGOs are disproportionately represented when compared to other religions. "More than 70 percent of religious NGOs at the UN are Christian, where the Vatican enjoys a special observer status, as a state and a religion."[5] While some have argued that the UN is too secular, the study actually critiques the UN for pandering to Christians.

Around 4.2 million people are engaged in pastoral activity in the Catholic Church, and about 1.5 million of them are full-time workers such as priests, monks, nuns, teachers, and missionaries. The Church is also a political entity with official ambassadors—known as Nunciatures—to 177 nations. "The Vatican is the oldest uninterrupted diplomatic service in the world." The Church has a diplomatic influence that no other religious organizations share.[6]

With a global presence comes a global infrastructure. Through television, radio, internet, and traditional publishing, the Church is able to connect its members to the Holy See. Many of these media are sponsored by the Church, but some of the best and most influential

5. Maria Tadeo, "Christianity Dominated United Nations, Concludes Study," *The Independent*, January 1, 2014, located at http://www.independent.co.uk/news/world/politics/christianity-dominates-united-nations-concludes-study-9032598.html.
6. O'Brien and Palmer, *The Atlas of Religion*, 108.

are fully independent, enabling them to critique without fear of retribution.[7]

A Surprise Ending

The 2013 resignation of Benedict XVI caught the Christian world off guard. As a historically astute academician, Benedict knew precisely how odd this sudden move looked. In order to appreciate the uniqueness of his resignation, we should step back and take a brief look at those who resigned before him in Roman Catholic history.

The last pope to quit on his own accord was Pope Celestine V, in 1294. Celestine was a simple, pious man in his 80s when elected. However, he was quickly caught in a struggle for power as King Charles II of Naples used the old pope as a pawn, making him appoint his choice men to key positions. After only five months, Celestine abdicated, not even once visiting Rome during his papacy because King Charles kept him under his thumb in Naples.

The strange sequence of events did not end there. Celestine's successor, Boniface VIII, locked up Celestine—the retired pope—in a castle. Shortly thereafter, old Celestine died. Questions swirled. Did Boniface have him murdered? Was it even legal for Celestine to resign in the first place? Was Boniface's election legitimate?[8]

The next papal abdication was every bit as scandalous. In perhaps the most complicated chapter in Roman Catholic history—the Western Schism—there happened to be three popes ruling Western Christendom at the same time: one in Rome, one in French Avignon, and one in Pisa. The Council of Constance (1414–1418) settled the matter by getting the popes to resign and electing a new one.

---

7. See John Allen Jr., *The Catholic Church* (Oxford: Oxford University Press, 2013), 78.
8. See John O'Malley, *A History of the Popes: From Peter to the Present* (New York: Rowman and Littlefield, 2010), 132–35.

The central question of the Council of Constance was whether a council can dismiss a pope (or popes) from office. The view that won the day was "conciliarism"—a council indeed has the authority to depose popes. The conciliarist solution to the Council of Constance left the door open to other popes potentially being dismissed by councils. It severely destabilized the authority of the papacy. Conciliarism is a system of checks and balances used by Orthodox Christians and many Protestant denominations to the present day. If a church leader overextends his reach, he can be deposed. Popes who came along after the Council of Constance resented this system of governance. After all, this is the main issue that had separated the Catholic Church from the Orthodox Communion centuries before. How could a pope rule as "vicar of Christ" with a bunch of cardinals and bishops breathing down his neck, examining his every move, keeping him in check?

The issue was not finally settled until the First Vatican Council in 1869–1870, when papal infallibility was officially promulgated. Conciliarism lost. A strong, centralized papacy became canon law.[9] One reason conciliarism finally lost the long battle was because the pope of that council, Pius IX, had firm control of the church. His papacy is still the longest of all time. He spent nearly thirty-two years in power.

The First Vatican Council effectively dashed any Orthodox or Protestant hopes for a reunited Christendom. Even some Catholics—known today as "Old Catholics"—opposed the declaration of papal infallibility. In protest they formed another denomination. Papal infallibility remains the central issue separating Catholics from Orthodox and Protestants believers today.

9. See papal infallibility as defined by the Roman Catholic *Code of Canon Law* here: http://www.vatican.va/archive/ENG1104/_P2H.HTM.

The Council of Constance remains a critical moment in the history of Christianity for other reasons. Not only is it the last time a pope resigned, it was also a precursor to the Protestant Reformation. Participants in the Council summoned the progressive Bohemian priest, Jan Hus—a reformer—and burned him at the stake for heresy after guaranteeing him safe passage. When one of his friends—Jerome of Prague—came to Hus's defense, he too was tried, convicted and burned for heresy. Hus's death spawned a series of wars—the Hussite Wars—that fueled the fires of rebellion. Those rebellions expanded significantly when Martin Luther began to read and sympathize with Hus.

With some pretty dismal history in mind, one asks, Why did Benedict resign the papacy on February 28, 2013? Of all people, he would know that when popes resign, things go badly. However, as history is showing us, Benedict may have done something brilliant. He may have established a much-needed precedent that, in time, could improve the church. As a pope ages and becomes ineffective, he could properly resign, passing the baton to a younger, more energetic man up to a very heavy task. Allowing a pope the ability to resign would also send a message that the twenty-first century papacy is focused more on spiritual matters than on temporal ones.

There was a risk in Benedict's move, however. Some have viewed his resignation as a weakening of papal supremacy. The office's declared infallible authority could be undermined in a situation of two or three living popes, much like what happened with the Avignon debacle.

A New Beginning

On March 13, 2013, the world met Jorge Bergoglio, an Argentine with Italian ancestry. He should have been known better than he was since he was runner-up in the voting back in 2005 when Cardinal

Joseph Ratzinger was elected.[10] However, in the days leading up to his election there was little discussion of him. Once elected, he took the name *Francis*, an unprecedented regnal name for a pope. He was identifying himself with St. Francis of Assisi (1181–1226), perhaps the most popular Roman Catholic saint since apostolic times. It was a strategic choice. Pope Francis wanted to connect himself, explicitly, with the poor and suffering. Indeed, shortly after becoming pope he began a campaign against unrestrained capitalism, calling the current economic world order "a cult of money."[11]

It is very clear that Pope Francis set about to reform the church from day one of his papacy. After being elected he made an extraordinary move. Standing on the balcony of St. Peter's Basilica, flanked by cardinals, he made a humble request that the people might pray for him. He then humbly bent over as the crowd fell silent. In the early days of his papacy he began urging fellow clergymen across the world to avoid ostentation, for example, by buying more "humble" cars. When he was the Archbishop of Buenos Aires, Francis was known to rely on public transportation and his own two feet. *Esquire* magazine drew attention to his humility when they named him their "Best Dressed Man of 2013" because of his avoidance of "opulent jewelry and fur-lined capes of yore" and, of course, the red papal shoes.[12]

Francis inherited the Petrine "keys to the kingdom" at a time when the Vatican was reeling. His cheerful, forthright approach to

10. John Allen Jr., "Profile: New Pope, Jesuit Bergoglio, Was Runner-Up in 2005 Conclave," *National Catholic Reporter*, March 3, 2013, located at http://ncronline.org/blogs/ncr-today/papabile-day-men-who-could-be-pope-13. For my section on Pope Francis I have relied on Allen's research, as he is the premier reporter in the English-speaking world for events inside the Vatican.

11. Lizzy Davies, "Pope Francis Attacks 'Cult of Money' in Reform Call," *The Guardian*, May 16, 2013, located at http://www.theguardian.com/world/2013/may/17/pope-francis-attacks-cult-money.

12. Max Berlinger, "The Best Dressed Man of 2013: Pope Francis," *Esquire*, December 27, 2013, located at http://www.esquire.com/blogs/mens-fashion/pope-francis-style-2013.

the media, and to the public in general, was refreshing after the rather cerebral papacy of Benedict, a brilliant German professor from Tübingen—one of the most respected theological institutions in the world. Francis's papacy commenced as many dark clouds converged upon the Vatican: charges of corruption in the curia, a "gay lobby" in the Vatican, charges of money laundering in the Vatican bank, and, perhaps most of all, the hemorrhaging of credibility due to child sex abuse lawsuits and cover-ups. Calm and composed in public, Francis's actions displayed a firm resolve unwilling to settle for the status quo. He fired individuals associated with corruption inside and outside the Vatican, including prominent clerics such as the notorious "Bishop Bling" from Germany, and all but one of the cardinals in charge of the Vatican bank.[13]

To get a sense of what was going on in the mind of Pope Francis shortly after his elevation, one can look at his 2013 apostolic exhortation *Evangelii Gaudium*, or "The Joy of the Gospel." At nearly fifty thousand words, the document shows just how committed he is to reforming the church and inspiring Catholics to recover the unique joy available to those who are in Christ Jesus.

Evangelii Gaudium is written for a church that is "bruised, hurting and dirty because it has been out on the streets." Francis wants to steer away from "a Church which is unhealthy from being confined and from clinging to its own security."[14] The naval gazing of the curia must change: "excessive centralization, rather than proving helpful,

13. "Bishop Bling" is Franz-Peter Tebartz-van Elst, bishop of Limburg. See Eric Lyman, "Pope Francis Shakes Up Vatican Bank, Sets Financial Cap for Sainthood," *The Washington Post*, January 15, 2014, located at http://www.washingtonpost.com/national/religion/pope-francis-shakes-up-vatican-bank-sets-financial-cap-for-sainthood/2014/01/15/2ecf5d20-7e21-11e3-97d3-b9925ce2c57b_story.html. See also John Allen Jr., "A Revolution Underway with Pope Francis," *National Catholic Reporter*, August 5, 2013, located at http://ncronline.org/news/vatican/revolution-underway.

14. *Evangelii Gaudium*, section 49. For the complete document in English see http://www.vatican.va/holy_father/francesco/apost_exhortations/documents/papa-francesco_esortazione-ap_20131124_evangelii-gaudium_en.html.

complicates the Church's life."[15] Reflecting on the problems that have bedeviled the church recently, he asks, "Whom are we going to evangelize if this is the way we act?"[16]

The pope encourages the church to look out rather than in. He wants his flock to think about higher things: they should love God, which will, in turn, cause them to reach out and "have an impact on society."[17] Christians should be the hands and feet of Jesus, begging for justice and mercy in a profligate world: "How can it be that it is not a news item when an elderly homeless person dies of exposure, but it is news when the stock market loses two points?"[18] "An economy of exclusion and inequality" is immoral. Humans must rise above the mentality of "survival of the fittest, where the powerful feed upon the powerless."[19] Pastors are urged to "hear the cry of the poor," since "a lack of solidarity towards his or her needs will directly affect our relationship with God."[20]

The unmistakable heart of *Evangelii Gaudium*, however, is a concern for the life of the church and the evangelization of the world. Pastors should prepare better sermons, designed to meet people where they are. The homily is not for entertainment. It should be "brief and avoid taking on the semblance of a speech or lecture. . . . This means that the words of the preacher must be measured, so that the Lord, more than his minister, will be the center of attention."[21] The Eucharist should be seen not as an exclusive prize for the righteous, but as "a powerful medicine and nourishment for the weak."[22] Preachers should practice "*lectio divina* (divine reading) . . .

15. Ibid., section 32.
16. Ibid., section 100.
17. Ibid., section 180.
18. Ibid., section 53.
19. Ibid., section 53.
20. Ibid., section 187.
21. Ibid., section 138.
22. Ibid., section 47.

reading God's word in a moment of prayer and allowing it to enlighten and renew us."[23] The Bible should lead us to ask, "Lord, what does this text say *to me*? What is it about my life that you want to change by this text?"[24] When the church connects to God, and when the focus is on others rather than on ourselves or on the institution of the church, then we will experience "the joy of the gospel." And for those who allow the salvation of Jesus into their lives, they "are set free from sin, sorrow, inner emptiness and loneliness."[25]

Much has been made of the differences between Benedict and Francis. That way of thinking only goes so far. They are quite different in style, but in substance they are remarkably similar. Like Francis, Benedict was also concerned about evangelizing the world, although he was particularly focused on how to reach Western Europe amid the trends toward secularization. Both of them oppose unbridled capitalism as a force of destruction. Both of them display strength yet also deep humility; Benedict's resignation must be seen as one of the most humble papal acts in history. Francis's humility is on display when he washes the feet of a Muslim girl or gives prepaid calling cards to immigrants and refugees.

However, make no mistake: these men have differences. Francis comes from, in his words, "the ends of the Earth," while Benedict was in the Vatican's control room for over thirty years as Prefect of the Congregation for the Doctrine of the Faith and then as Pope.[26] Benedict's career was an academic one. And while Francis, too, spent much of his life in academia, his career went more in the direction of pastoral ministry. Francis's pastoral bent seems to be what Catholics

---

23. Ibid., section 152.
24. Ibid., section 153.
25. Ibid., section 1.
26. "Transcript: Pope Francis' First Speech as Pontiff," *NPR*, March 13, 2013, located at http://www.npr.org/2013/03/13/174224173/transcript-pope-francis-first-speech-as-pontiff.

and non-Catholics alike are responding to so favorably. Francis is also more accessible, surprising reporters by stopping to have long conversations about virtually anything they want to ask. Benedict was much more cautious than that.

Since the Second Vatican Council in the early 1960s, the Catholic Church has often been characterized as a pendulum swinging from conservative to progressive. And while this dichotomous "taxonomy"—in the words of George Weigel—has become commonplace, it is not without detractors.[27] Nevertheless, dislodging this understanding from the Catholic and public mind has proven terribly difficult. In the standard account, Pope John XXIII caught everybody off-guard by calling for "*aggiornamento*" ("updating" or "refreshing") in the Church, leading to significant renewal during a period of massive social upheaval. The era of traditionalism and conservatism was over. John's successor, Paul VI, was equally "ecumenical" and reform minded as the Second Vatican Council overhauled the teachings and posture of the Church. John Paul I reigned only one month, but his successor, John Paul II—elected in 1978—represented a resolute turn to the right. Liberal theologians such as Hans Küng would make their careers bemoaning the gains that were lost in the seismic, conservative shift. Benedict, as John Paul's right-hand man, maintained that trajectory.

Pope Francis, however, represents a return to the euphoria that accompanied the Second Vatican Council. Theologically he is open, personally he is acceptable and full of humility, geographically he represents the heart of today's Roman Catholic Church—Latin America. Therefore, he is seen as a man closer to the Church since the Church is today anchored in the southern hemisphere. He is man who understands the poor, in a way a German or Italian simply

---

27. George Weigel, *Evangelical Catholicism: Deep Reform in the 21st-Century Church* (New York: Basic Books, 2013), 10–11.

cannot. The new pope is seen as a man of the people. And the world, not just the Roman Catholic Church, has taken notice.

Authority

The most important difference between Catholics and non-Catholics is the issue of authority. The litmus test boils down to the pope. If you are a Catholic, you consider the bishop of Rome the authority in matters of faith and religion.

Pope Francis is the 266th successor in a long chain running back to early Christian times. Catholics believe the apostle Peter was the first pope, put in charge by Jesus's explicit command in Matt. 16:18–19:

> You are Peter, and on this rock I will build my church, and the gates of Hades will not overcome it. I will give you the keys of the kingdom of heaven; whatever you bind on earth will be bound in heaven, and whatever you loose on earth will be loosed in heaven.

Catholics believe this scene to be crucial for papal claims of authority. Whoever is in the position of the bishop of Rome, as the successor to Peter, has jurisdiction over the kingdom of God on earth. It is a position described in the Catechism of the Catholic Church as "vicar of Christ." The pope has "full, supreme, and universal power over the whole Church, a power which he can always exercise unhindered."[28] Protestants and Orthodox Christians reject this very high view of the papacy, but nonetheless respect the office due to its esteemed heritage as one of the five great patriarchs of a once-united Christendom (alongside Jerusalem, Antioch, Alexandria, and Constantinople).

The Catholic hierarchy is massive, with numerous levels of authority. Church teaching holds that when Peter was given authority by Christ, a great system of apostolic succession—also

---

28. "Catechism of the Catholic Church," section 882, located at http://www.vatican.va/archive/ccc_css/archive/catechism/p123a9p4.htm.

known as episcopal succession—was set into motion. Apostolic succession is not unique to the Roman Church. Orthodox Christians and many Protestants such as the Anglicans share this "episcopal" understanding. The long chain of authority began when the Lord Jesus ordained his apostles for supervision of the church. The apostles ordained other leaders in various capacities such as evangelists, elders, and deacons. Those that the apostles ordained conferred their authority onto others, and on and on the process went down to the present. In this line of thinking, whoever is an ordained a clergyman is a part of that veritable line of succession going all the way back to the Lord Jesus himself, and ultimately to God, whose authority is shared by his son.

It is hard to imagine running a company that oversees a population roughly equivalent to three times the population of the United States of America, or the entire population of India. But many offices in the Church share the load. In terms of administration, the most significant roles are that of bishops and cardinals. Bishops manage the world's two thousand dioceses, ordain new clergy, gather together to make regional decisions, and travel to Rome—traditionally every five years—to report to the pope.

Most of the two hundred or so cardinals are also bishops. Cardinals are recognizable due to their blood-red colored vestments, signifying a willingness to be martyred for the Church. They are organized into the College of Cardinals, which serves as an advising apparatus to the pope. Most importantly, however, cardinals under the age of eighty are entrusted with the vital task of electing each new pope. As the Catholic Church has become so global in recent memory, the college has diversified somewhat, but certainly not on par with membership. Today, over half of the cardinals are from Europe. Nearly a quarter of them are from Italy—more than twice the number of cardinals from North America.[29]

The Roman Curia (court) is the administrative cabinet and governing body of the Holy See. Until 1870 the pope was the political ruler of the Papal States, a concoction of territories in the Italian peninsula. Since the late eighteenth century, however, the pope's political jurisdiction has been reduced to Vatican City State, a small enclave in the city of Rome with less than one thousand people in it. While the pope's leadership is almost exclusively that of being spiritual head of the Roman Church, his political influence can be massive. For example, it is widely held that Pope John Paul II played a critical role in the collapse of Communism in eastern and central Europe that began in Poland—his home country—in the 1980s.

While the pope is considered to be the infallible authority in the Roman Catholic Church, his leadership does not go untested from within. In December 2013 a series of news stories from reputable reporters described a tug of war going on between Francis and some powerful members of the curia. The debate centered on Francis's desire to change the old curia system and replace it with something else, although it is unclear what exactly he has in mind. What is clear is that he has repeatedly expressed consternation at a system he views as overly complicated and in grave need of reform. Seeking a more "pastoral" administration, he has "reshuffled" the Vatican's core in what was viewed as a "powerful sign of change." One influential American member of the curia—Cardinal Raymond Burke—publicly questioned Francis's decisions, and characterized the pope's writings as "suggestions" rather than as official church teaching.[30] Burke is a well-known ultraconservative who has spoken out repeatedly against abortion and same-sex marriage. He was a close confidant of

29. See the Vatican's statistics, located at http://www.vatican.va/news_services/press/documentazione /documents/cardinali_statistiche /cardinali_statistiche_continenti_en.html.

30. See David Gibson, "Pope Francis' Vatican Reforms May Prompt Curial Pushback," *National Catholic Reporter*, December 17, 2013, located at http://ncronline.org/news/vatican/pope-francis-vatican-reforms-may-prompt-curial-pushback.

Benedict and John Paul II. However, his public spat with Francis led to a major curtailing of his power. In the *New York Times* it was speculated that Burke's "removal from the Congregation for Bishops will sharply reduce his influence, especially over personnel changes in American churches."[31] Francis sent a clear message that public opposition to his leadership—even among the most senior members of the curia—would not go unnoticed. When Francis appointed his first round of cardinals, the United States was conspicuously snubbed, perhaps a slap on the wrist that was a sign of things to come. Rather, Francis appointed nine Europeans (mainly Italians), five from Latin America and the Caribbean, two from Africa, two from Asia, and a Canadian.[32]

Conclusion: The Eternal City

While Francis's first round of appointments to the cardinalate in 2014 did not accurately reflect a changing of the guard in world Catholicism from Western Europe to the Global South, the reality is that the numbers are, in fact, quickly moving in that direction. The "eternal city" has a human endowment in excess of a billion people, and the fertility trends of the majority world are like tailwinds propelling it. Indeed, Rome will remain the *axis mundi* of the Christian world for the foreseeable future due to its constituency being 70 percent—and rising—from the majority world. Any thought of Rome's declining influence in the world is nonsense.

Vatican insider John Allen Jr. discussed his perception of the future of the Catholic Church in light of its "rising Southern tide."[33] In

---

31. Jim Yardley and Jason Horowitz, "Pope Replaces Conservative U.S. Cardinal on Influential Vatican Committee," *New York Times*, December 16, 2013, located at http://www.nytimes.com/2013/12/17 /world/europe /pope-replaces-conservative-us-cardinal-on-influential-vatican-committee.html.
32. See "Pope Francis Creates 19 New Cardinals," *Vatican Radio*, February 22, 2014, located at http://www.news.va/en/news/pope-francis-creates-19-new-cardinals.

his view, the Catholic Church is moving in a decidedly southern direction. In the foreseeable future, the clear trends within the global Roman Catholic Church are that it will be:

- *Morally conservative*: the liberals will lose many of the "hot button" battles, even with Pope Francis at the helm, because the great "southern consensus" is "remarkably traditionalist."

- *Liberal on social justice*: Southern Catholics are "suspicious of capitalism and free markets." Francis has been explicit that the current economic system in place in the Western world is immoral. Liberation theology, and its preferential option for the poor, resonates with the vast majority of Catholics who struggle to make a living.

- *Biblical*: "higher criticism" and other academic trends so prominent in the Western university will lose out to a more literal understanding of the Bible. Southern Catholics are not so concerned with ivory tower, Euro-American debates that are aimed more at advancing academics than with obeying the divine word of God.

- *Concerned with pluralism, not secularism*: People in Asia, Africa, and Latin America tend to be religious. While Westerners focus on the recession of faith, Global South Christians focus more on how Christianity can influence, and compete with, the world's religions.

- *Young and optimistic*: The median age of Europeans and Americans is around forty years. In Asia it is twenty-nine. In Latin America it is twenty-seven. In Africa it is nineteen. The future of Christianity

33. John Allen Jr., *The Future Church: How Ten Trends Are Revolutionizing the Catholic Church* (New York: Doubleday, 2009), 433–35.

is young and fertile. African women have, on average, five children. The Catholic Church will benefit mightily from exponential growth.

- *Alien to Europeans and Americans*: Gay marriage will not be as important a topic as polygamy. For example, in Kenya and Nigeria, 98 percent of the public claimed homosexuality can "never be justified."[34] The central topics will be miracles, witchcraft, and poverty. In Ethiopia, 74 percent of Christians have witnessed an exorcism. More than half of Africa's Christians expect Jesus to return to earth during their lifetime.[35]

While Christianity's great recession continues in the West, the central problems facing Global South Christians are how to handle excessive and rapid growth.

To whom does Christianity belong? Statistically, about half of it belongs to Rome. And the profound influence of the eternal city will continue to live on in many parts of the world, and in complex ways. It is not an understatement to say that the influence of the Vatican is at an all-time high, globally. While the Catholic numbers continue to surge, it is crucial that Protestants and Orthodox Christians get to know their Catholic sisters and brothers. For many people in the world, the Catholic Church *is* the face of Christianity. The rest of the world *needs* a Catholic Church that is ecumenical, healthy, and engaged. The Catholic world, being so strong in the Global South, is uniquely positioned to be a force for good in the future.

---

34. "Attitudes Toward Homosexuality in African Countries," PewResearch, November 13, 2006, located at http://www.pewresearch.org/daily-number /attitudes-toward-homosexuality-in-african-countries/.

35. For statistics on Jesus's return see PewResearch, "Tolerance and Tension: Islam and Christianity in Sub-Saharan Africa," April 15, 2010, located at http://www.pewforum.org/2010/04/15/executive-summary-islam-and-christianity-in-sub-saharan-africa/. For Ethiopia and exorcism, see chapter 2 of the "Tolerance and Tension" report, located at http://www.pewforum.org/files/2010/04/sub-saharan-africa-chapter-2.pdf.

Protestants and Orthodox Christians need to engage Catholics in order to provide solutions to human and ecological problems. Few organizations, indeed few nations, have the influence of Rome. With power comes responsibility. A Roman Catholic Church with a global reach has endless possibilities. The world's Christians should be cheering for Rome to be the best church it can possibly be.

Finally, a word about ecumenism. In the twentieth century, the ecumenical movement was led by Euro-American Protestants. Perhaps it is time for Rome to step forward and take a more vital role in the global ecumenical task. While the theological agenda of Western Protestantism continues to move in contrast to the agenda of the Global South, it seems high time for the Catholic Church to take the ecumenical controls for a while. Not only would the Orthodox churches become much more enthusiastic in response to Catholic leadership in the global ecumenical movement, but Christians in Asia, Africa, and Latin America might respond to ecumenism more favorably. As it stands, the most important outlet of the global ecumenical movement—the World Council of Churches—seems stuck in the waning twilight of old-line Protestantism. An ecumenical agenda that includes a much more prolific role for the Roman Catholic Church would help bring the ecumenical focus back to the organic union of the world's Christians. The Catholic Church might have to revisit traditional issues such as papal infallibility, the Creed, and the 1054 schism. While it would be painful to have those discussions, global Christianity needs those conversations to take place. Indeed the reunion of Christianity is contingent on those conversations taking place.

8

Protesters

Acts 15:39–40

They had such a sharp disagreement that they parted company. Barnabas took Mark and sailed for Cyprus, but Paul chose Silas and left.

In the early sixteenth century, a German monk named Martin Luther launched a scathing critique of his church, especially its questionable fundraising methods to build Saint Peter's Basilica in Rome, the greatest Roman Catholic Church building in history. Construction began in 1506 and the church needed a steady flow of capital. Luther's main qualm was not necessarily with the construction of a beautiful church to surpass all others. Rather, his complaints were of a theological nature. He was disturbed by the selling of indulgences, a fundraising mechanism by which Rome offered afterlife benefits for those willing to contribute. Johann Tetzel—the grand commissioner for indulgences in Luther's region—put it this way: "When the coin in the coffer rings, the soul from purgatory springs." Luther thought the concept absurd at best and heretical at worst. His emphasis on justification by faith alone would not tolerate a system that depended on the saints and a "treasury of merit" they had built up through the centuries. No, the saints could never save us. In Christ alone was salvation found. Luther began speaking out publicly against these parchment guarantees of forgiveness, and penned his famous *Ninety-Five Theses*. He posted the document on Wittenberg's castle church door on October 31, 1517. The mighty protest that would split Western Europe had begun.

Many influential leaders, both religious and political, thought Luther was on to something. Political alliances that had simmered tenuously for generations began to give way. Medieval Christendom began to crumble as political rulers questioned the whole idea of sending tax revenues to Rome. Why not keep that money and invest it locally? Luther was more concerned with theological reform, but for others in high places it often came down to money, power, and self-preservation. Luther provided a new way of thinking, and he captured the imagination of many around him. His extraordinary courage, some would say recklessness, began to empower others, and massive change ensued.

Within a surprisingly short period of time, the protests spread, and became less about indulgences and more about emancipation from a church that was perceived as having a stranglehold on its members. They escalated further into protests against systems of government, economic systems, and authority in general.

Ulrich Zwingli's protests caught on in Switzerland and set the stage for one of the most durable theologians of all time—John Calvin—who set the agenda for reform in Geneva. Heinrich Bullinger was left with the mantle of authority in Zurich after Zwingli was killed in battle fighting for his understanding of reform. Other reformer groups such as Anabaptists began to rise up in protest against earlier reformers. They were opposed and persecuted. Wars broke out. Cities divided. Entire societies were unsettled as many different conceptions of reform spawned ever new protests.

Even in Luther's city different conceptions of reform erupted into bitter, public confrontations. German peasants thought Luther had given them permission to rise up against the upper classes and attain a greater measure of freedom. Thomas Müntzer, a leader in the Peasants' Revolt, advocated a literal reading of scripture—that all Christians should share their possessions. But they miscalculated terribly. Luther turned against them, authorizing their brutal suppression in his rancorous treatise *Against the Murderous, Thieving Hordes of Peasants*. He wrote,

> They are starting a rebellion, and violently robbing and plundering monasteries and castles which are not theirs. . . . Rebellion is not simple murder, but is like a great fire, which attacks and lays waste a whole land. Thus rebellion brings with it a land full of murder and bloodshed, makes widows and orphans, and turns everything upside down. . . . Therefore let everyone who can, smite, slay and stab, secretly or openly, remembering that nothing can be more poisonous, hurtful or devilish than a rebel. It is just as when one must kill a mad dog; if you do not strike him, he will strike you, and a whole land with you.[1]

Luther's persuasive abilities, combined with his connections to the aristocracy, spelled disaster for the peasants. They were not trained fighters, and were slaughtered in battle after pitiful battle. Historian Diarmaid MacCulloch calls it "Europe's most massive and widespread popular uprising before the 1789 French Revolution."[2]

---

1. Martin Luther, *Against the Robbing and Murdering Hordes of Peasants*, in *Martin Luther: Documents of Modern History*, ed. E. G. Rupp and Benjamin Drewery (London: Edward Arnold, 1970), 121–126.
2. Diarmaid MacCulloch, *The Reformation: A History* (New York: Penguin, 2003), 158.

The Protestant Principle

Paul Tillich, one of the foremost theologians of the twentieth century, coined an apt expression: "The Protestant Principle."[3] What he meant by that term was that Protestants have it in their very nature to protest. They were born by protest. It is what they naturally do. And there are implications that come with this posture of protest. Decisions are never final; they must be challenged. Expressions of faith will be plagued by voices of dissent. Even creeds do not escape critique. Faith is never concrete, but always fluid, always transient, always standing "under the prophetic judgment and not above it." Criticism should be *expected* in a context of protest and dissent. In Luther's mind, even the pope himself should be protested.

Rebellion is hardwired into the machine of Protestantism. And some consider this idea the genius of Protestantism; it is organic and alive, it self-corrects. Luther called this phenomenon *ecclesia semper reformanda est*, a church that is always reforming. However, this is precisely why Protestantism fragmented quickly. Within a few decades of Luther's initial protest, the dissent had expanded and created myriad stripes of Lutherans, Reformed Christians, Anabaptists, and Anglicans. And these groups splintered. And the splinters found reasons to protest against others within their movements. And so it went, and so it goes.

As I write, the Presbyterian churches in the United States are splitting again. A new group is being formed called ECO (A Covenant Order of Evangelical Presbyterians). Dissatisfied with the progressive direction of the Presbyterian Church USA (PCUSA), they have decided to create a new denomination, even at a punishing cost. One megachurch in California paid $8.89 million to the PCUSA just for the right to break away. However, their pastor—John

3. Paul Tillich, *Dynamics of Faith* (New York: Harper and Row, 1957), 28–29.

Ortberg—and 93 percent of the membership thought it was worth the price.[4] Moving themselves out from under the PCUSA umbrella is their way of protesting. They are standing up for what they believe. And they are quite willing to put their money where their mouths are. The Presbyterians are far from being alone. The Anglican Communion has been flirting with a massive conservative/progressive split for over a decade, particularly as the robust Anglican churches of Africa continue to protest against the Western churches' position on homosexuality. Lutherans are splitting as well. For example, in the year 2000 the Lutheran Congregations in Mission for Christ (LCMC) split from the Evangelical Lutheran Church in America (ELCA). Their reasoning was that the ELCA had violated the historic Lutheran Confessions and had compromised on the authority of scripture.[5]

Roman Catholic and Orthodox churches have problems, but arbitrary splitting is not one of them. Their members can dissent up to a point. Eventually the individual must swallow his complaint and get on board with the rest of the church. Continued protest is not a virtue after that. For Protestants, however, protesting defines the church. The institution is at its finest hour when up in arms over something that appears wrong-headed, unjust, or patently false. Luther was willing to die for his cause. And Protestants have inherited Luther's fundamental value—protesting keeps the church on track, keeps it honest, keeps it pure. With the Bible in hand as the arbiter of truth, Protestants are empowered to state their opinion until proven wrong. Luther's famous burst of courage at the Diet

---

4. See Sarah Pulliam Bailey, "John Ortberg's Menlo Park Presbyterian Votes to Leave PCUSA Despite million Fee," *The Washington Post*, March 5, 2014, located at http://www.washingtonpost.com/national/religion/john-ortbergs-menlo-park-presbyterian-votes-to-leave-pcusa-despite-8-million-fee /2014/03/05 /4b47614c-a4b3-11e3-b865-38b254d92063_story.html.
5. See the LCMC website at http://www.lcmc.net/statement-of-faith/231.

of Worms in 1521 is the quintessential moment of conviction for Protestants. He faced a hostile inquisitor in Johann Eck, who demanded that Luther recant his writings and his heretical views. Luther refused. And then he challenged Eck, "Unless I am convinced by the testimony of the scriptures or by clear reason . . . I am bound by the scriptures I have quoted and my conscience is captive to the Word of God. I cannot and I will not retract anything, since it is neither safe nor right to go against conscience. I cannot do otherwise. Here I stand. May God help me. Amen."[6] On this watershed moment, MacCulloch commented eloquently, "This can stand for the motto of all Protestants—ultimately, perhaps, all of Western civilization."[7]

Key Aspects of Protestantism

The Roman Catholic Church claims the allegiance of 50 percent of the world's 2.2 billion Christians.[8] Protestantism claims about 40 percent, that is, around 800 million members. The remainder belongs to the Orthodox fold.

Defining Protestantism is no easy task. In the most basic sense, Protestants are Christians who are neither Orthodox nor Roman Catholic. However, there are tens of thousands of Protestant denominations, fellowships, and groups. There is no standard typology for Protestantism. One thing is clear, however: Protestantism has changed dramatically in the last century. The main reason for this is the sudden and staggering growth of Pentecostalism. In the late 1800s and early 1900s several Pentecostal revivals suddenly broke out in various places across the world such as Los Angeles,

---

6. Carter Lindberg, *The European Reformations*, second ed. (Oxford: Wiley-Blackwell, 2010), 84.
7. Diarmaid MacCulloch, *The Reformation*, 131.
8. For the global Christian population, see "Global Christianity—A Report on the Size and Distribution of the World's Christian Population," *PewResearch*, December 19, 2011, located at http://www.pewforum.org/2011/12/19/global-christianity-movements-and-denominations/.

India, Brazil, Chile, Wales, South Africa, and later in East Africa. While at the time it was dismissed by more mainline Christians as outlandish and even heterodox, the movement continues to grow rapidly. This unforeseen trend has deeply impacted the contours of world Christianity. Pentecostalism is today a major strand of Protestantism, and has surpassed many of the denominational fellowships that once criticized it, as demonstrated by the populations of some of the major worldwide Protestant fellowships:

- Pentecostal (rooted in the global Pentecostal revivals): around 280 million members[9];

- Methodist (rooted in John Wesley): around 80 million members[10];

- Reformed/Presbyterian (rooted in John Calvin): around 80 million members[11];

- The Anglican Communion (rooted in the Church of England): around 80 million members[12];

- Lutherans (explicitly identify with Martin Luther): around 70 million members[13];

- Baptists (rooted in English Puritanism): around 50 million members[14].

Each of these movements includes dozens of denominations within them. The Anglican Communion is unique in that the archbishop

9. Ibid.
10. See World Methodist Council, located at http://worldmethodistcouncil.org/about/member-churches/.
11. See World Communion of Reformed Churches, located at http://wcrc.ch/our-story/.
12. See Anglican Communion, located at http://www.aco.org/tour/.
13. See The Lutheran World Federation, located at http://www.lutheranworld.org/content/about-lwf.
14. David Bebbington, *Baptists through the Centuries: A History of a Global People* (Waco, TX: Baylor University Press, 2010), 3. See also Baptist World Alliance, located at https://www.bwanet.org/.

of Canterbury (UK) serves as a symbolic head of the associated denominations. The others have no such central figure.

With a population of 800 million spread all over the world in hundreds of denominations, networks, and groups, it would seem that identifying a core Protestant collection of beliefs is impossible. There are, however, several key tenets that have survived the test of time, and most of them can be traced back to the central claims of Martin Luther and the early reformers. There are reasons why the Roman Catholic Church could not make room for the reformers, and thus would not countenance their existence without a fight. Over time, the Protestants were indeed pushed out of the Roman fold because of these core commitments. Luther and company's most coveted ideas still reverberate in the many manifestations of Protestantism today:

1. *Sola scriptura* (only scripture): the Bible is the sole authority. Any religious authority is rooted in the scriptures. If a religious leader teaches something in conflict with the Bible, then that person's teachings must be rejected. This crucial idea is the reason Protestants are eager to translate the scriptures into the languages of the ordinary people. The only problem with this reasoning is that Protestants struggle over how best to interpret scripture. If the Bible is the authority, then whose interpretation has authoritative power?

2. Priesthood of all believers. This idea from 1 Peter 2 and other scriptures emphasizes that each person is a priest, and God's people are collectively "a royal priesthood." The notion of an earthly priesthood akin to the Levites in the Old Testament is fundamentally mistaken. The New Testament knows no such priesthood. Jesus ordains all who are baptized by water and spirit to be his priests, and thus valid representatives of the

gospel.[15] One question that Protestants have had to deal with, however, is that if everyone is a priest, then who is the laity? The church, potentially, becomes a body of individual leaders with no followers. It therefore comes as no surprise that there are thousands of Protestant denominations.

3. *Sola fide* (only faith): Christians are justified (or, saved) by their faith and not by their works. This fundamental teaching from Paul is the very bedrock of his entire theological system. The idea is unpacked carefully in Romans and Galatians, precisely the two works around which Luther shaped his theological corpus. Historically, Protestants have tended to privilege faith over works, thereby marginalizing the message of the book of James—that faith without good works is dead. Critics have argued that Protestants made salvation an intellectual decision. Can the "sinner's prayer" really save a person, even if they do not go on to live a Christian life? This question stems not just from Luther, but from a reading of the apostle Paul himself. Nevertheless, Protestants continue to hold the line: salvation is by faith in Christ, and good works are a response to that deep conviction.

4. Direct access to God. Protestants have no intermediaries between the believer and God. They believe Christ's death, burial, and resurrection opened access to God. Whereas the Israelites had to access God through the priests and the sacrificial system, Protestants believe they can access God directly and immediately. Similarly, when Catholics and Orthodox Christians pray through saints, through icons, through the Virgin Mary, or through a priest, they are fundamentally misunderstanding the whole reason for Christ's coming. As Heb.

15. A Catholic scholar, Garry Wills, has recently published a book challenging the notion of a priesthood. See Garry Wills, *Why Priests? A Failed Tradition* (New York: Viking, 2013).

4:16 teaches, "Let us then approach God's throne of grace with confidence, so that we may receive mercy and find grace to help us in our time of need."

5. Suspicion of a centralized authority. The early Protestants deeply resented the papacy. When Luther was denounced by the pope he fired back with profanity, referring to the pope as the Antichrist, an enemy of God, and a "fart-ass."[16] Luther reasoned that there must always be a suspicion directed at the person claiming to represent God. Christians must turn to the Bible and figure out for themselves what is being asked of them. The individual Christian has an unmistakable dignity and responsibility to God alone.

These five convictions run deep inside the hearts and minds of Protestants. They are nonnegotiable. They are the reasons why Protestants and Catholics will not unite for the foreseeable future. They may cooperate and even admire one another from afar, but full unity is a conversation for another time, in the distant future.

Roman Catholics and Orthodox Christians tend to think of their church as a large family. They are all in it together. They may have disagreements, but it would be preposterous to leave. They may complain about their church, but there is simply no mechanism for breaking away from it in order to start a new church outside of the old church. To be a member of a family means to work through conflict, as a body. If a member finds herself at variance with the church, then she must find a way to work through it, but she cannot leave. It would be akin to leaving one's biological family. For all intents and purposes, leaving is not an option.

---

16. Martin Brecht, *Martin Luther: The Preservation of the Church, 1532–1546*, vol. 3 (Minneapolis, MN: Fortress Press, 1999), 360.

Protestants do not share this genetic attachment to the church. It is entirely feasible for them to transition into another community of faith. Protestants have established a framework that allows for religious switching.[17] It is not terribly odd to do so. The Protestant cornerstone is that the individual is emphasized at the expense of the community. The health and welfare of the person is the primary concern. Thus, if the community and the individual happen to clash, then there are options for dealing with the problem. One does not *have* to stay. It is very liberating, but it can also be very costly.

In many ways, Protestants are simply imitating Luther when they stand up to the institution and remind it of the dignity of the voice of opposition. The voice of the protester is credible because it emphasizes the individual over against the corporate. However, the cost is that religious authority in Protestantism is much weaker than in the Orthodox and Catholic institutions.

Another complication is that splintering off from the main can leave a person virtually homeless in an ecclesial sense. Is one a Lutheran or a Presbyterian? Does it really even matter in a context when one can easily switch, or start another church as an act of defiance?

In the minds of Protestants, what one loses in religious community he or she gains in the dignity of the protest. It is empowering to stand against the system—to rage against the machine—when the system gets it wrong. In fact, Protestants agree, this process of confronting the system keeps the church on its toes, *semper reformanda*. Splitting off may be painful for individuals, but ultimately it keeps the corporate church more pure.

Protestants are painfully aware of this ambivalence, but the bottom line is freedom. When the benefits of having religious autonomy

17. For more on religious switching, see Robert Putnam and David Campbell, *American Grace: How Religion Divides and Unites Us* (New York: Simon and Schuster, 2010).

are weighed against the benefits of having a lifelong religious community, Protestants choose the former. Certainly Protestants do have great admiration for the Catholic and Orthodox sense of community exemplified in a national church (as many Orthodox denominations are organized) or in a Roman Catholic identity. But when faced with the choice, Protestants understand the price of freedom and they are willing to pay for it. Thus, in a sense, Protestants live from split to split. However, in the interim—in the time between splits—Protestants do their best to live together in an apprehensive state of harmony, in spite of conflicting beliefs that may eventually erupt and spawn another wave of protest.

Christianity's southern shift has brought the Protestant principle with it. When Protestants missionized people in the Global South, quite naturally, this proclivity to protest was embedded in their message. In the next section, two important movements—Iglesia Ni Cristo and Ethiopianism—illustrate how the empowering of the individual and the proclivity to protest has played out in southern Christianity.

Filipino Protesters: The Case of the Iglesia Ni Cristo

Iglesia Ni Cristo (INC) originated in the Philippines in 1914 under the leadership of Felix Ysagun Manalo (1886–1963).[18] With a membership in the millions—around 2.3 percent of the Filipino population—it is considered the largest indigenous church in the Philippines.[19]

---

18. For Iglesia Ni Cristo, see Hirofumi Ando, "A Study of the Iglesia Ni Cristo: A Politico-Religious Sect in the Philippines," *Pacific Affairs* 42, no. 3 (1969): 334–45; Ann C. Harper, "The Iglesia Ni Cristo and Evangelical Christianity," *Journal of Asian Mission* 3, no. 1 (2001): 101–19; Adriel Obar Meimban, "A Historical Analysis of the Iglesia Ni Cristo," *The Journal of Sophia Asian Studies* 12 (1994): 98–134; and Julita Reyes Santa Romana, "The Iglesia Ni Kristo: A Study," MA thesis, University of Manila, 1954.

In 1902 Felix Manalo began to have doubts about the Roman Catholic Church after witnessing a Protestant-Catholic debate on venerating religious images. Two years later he converted to Methodism and began training for ministry. His doubts persisted, however, and he changed denominations repeatedly, searching for the true church. In 1908 he joined the Christian Church (Disciples of Christ) which impacted him with its restorationist, "back to the Bible" approach, and its insistence on water immersion for believers rather than infants. In 1911 he joined the Seventh-Day Adventists, but after a turbulent period of ministry he was dismissed for unclear reasons.

In 1913, after a brief period of calling himself an atheist, Manalo isolated himself for three days. He emerged claiming he would found a new church based on *scripture alone*—that quintessentially Protestant virtue—without any foreign influence. On July 27, 1914 he registered his church with the government and it grew exponentially over time. Manalo led the church for forty-nine years. When he died in 1968 his son Eraño de Guzman Manalo (1925–2009) took the reins of leadership. Upon the death of Eraño in 2009, his son Eduardo (1955–present) became executive minister.

Some of the teachings of the INC have sparked controversy. In 1922 Manalo claimed to be the angel from the east in Rev. 7:1–3. He taught that all churches lived in error since apostolic times, and he was ordained to restore the true church. Two passages from Isaiah are critical for INC self-understanding: 43:5–6 and 46:11–13. They claim these passages prophesy the movement's rise in "the East," meaning the Philippines. The "man of purpose from a far country" is Felix Manalo, the Last Messenger of God. The INC is

---

19. Raul Pangalangan, "Religion and the Secular State: National Report for the Philippines," International Center for Law and Religion Studies, Brigham Young University, 2010, located at http://www.iclrs.org/content/blurb/files/Philippines wide.pdf.

non-Trinitarian, arguing that while Jesus is indeed God's son and the redeemer of humankind, he is a created being. It has a separatist culture: church attendance is expected twice per week, all teaching is tightly controlled, and some members live in INC-owned housing. It claims to be the only true church that offers salvation. Repeated clashes with the Roman Catholic Church have attracted national attention for the INC.

While the precise number of INC members is debated, clearly it has impacted Filipino society in areas such as education, health, and politics. It is an indigenous movement, borrowing liberally from Filipino culture in areas such as vernacular preaching and folk hymnody. Its largest and most respected educational institution—New Era University—accepts church members as well as nonmembers. INC has shown an impressive ability to sway elections since members are expected to "be perfectly united in mind and thought" (1 Cor. 1:10) when casting votes. Its chapels are large, well-constructed, and distinctive. Its television and media presence is significant. INC has a vibrant missionary program, notably to the Western world, and an array of ministries in the Philippines and abroad.

The INC is an apt reminder of Protestantism's ambivalence. It began as one man's protest against Catholicism. Empowered by his protest he found another church, only to protest again. The protesting continued until Manalo was able to create a church of his own. No longer under any earthly authority, he had effectively supplanted the authority of the papacy—or any other denominational hierarchy—by emphasizing the autonomy and the power of the individual. Thus a new movement was created, until the next major protest fractures it into pieces. It is impressive when one individual is able to spawn a movement so influential in a particular society, but such is the history of Protestantism. What begins as an attempt to protest the authority of one man or institution ends up being an attempt to assert the authority of another, in this case Felix Manalo, his son, and his grandson. They become the new authority. And, in time, new protests will inevitably emerge. The irony is profound.

An African Protest: The Case of Ethiopianism

Ethiopianism was a religious and political movement that emerged in Africa in the second half of the nineteenth century and served as an important catalyst for the African Initiated Churches—the AICs.[20] In the first half of the twentieth century, the movement lost much of its religious character and merged into larger Pan-African ideals for political independence. What we have in Ethiopianism is a case study in how a movement can mushroom to the point that it affects entire civilizations, much like what happened in Europe's case. The Protestant Reformation radically transformed a continent, and Ethiopianism was Africa's version of that phenomenon.

The term Ethiopianism comes from Greek word *aithiops* meaning "black face." This word was used in the Septuagint (Greek translation of the Hebrew Old Testament) to translate *Kush*—a geographic term that usually referred to Ethiopia and Sudan, but came to be associated with black Africa in general. In scholarship, Ethiopianism is generally used as a historic term, from the late 1800s and early 1900s, to connote "black nationalism."

The roots of the movement are many. The most obvious is the appropriation by Africans of Ps. 68:31 (KJV), "Princes shall come out of Egypt; Ethiopia [meaning Africa] shall soon stretch out her hands unto God." This verse came to be associated with black dignity, self-

---

20. For Ethiopianism, see Ogbu Kalu, ed., *African Christianity: An African Story* (Trenton, NJ: Africa World Press, 2007); Kalu, *African Pentecostalism: An Introduction* (Oxford: Oxford University Press, 2008); and Bengt Sundkler, *Bantu Prophets in South Africa* (Oxford: Oxford University Press, 1961).

governance, and independent churches. The ideology was inspired by the glories of Africa's ancient past: powerful kings and empires, the cultural achievements of Egypt and Ethiopia, and the importance of Africa in the Bible. Liberated black "returnees" (former slaves, activist intellectuals, and others) who migrated from England and America to Sierra Leone and Liberia were another major tributary to the larger movement. Their return motivated the idea that Africa would be evangelized by her own kinsmen. These migrations created a cosmopolitan, globally interdependent ethos for the Ethiopianist movements. Africans were returning from all corners of the world for the betterment of the homeland.

At its inception, Ethiopianism was enmeshed in both Christianity and black independence. The earliest voices of protest came from highly educated church leaders—mainly Methodist and Anglican—in Africa and the West. Among the early voices were Mangena Mokone, Joseph Mathunye Kanyane Napo, James Mata Dwane, and Samuel James Brander. The key political theorist in the movement was Edward Wilmot Blyden, the father of Pan-Africanism. Many of the early leaders split off from Western mission churches and founded African-led churches, often incorporating terms such as *Ethiopian* or *Cush* into their church titles. It was classic Protestantism with a context quite similar to Luther's. Achieving ecclesial independence just might mean political independence as well. Luther was able to free his beloved German people from the Roman chokehold. Leaders of the Ethiopian movements aspired to evade the coming yoke of the West in the midst of the infamous scramble for Africa in the late nineteenth and early twentieth centuries.

Ethiopia's defense of its land against Italian invaders at the Battle of Adwa in 1896 proved that Africans could defeat white colonial powers. This African self-assertion was feared in the West. In 1906, the *New York Times* published an article that summarized those fears:

"Ethiopian Movement Imperils White Rule."[21] The article referred to Africans as "Kaffirs," a derisive term, and decried the fact that they were getting educated in the West. Ethiopianist uprisings were strongest in South Africa, causing alarm to the point of violent suppression.

Ethiopianism demonstrates one of the great strengths of Protestantism: the dignity of the individual and the critique of an institution that violates this principle. The leaders of the Ethiopianist movements recognized that the status quo—white rule—was unfair and had to be protested. These protests empowered Africans across the continent in the twentieth century. And it is a very important point that when African nations began achieving independence in the 1950s, the churches grew exponentially. Christianity assisted black independence, both politically and ecclesially. Africans returned the favor and crafted Christianity in their own image.

Conclusion: Purity or Unity?

Why are there one hundred different Presbyterian denominations *in South Korea*?[22] Why are there seventy Baptist denominations in the United States?[23] Why do Protestant movements tend to proliferate and fragment, seemingly without end? The answer has to do with authority. Protestants, for all of their heroic protests against social ills and injustices, they always face a choice. Stay in the church and accept the inadequacies of that church, or move on and craft a new church that is purer, more authentic, or more appealing to the individual.

21. "Ethiopian Movement Imperils White Rule," *New York Times*, March 4, 1906, located at http://query.nytimes.com/mem/archive-free/pdf?res=F00B13F63B5A12738DDDAD0894DB405B868CF1D3.
22. See "Korea, Republic of," at *Reformiert Online*, located at http://www.reformiert-online.net/weltweit/land.php?id=75&lg=eng.
23. William Brackney, *Baptists in North America* (Oxford: Blackwell, 2006), 270–71.

It is an Achilles' heel; the greatest strength becomes, tragically, the source of the downfall. However, Protestant durability should not be underestimated. As the Protestant institutions decay, reform is always around the corner. Christianity always remains relevant. While the Catholic and the Orthodox struggle to keep up with the times, Protestants are always ahead of the curve, nimbly adjusting and readjusting in order to meet the needs of the people.

In the twentieth century, Protestants became keenly aware of their divisions, and how those divisions seem so contrary to the unity Jesus prayed for in John 17:23, "That they may be brought to complete unity." Jesus established one church, and it seems scandalous that Christians are so divided over so many things. However, it is equally scandalous when the church refuses to reform—even when it is so clear that it needs to reform. Thus is the predicament of the world church: unity or purity. Protestants tend to emphasize their purity while Catholics and the Orthodox emphasize their own unity. It seems as though we are at a stalemate in world Christianity. One can be Orthodox, Catholic, or one of thousands of Protestant groups.

But what if a movement came along that found a way to navigate these tensions? What if Christians managed to repair the damage that division has caused? What if the Orthodox bishops met with the Roman Catholic bishops and set an example for the Protestants by coming closer into fellowship? My best guess is that the Protestants would take notice, and become inspired by something so obviously, undeniably Christian. How could one possibly deny the rightness of Christian unity?

To whom does Christianity belong? To the purists or to the ecumenists? To the protesters or to the protested against? To the state-church hierarchies or to the revolutionaries? To the massive cathedrals in Russia or to the underground networks in China?

Perhaps it is time for the protesters to protest against Christian division, "so that they may have the full measure of my joy within them." (Jesus' words, in John 17:13)

9

Secularization

Colossians 1:6

The gospel is bearing fruit and growing throughout the whole world—just as it has been doing among you since the day you heard it.

Although we were a bit late, we were excited to attend the advertised piano concert at a beautiful, historic church building in downtown Stockholm in the summer of 2013. My wife and I quietly opened the huge wooden doors only to see a handful of people, maybe six or seven, sitting and listening to beautiful music being played by the expert hands of a middle-aged woman. We walked up the aisle and sat near the front so we could see her dexterity in full display. A disheveled woman clandestinely tried to sell flowers to a perplexed tourist, but was promptly shooed away by the church sexton.

Was this merely a rehearsal? No, it was reality. In Sweden, hardly anyone attends church anymore, even when they provide an impressively trained pianist to try to reach out on behalf of the church.

Christianity has declined so far in Sweden that it is now widely considered one of the most irreligious countries in the world.[1] Estimates are that only 2 percent of the Church of Sweden members even attend worship services anymore, and around 85 percent of the population identify themselves as nonbelievers.[2] Folke Olofsson, a Church of Sweden priest, wrote a moving essay entitled "A Grief Observed—On Being a Priest in a Dying Church." In it, he acknowledges that some people argue Christianity is still alive in Sweden—just underneath the surface. He responds, "The only thing I can say is: I was there, I saw it with my own eyes and that is bad enough."[3] He continues,

> Since my fifteenth year . . . I have been a communicant member of the Church of Sweden. I have gone to communion regularly for forty-five years in what I thought was the *real* church. During these years I have *at the inside* lived with and through all the changes that have taken place, I have seen them being prepared, I have heard the arguments, listened to the debates, seen the campaigns, encountered the propaganda, the threats, the intimidations, the promises, the deceits, the lies, the marginalization and the elimination. I have seen how the church has changed; how it has been occupied and taken over . . . I have seen all the small steps leading to where the Church of Sweden is now. And I have not been able to stop it. . . . And I have had enough. "You have lost," as an English friend said to me over the lunch table. Am I depressed or even dejected? Yes. . . . Am I sick and tired of being a priest in a church which may no longer be a real church? Yes!

Many scholars are joining the chorus: Christianity in Western

1. Sociologist Phil Zuckerman considers "Denmark and Sweden . . . probably the least religious countries in the world, and possibly in the history of the world." Phil Zuckerman, *Society without God* (New York: New York University Press, 2008), 3–4.
2. Statistics come from Maarit Jantera-Jareborg, "Religion and the Secular State in Sweden," in *Religion and Secular State in Sweden* (Provo, Utah: The International Center for Law and Religion Studies, Brigham Young University, 2010), 669–86. Located online at http://www.iclrs.org/content/blurb/files/Sweden.1.pdf.
3. For Olofsson's full-length essay, see http://kalin.nu/english/olofsson.htm A shorter version of the essay was published in the November 2004 issue of *Touchstone* journal: http://www.touchstonemag.com/archives/article.php?id=17-09-032-f.

Europe is on life-support. Friedrich Nietzsche's eerily prophetic words in 1882 seem to have come true: "God is dead. God remains dead. And we have killed him."[4]

Similarly dismal views are being expressed by Christians and scholars in books, magazines, conferences and churches, and they are all asking the same question: What happened to Christianity in Western Europe? In the UK, for instance, the *Independent* featured an article in 2011 with the provocative title, "Will the Last Person to Leave the Church of England Please Turn out the Lights?"[5] Also in 2011, a scientific, census-based analysis forecasted that Christianity may soon die out altogether in Australia, Austria, Canada, the Czech Republic, Finland, Ireland, New Zealand, Switzerland, and the Netherlands.[6]

It is a whole different story in the Global South. In 2013, Guatemalan president Otto Molina openly proclaimed Christ as "Lord of the Nation."[7] In Juarez, Mexico, an evangelical church recently built a life-size rendition of Noah's Ark in order to reach out to the community.[8] Evangelical Christians in Hong Kong opened up a massive Noah's Ark theme park in 2009, complete with a life-sized ark, 180-degree wide screen theater, a reconstruction of the Holy of

4. Friedrich Nietzsche, *The Gay Science*, ed. Bernard Williams, trans. Josefine Nauckhoff (Cambridge: Cambridge University Press, 2001), 120.
5. Adrian Hamilton's article appeared Monday April 18, 2011, located at http://www.independent.co.uk /voices/faith /will-the-last-person-to-leave-the-church-of-england-please-turn-out-the-lights-2269185.html.
6. See D. M. Abrams, H. A. Yaple, and R. J. Weiner, "Dynamics of Social Group Competition: Modeling the Decline of Religious Affiliation," in *Physical Review Letters* 107, no. 8 (August 16, 2011).
7. Jessica Martinez, "Guatemalan President Names Jesus Christ Lord of Guatemala," *Christian Post*, August 26, 2013, located at http://www.christianpost.com/news/guatemalan-president-names-jesus-christ-lord-of-guatemala-103040/.
8. Jessica Martinez, "Mexican Church Builds Life Size Noah's Ark as Symbol of Hope for Community," *Christian Post*, August 29, 2013, located at http://www.christianpost.com/news/mexican-church-builds-life-size-noahs-ark-as-symbol-of-hope-for-community-103346/.

Holies, and galleries geared toward a creationist understanding of the world.[9] For $200 one can reserve a deluxe room.

In the Global South, churches are struggling to keep up with a massive Christian boom. Prominent Catholic journalist John L. Allen Jr., writes, "The biggest pastoral and administrative headache for many Southern Catholic leaders is managing growth, not contraction."[10] He writes that in Latin America, seminary enrollments have risen by around 440 percent in the last twenty-five years. Even still, "substantial increases in priests have not been enough to keep pace with the growth of the Catholic population."[11]

Secular: A Loaded Word

Secularization is an important idea, but the word is not entirely straightforward. Scholars mean different things when they talk about it. In a landmark work, *Rethinking Secularism*, the editors describe the problem:

> Secularism . . . is only one of a cluster of related terms. Reference to the secular, secularity, secularism, and secularization can mean different things in confusing ways. There is no simple way to standardize usage now by trying to ensure an association of each term with only one clearly defined concept. . . . The very use of the term "secular" signifies that we are buying into a secular/religious distinction that in some way defines not only the secular sphere itself but also the realm of the religious. However one defines secularity and secularism . . . it involves religion. It is either the absence of it, the control over it, the equal treatment of its various forms, or its replacement by the social values common to a secular way of life.[12]

---

9. See the Noah's Ark theme park website at http://www.noahsark.com.hk/eng/index.php.
10. John L. Allen Jr., *The Future Church: How Ten Trends Are Revolutionizing the Catholic Church* (New York: Doubleday, 2009), 28.
11. He cites the work of Edward Cleary for this statistic. See ibid., 29.
12. Craig Calhoun, Mark Juergensmeyer, and Jonathan Van Antwerpen, eds., *Rethinking Secularism* (Oxford: Oxford University Press, 2011), 5.

The authors point out that the etymological root to the Latin word *saeculum* simply means "century" or "age." However, over time, the word *secular* evolved to refer to members of the Christian clergy who served in parishes—rather than the clergy who joined monasteries and religious orders. A "secular" priest was therefore one who worked in the world. A cloistered nun or monk was not considered "secular" because she or he avoided "the world" by remaining separate, as in a monastery. It is very ironic that while the word *secular* once referred to a type of clergy, it now refers to a person or institution that is not religious.

The word *secular* has come to signify something irreligious, but it plays out in myriad ways. The French Revolution was an attempt to secularize by marginalizing, indeed punishing, the Catholic Church. Between the years of 1789 and 1801 the state enacted a number of policies to undermine the church: "laicization"—turning clergy into employees of the state, reclaiming land from the Church, converting churches into "Temples of Reason," and widespread persecution of priests, including executions. In Mustafa Kemal Ataturk's Turkey, in the 1920s, Islam was formally removed from its once privileged position as the religion of the state. In 1940s India, Jawaharlal Nehru, the first prime minister after independence, wanted to promote religious tolerance by marginalizing religion. He thought secularism was a "pillar of modernity," and thus by advocating secularity, religion's importance would decline. To Nehru, the diminishing of religion would lead to a more just, equal, and tolerant society.[13] Gandhi disagreed with him in fundamental ways on these issues.

13. See discussion of Nehru in ibid., 6–9.

Secularism: Two Very Different Interpretations

In recent decades, in the United States, a great debate exists over religion's influence in society. On one extreme of the spectrum is the Religious Right, a group of Americans who believe that God and country are one; for the nation to forsake God would be immoral and unpatriotic. On the other end is what we might be called radical secularism, the belief that religion and state institutions should be cleanly separated. Secularists will argue that America is home to many religions, and in order to respect all of them, the nation must privilege none of them. There are numerous positions in between, and combinations of secular/religious can become complex. Looming over all the discourse, however, is a volatile question that elicits passionate responses: Is America becoming secular in the way many Western European nations are? It is an important question because America is the largest Christian-majority nation in the world, and its influence on world Christianity is incalculable at this point in time. What Americans decide on these matters will, no doubt, influence how many other nations respond.

I am convinced Europeans and North Americans have very different understandings of the word *secular*. The reason is because Americans do not really understand the concept of state church. But Europeans understand it well. Some even struggle to think of church and state as separate entities. When British scholar Linda Woodhead was asked, "What should change, Church or society?" Her response is telling:

> The reason I was dumbfounded was that I had never thought of the Church like that—as separate from society. The more I reflected on it, the less sense it made to think of the Church of England without England. . . . Rather than ignoring or repressing the Church of England's deep insertion into society, the time seems ripe for rediscovering it as its saving asset. . . . Once the Church starts to exist

for the benefit of activists alone, it ceases to be a Church, and becomes a sect.[14]

For her, a church without the state is virtually incomprehensible.

For Americans, secularization is a society-wide drift away from Christianity. Europeans, however, have in mind a gradual divorce of church and state. These two mammoth institutions that have defined European civilization since the days of the Holy Roman Empire are going their separate ways, slowly but surely. And, for the most part, Europeans seem to welcome the process after all these years of living under its authority: one must get baptized in the church, file paperwork with the church, get married in the church, go through catechism in the church, and pay taxes for the church to be maintained and staffed. It was all part of life, and Western Europeans welcome a new era of separation in the name of freedom. People should have the freedom to marry however they want, freedom to divorce, freedom to donate to whatever religion they choose, freedom to reject the church without feeling social shame, freedom to make individual decisions about whether children should be taught religion in school. These are old issues in the United States, and most of them have been settled for generations. But they are still being sorted out in Europe, where, in many cases, the church and the state are still quite interdependent.[15]

Understanding the Scholarly Discourse

The secularization thesis, popularized by important social theorists such as Marx, Freud, Weber, and Durkheim, is that modernization

14. Linda Woodhead, "Measuring the Church's Social Footprint," *Church Times*, February 14, 2014, located at http://www.churchtimes.co.uk/articles/2014/14-february/features/features/measuring-the-church-s-social-footprint.
15. See Rodney Stark, *The Triumph of Christianity* (New York: HarperOne, 2011), 377. Stark shows the various ways that Western European nations privilege, subsidize, and further endow their traditional state churches.

would lead to a marginalization of religion. As the needs of people are met, religion will melt away. As science discovers more, humans will see that our world is not magical or spiritual—it is material. And religion stifles the search for truth. Religion is seen as a massive, unyielding force impeding human progress. It provides false answers. People are urged to pray that God will come to the rescue. In science, people figure out the truth of the matter, leading to real solutions. Anthropologist pioneers Tylor and Frazer critiqued religion on this point. Science does not make the blunders so common in religious thinking. Science offers facts. Religion offers explanations riddled with magical creatures and untestable absurdities.

Secularization discourse can be rancorous, highly complex, and provocative.[16] In one of the best overviews of the topic, Mary Eberstadt argues, "Everyone has a dog of one kind or another in the fight over secularization—ardent secularists and pious churchgoers alike."[17] There is today an entire industry devoted to studying secularization, its causes, its prospects, and whether it is even a real thing. The Social Science Research Council in the United States has devoted years to the topic, resulting in excellent books and a major online research initiative, *The Immanent Frame*.[18]

What complicates secularization discourse is that eminent scholars of religion take hard, contradictory positions on the topic. For example, historian Callum Brown argues, "It is in my lifetime that the people have forsaken formal Christian religion, and the churches have entered seemingly terminal decline. . . . From 1956, all indices

---

16. For an excellent description of how the debate plays out in scholarly discourse, see Robert Wuthnow, *Boundless Faith: The Global Outreach of American Churches* (Los Angeles: University of California Press, 2009), 47–51.

17. Mary Eberstadt, *How the West Really Lost God: A New Theory of Secularization* (West Conshohocken, PA: Templeton Press, 2013), 6.

18. See especially Calhoun, Juergensmeyer, and Van Antwerpen, *Rethinking Secularism*. See *The Immanent Frame* at http://blogs.ssrc.org/tif/about/. See also NYU Press's upcoming book series *The Secular Studies Series*, ed. by Phil Zuckerman.

of religiosity in Britain start to decline, and from 1963 most enter free fall."[19] Brown argues it is critical that we understand this process from a historical perspective because it is an undeniable reality. Britain is secular. Similarly, Robert Putnam and David Campbell argue, "Americans have become somewhat less observant religiously over the last half-century."[20]

On the opposite side, however, there are equally influential scholars who completely disagree with these ideas. For instance, sociologists Rodney Stark and Peter Berger take the view that Western Europe was never very religious. Christianity was a political entity, as kings baptized entire populations without really evangelizing them. Stark writes, "It's not that Scandinavians, for example, have stopped going to church; they never did go."[21] And in his estimation, the United States is as religiously robust as ever, if not more so.[22] Stark refers to any talk of "the end of Christian America" as being patently "absurd." He writes, "Americans show no signs of losing their belief in supernatural beings."[23] In Stark's view, it would be preposterous to advance a metatheory of secularization that it is somehow linked to modernity, rationality, or increased wealth. Both he and Berger believe the future of the world looks much more religious than irreligious, especially since once-powerful Marxist blocks such as China and Eastern Europe continue to ease restrictions on religion.

Statistics are used by both sides to support their theses. However, they do not really paint a consistent picture. For example, the impressive Eurobarometer survey, which addresses public opinion in

19. Callum Brown, *The Death of Christian Britain* (New York: Routledge, 2001), 30, 188.
20. Robert Putnam and David Campbell, *American Grace: How Religion Divides and Unites Us* (New York: Simon and Schuster, 2010), 79–80.
21. Stark, *Triumph of Christianity*, 376.
22. See for example Rodney Stark, "Secularization, R.I.P.," *Sociology of Religion* 60, no. 3 (1999); and Peter Berger, ed., *The Desecularization of the World* (Grand Rapids, MI: Eerdmans, 1999).
23. Stark, *Triumph of Christianity*, 370, 372.

the European Union and EU candidate countries, does not really clarify what Europeans think about religion, but it does point to complexity.[24] For instance, Europeans still "think about the meaning and purpose of life" in large numbers. "Only 8 percent declare that they never have such philosophical reflections." Greeks and Cypriots think most often about life's meaning whereas Austrians and Hungarians ponder these matters the least.

The vast majority of Europeans have religious and spiritual beliefs, although not in overwhelmingly Christian ways. In 2010, around 20 percent of Europeans claimed there is no "spirit, God, or life force."[25] Around 77 percent believe in "a God" (51 percent) or a "spirit or life force" (26 percent). In descending order, Romania (92 percent), Malta (94 percent), Cyprus (88 percent), Greece (79 percent), Poland (79 percent), Italy (74 percent), Portugal (70 percent), and Ireland (70 percent) are the EU nations where most people "believe there is a God." All of them claim to believe in a God at a rate 70 percent or higher. Conspicuously, no Protestant nations believe in a God at a rate above 50 percent. The highest is Germany, at 44 percent, and this is accounted for by the fact that Protestants only slightly outnumber Catholics in Germany; thus Catholics offset the Protestants' lack of belief.

Among European Union and EU candidate Protestant-majority nations, there is reason to think belief in a God will soon become something of the past. Protestant nations have very low rates when asked if they believe in a God: the UK (37 percent), Denmark (28

24. See the 2005 Eurobarometer survey, "Social Values, Science and Technology," located at http://ec.europa.eu/public_opinion/archives/ebs/ebs_225_report_en.pdf. See section 1.2, "Religious and Spiritual Beliefs."

25. Data comes from Eurobarometer "Biotechnology" report in 2010, located at http://ec.europa.eu/public_opinion/archives/ebs/ebs_341_en.pdf. I used the 2010 data here because it was the most recent data I could find. The most recent *analysis* is from 2005, which is why I used it in the previous paragraph. Between 2005 and 2010 few significant changes occurred, except in the case of Portugal, which dropped from 81 percent to 70 percent when respondents were asked whether they believe in a God.

percent), Finland (33 percent), Iceland (31 percent), Norway (22 percent), Sweden (18 percent), and Estonia (18 percent). Sweden and Estonia may be the most secular nations on earth. However, the nations with the highest rates of atheism—defined as "You don't believe there is any sort of spirit, God or life force"—are France (40 percent), Czech Republic (37 percent), Sweden (34 percent), and the Netherlands (30 percent). One interesting nation here is EU candidate Turkey, with a population over 99 percent Muslim. Turks believe in a God at a rate of 94 percent; only 1 percent of them do not believe in any kind of God or spirit.

In Europe, Protestant nations are moving away from faith much quicker than Catholic or Orthodox nations, with Scandinavia being "ground zero of secularization."[26] There are many theories for why this is happening. One is that when churches become more lax in their requirements, commitment levels fall. There is good evidence for making this case. An obvious example is Mormons: tighter controls on membership conduct seem to result in higher rates of participation. Similarly, Pentecostals and other conservative Protestants are not losing as much ground in their numbers. Rodney Stark argues that "lazy, monopoly churches," offer an "extremely inexpensive religion, stripped of moral demands." They have become "obstructionist" and disallow religious competition from coming in and shaking things up.[27] And there is a growing body of research making this point, such as Laurence Iannaccone's "Why Strict Churches Are Strong" and Dean Kelley's *Why Conservative Churches Are Growing*.[28]

26. Eberstadt, *How the West Really Lost God*, 48.
27. Stark, *Triumph of Christianity*, 376, 379.
28. Laurence Iannaccone, "Why Strict Churches Are Strong," *The American Journal of Sociology* 99, no. 5 (March 1994): 1180–1211. Dean Kelley, *Why Conservative Churches Are Growing* (Macon, GA: Mercer University Press, 1996).

However, the so-called mainline Protestant traditions—Anglicans, Lutherans, Presbyterians—"are in dire straits" all over the Western world. Mary Eberstadt has asked pointedly, "Is Protestantism really the cause of secularism?" Her conclusion is thus: "One way of understanding 'secularization' is this: it is the phenomenon through which Protestants, generally speaking, go godless and Catholics, generally speaking, go Protestant."[29] And Protestants decline faster when they stray from tradition. "Both within the churches as well as between churches, what is traditional tends to be strong." Where do we put the blame for all this? She argues it is the fault of the Reformation. It "had one clear consequence: it has weakened the churches that attempted it." They stopped emphasizing family, they had fewer children, their memberships grayed, their pews emptied, and their finances declined since worshipers failed to replace themselves. It is a familiar tale in nations where fertility rates hover at two children per woman or less.[30]

Bishop Simo: Case Study in Finland

In 2013 I interviewed Simo Peura, a bishop in the Finnish Evangelical Lutheran Church.[31] As he is also a competent scholar, I wanted to get his perspective on why Western Europe secularized so quickly and why the Nordic countries in particular seem to have cut their ties with traditional Christianity. After a brief history lesson, we began to get into the main reason I wished to visit.

Bishop Simo began by expressing his view that Americans think about the church as "free market capitalism." And he does not like the idea at all. Americans preach sermons that they think will grow

---

29. Eberstadt, *How the West Really Lost God*, 53.
30. Ibid., 153–54.
31. Interview with Bishop Simo Peura, November 1, 2013, at BEXCO (Busan Exhibition and Conference Center), Busan, South Korea.

the flock. In his view, the gospel should be proclaimed "as it is" and people can then decide whether they want to respond. Americans, however, "preach in such a way as to impress the audience," which is not good because they cannot preach their convictions. Rather, they have to preach in a way that will attract more business.

The Finnish church is very different. Eighty percent of the population is Lutheran. People pay membership fees, and the state collects taxes. People are not obligated to pay the church. In fact it is quite easy to surrender one's membership. Employees of the church are paid by the state. And the church pays a certain sum of money to the state to cover the costs of collecting and distributing. I asked the bishop if memberships were going up or down and he said they had gone down roughly 1 percent "in the last few years" which, obviously, may threaten parish budgets in the future. He did not seem overly worried about this problem, however. But he did state that the Finnish system has a tragic flaw here, because "you don't have to worry about your flock if they start to turn away." In other words, "Finland pastors don't have pressure like in a business." I was reminded of Stark's "lazy church" argument: "The money continues to come whether or not people attend, so there is no need for clergy to exert themselves," and religion becomes "a type of public utility."[32]

What really concerns the bishop, however, is the church losing its young people. Youth do not seem to recognize that they need the church's voice to help them. "The problem today is individualism," he said. I brought up Luther's commitment to *sola scriptura*—that the individual should have the freedom to make her own individual decisions based on her own interpretation of the Bible. However, the bishop warned, the problem is not that people want to interpret the Bible. The problem is that the people feel they can be Christian

32. Stark, *Triumph of Christianity*, 377.

183

without the church. They feel like they can connect with God without the collective wisdom of centuries of faith. Young people are short-circuiting the process, believing they can access God without the community of the faithful.

In light of the absence of youth, I asked the bishop about the future of his church. His response was that there is great hope . . . in Africa. He said he went to Tanzania recently and was amazed at the growth in the Lutheran churches there. He said the Finnish churches need to learn from their African counterparts.

However, when it comes to Finland, "only 2 percent of the members participate in Sunday services," and "that number is still falling downward all the time." Almost without exception the people look to the church when a person dies because they want a church funeral. He stated that this may mean that people "at the end of the day, believe in heaven and hell." The church tries to appeal to the people: children clubs, confirmation classes, camps, young mother groups. They try to get volunteers to sign up and get involved. But the numbers are working against them. There are other factors working against them as well: "Many people . . . don't like what the church represents. For example, what to think about gay people? The Finnish church has been conservative. There are no blessings for same-sex couples."

I asked the bishop to identify the most important challenges facing his church and he provided three: 1) the church must figure out how to get people more engaged, especially volunteers; 2) the church must come up with more robust worship services because "they are irrelevant today"; and 3) the Finnish church should realize that it is now a mission field. "Tanzania used to be the mission field for Lutherans from Finland. But today we in Finland are the mission field."

In conclusion, the bishop said the Nordic churches are in a deep crisis. "In a generation or two—even today in many cases—the children will not understand the Christian connection because Christian teaching is failing." He said there is a vast, Christian background that the Nordic nations are forgetting. In a short time, these nations will not recognize the wonderful social programs they have were in fact brought about because of Christianity.

Rev. Dr. Jutta: Case Study in Germany

In chapter 4 I discussed a few aspects of a long interview I had with Rev. Dr. Jutta Koslowski, a Protestant pastor from Germany, but here I recount it more fully. Jutta described many of the same tensions that Bishop Simo did. But in a few key areas she disagreed with him. For instance, when I asked Pastor Jutta about "reverse missions" from Africa, she replied strongly, "Germans and Africans are very different. Besides, the African churches are African in nature and in membership. It is a poor excuse for German Christians to sit back and think that the Africans will re-evangelize Germany. This is something the *German* churches should do."[33] I brought up Stark's idea that perhaps Germany was never truly evangelized to begin with. She disagreed, claiming, "Christianity was rooted deeply in the society and culture for centuries, but it is now secularized. The reason? It is because of a crisis of authenticity in the church. The Second World War was the culmination point. The churches failed to carry out a message that was trustworthy." Jutta explained that the German churches were "packed" during the Second World War. The staggering declines happened only after the war because the churches failed to share a message. In addition, "The churches mingled with

---

33. Interview with Jutta Koslowski, November 6, 2013, at HanWha Resort, Busan, South Korea.

the Hitler regime. When Hitler fell, the church was vulnerable. It had been on the wrong side."

Jutta gave a fascinating explanation for the great decline of the German church. She claimed the church is extremely guilty and burdened by the events of the Second World War. However, at this point in the interview, she began to stare into the distance. I was struck by her loss of words here. She is a very articulate person, but this topic stopped her in an uncharacteristic way. Quietly, she said, "The spirit isn't in the churches anymore. The churches have not repented properly. Churches don't want to face the complicity. They do not want to face these difficult issues. There is regret, of course, but no repentance. This is the spiritual dimension." She questioned aloud whether God had withdrawn from the German church. She asked, "Is Christianity still God's partner on earth?" She brought up the Jews—they were God's partner but kept failing, so God established a new partner with the founding of Christianity. But after the Shoah, Christians were complicit in horrific crimes, causing Rev. Jutta to wonder whether God might be looking for a new partner again. "Maybe God is looking for people who are upright. Maybe God is looking for people who focus on ethical matters."

Jutta said it is hard to get into the pulpit and preach because of this ambiguity. "The churches have failed," she said. And the people feel a collective sense of failure about their church. She prepares weekly sermons for her parish of sixteen hundred people near Frankfurt, but "only four older ladies come to services." Sometimes even one or two of these ladies cannot make it, and she cancels the sermon.

As an American, I am amazed by the tragedy of the situation. Here is an articulate, highly educated, deeply religious woman preparing sermons for three or four people. Why does she do it?

Her answer was this: she believes in the church, but in the case of Germany, two things are needed urgently: repentance, and a radical change in theology. She said we are living in a crucial time. It is a time of science and medicine. And the paradigm shift will continue to occur, and churches must train differently, preach differently, construct theology differently. She said she agrees with Dietrich Bonhoeffer that all humans will experience salvation at the *eschaton*—the last days. Redemption is no longer at the center of her theology since, in the end, all will be saved.

I pressed her again on the issue of reverse mission, and whether Europe will open itself up to Christians who immigrate into her nation's borders, bringing their faith with them. But she held firm to her earlier position: "Reverse mission is a good idea. But I doubt whether it will go to Europe. Korean missionaries can work in China, but that won't work in Europe. There is still a huge amount of work to be done in China. Yes, I hope they can evangelize China. But I have no hope that Christianity in the Global South will take root in Germany." She argued that Western Europe needs a new Christianity that appeals to a "critical mind." The Christianity of the Global South has yet to sufficiently answer the penetrating questions of the Enlightenment. Thus, a theology for Germany, and for Europe, must be "intellectually mature."

I asked her about Pentecostalism and charismatic Christianity. She said it is "very marginal" in Germany, and will "never become mainstream." She said she is in communication with Pentecostals, and they claim to be growing. But she does not see growth. They constantly announce revival, but it is not happening. She reiterated her point: "Christianity in Europe will not be revived with the Global South styles of faith."

I asked her if a new theology for Europe would be pluralistic and she said no. She still believes in the beauty of the Christian message. But it must be renewed. "This does not mean to replace Christian theology with a new religion, but we need to privilege the aspects of our theology that are rooted in the Bible."

Although trained in theology, Jutta said her focus is on being a pastor. She said it is difficult. In fact, she stated, "Most of my colleagues try to hide that they are pastors." But she firmly believes in proclaiming the gospel, even in a land of deaf ears. People are curious by her desire to preach. "Pastors are on the front lines, receiving the bias against the church. There is no hostility against the church, it is more of a friendly reservation."

And that may be the greatest challenge posed by secularization: indifference, apathy, a "friendly reservation." In the future, the European churches will have to figure out how to make the gospel message necessary again. They will have to justify their existence. It is a problem reminiscent of New Testament times. How do you convince someone they need the message of Jesus Christ?

Conclusion: 10 Percent Full

Philip Jenkins has discussed Christianity in Western Europe as being a glass 90 percent empty. But, he cautions,

> We can also see it as 10 percent full, and in a continent as populous as Europe, even that small fraction is not negligible. Moreover, the events of September 11 and subsequent Muslim–Christian controversies have led some Europeans to pay renewed attention to Christian values and practices. It remains to be seen whether such innovations represent the seeds of new growth or the last gutterings of faith.[34]

With the Psalmist in Psalm 121, Europeans committed to Christ must be asking, "From whence cometh our help?" The answer: "Your help cometh from the Lord, which made heaven and earth." Will the Lord preserve Europe as he preserved Israel? Will the Lord "preserve thy

---

34. Philip Jenkins, *The Next Christendom: The Coming of Global Christianity*, rev. and expanded ed. (Oxford: Oxford University Press, 2007), xiii.

going out and thy coming in from this time forth?" Certainly, at the present, it seems far more people are "going out" than those who are "coming in." The theologian in me can only sit in wonder at what God might be doing to this land that only a hundred years ago was sending missionaries to the ends of the earth. Who would have thought today it would be in the state it is in, religiously speaking?

Is America next? Some think so. The years 1990 to 2012 have been called "The Great Decline." Political scientist Tobin Grant writes, "The drop in religiosity has been twice as great as the decline of the 1960s and 1970s."[35] Sociologist Mark Chaves has sounded the alarm: American Christianity is changing faster than we might have imagined. And it will change America, inevitably. In his view, seminaries are not attracting the quality of student that they used to, and fewer people choose the ministry as a career. Thus the clergy is aging. Liberal Protestants are swiftly joining the ranks of the "nones"—those who claim no religious affiliation. Ultimately, he writes, "If there is a trend, it is toward less religion."[36]

To whom does Christianity belong? Can Europe even claim it anymore? Frans Verstraelen argues, strongly, yes! He makes the case that Christians, scholarly and nonscholarly alike, should be paying careful attention to European Christianity *precisely because* it has survived—albeit tattered—the "onslaught of secularism." Christianity in Europe has been "tested and purified." And do not think for a moment that the rest of the world will avoid having to deal with secularization. It is coming. It will come to Asia, Africa, and Latin

---

35. Tobin Grant, "The Great Decline: 60 years of Religion in One Graph," *Religion News Service*, January 27, 2014, located at http://tobingrant.religionnews.com/2014/01/27/great-decline-religion-united-states-one-graph/.

36. Mark Chaves, *American Religion: Contemporary Trends* (Princeton, NJ: Princeton University Press, 2011), 110. See also the helpful article by Peter Foster, "American Is Turning Secular Much Faster Than We Realise," *The Telegraph*, February 20, 2014, located at http://blogs.telegraph.co.uk/news/peterfoster/100260301/america-is-turning-secular-much-faster-than-we-realise/.

America just as it came to Europe. Indeed, just as it is hitting the shores of North America.[37]

However, it is far too early to discuss secularization in Asia, Africa, and Latin America right now. Religiosity in those contexts is booming. As Asia experiences newfound religious freedom, Christianity continues to swell dramatically. As Africa becomes the new Christian heartland, Christianity's agenda for the twenty-first century will be set by pastors in Kenya and Nigeria rather than by bishops in Italy or England. And as Latin America deals with Pentecostal growth, churches will have to compete for members. But competition can be good for business. Irrelevant churches are forced to close shop as innovative, customer-driven ways of doing Christianity proliferate. The Roman Catholic Church will have to reinvent itself in order to prevent further hemorrhaging.

But, secularization in the Global South? No. It's way too early for that conversation. World Christianity is still reeling from the rather sudden secularization of Western Europe and Canada, and, increasingly, the United States.

Olav Fykse Tveit, the general secretary of the World Council of Churches, recently put it this way, "It is important not to see secularism only as negative; it is also a challenge: How are we to express Christian faith more authentically?"[38]

The future of Christianity hinges on whether it can meet that challenge.

---

37. Frans Verstraelen, "Jenkins' *The Next Christendom* and Europe," in *Global Christianity: Contested Claims*, ed. Frans Wijsen and Robert Schreiter (New York: Rodopi, 2007), 114–15.

38. See "We Have to Build Bridges," *World Council of Churches*, April 3, 2014, located at http://www.oikoumene.org/en/press-centre/news/201cwe-have-to-build-bridges201d-says-wcc-general-secretary-during-his-visit-to-finland.

10

Missions and Migration

Matthew 2:13

An angel of the Lord appeared to Joseph in a dream. "Get up," he said, "take the child and his mother and escape to Egypt."

Migration narratives are not new to the Christian faith. Abraham was called to migrate, as was Moses, Nehemiah, Jesus, the apostles, and so many people of faith since. The Gospel of Matthew explains that Mary and Joseph, with their baby, migrated to Egypt in order to escape a crisis that threatened the life of Jesus.

I cannot help but to think of the refugees who flood into the United States of America, from Latin America, to escape innumerable crises there: poverty, drug wars, hopelessness, and unemployment. They work hard in our strawberry fields and send their money back home to support wives, husbands, children, and parents.

Perhaps no other global issue compares to the gravity of this one: migration. People who live in hopeless contexts want to get out, so they move. And as they travel, they bring their faith with them.

Sometimes it is the only resource they have. In a way they have become missionaries, albeit unintentionally.

Migration and missions are issues that are tied together in the twenty-first century. They cannot be separated. Immigrants from hopeless contexts move to hopeful contexts. And whether headed to the United States, Spain, Canada, or the UK, the story is the same. People want a taste of what they perceive to be the promised land. Yet they are not willing to sever ties with the motherland—especially when it comes to religion.

A Missionary to Canada

In 1999 I received an invitation from the University of Calgary's Religious Studies Department to work on a PhD. It was the greatest piece of snail mail that I have ever received. However, I was not prepared for the great mountain of paperwork that had to be completed for my wife and me to relocate internationally. We packed our little 1995 Mazda Protégé and headed from Texas to the Great White North. We became, officially, international migrants.

Migrating to another nation is difficult, expensive, and complicated. And once arrived in the new land, the foreigner becomes vulnerable. One mistake and we get deported. I went through extremely intrusive physical exams where every cavity of my body was searched for any sign of disease. To whom shall I complain? I was a migrant. Besides, Canada cannot afford a bunch of sick immigrants, especially in a nation that offers socialized health care. I had to prove that I was healthy, smart, and had enough money to make my own way. With a little support, I would return the favor one day by paying my taxes. Hopefully, the investment Canada was making in me would pay dividends for them in the long run. In a nation of low fertility, they needed me as a source of revenue, as much as I needed them for an excellent education. They needed my labor, and my posterity. I needed their professors to educate me.

We were poor, renting the basement of a young couple. My wife worked as a nanny for a wealthy, young Korean couple. They often came home much later than they said they would. But who's complaining? It was work. She also drove an hour to work at Pots and Peppers selling kitchenware. I was grading papers for the university, for pennies. It was just part of paying my dues as I worked my way up the ladder. You must start somewhere, and we were on the bottom rung.

Suddenly, in came a gift from God. Little did I know, I was about to become a missionary. Americans are, on average, more religious than Canadians, or so the statistics say. And Americans from Texas are certainly more religious than the average Canadian. Like Europeans, Canadians are moving away from Christian faith—they are secularizing—at a quicker pace than in the United States. A young, enthusiastic, twenty-six-year-old minister with a passion for Jesus is not altogether common in Canada. Within my first year I was asked to pastor a church. It was a godsend. This little ecumenical Disciples of Christ/United Church of Canada congregation, Campbell-Stone United, asked if I would serve as their minister. They offered me a salary, a respectable array of benefits, and a pulpit for preaching the word of God. "But I'm working on a PhD; I don't know if I can commit the time you need." That's fine. They wanted a pastor, and they had not been able to find one. In fact they were on the cusp of closing their doors. Nobody was interested. This wonderful congregation brought me in and supported me as if I was a long-lost relative. "Let us know if we need to help you with a down payment for a mortgage." This is the world of Christianity. Trust is often instant. I accepted the position (but declined the mortgage help). I was a missionary.

I served that church for seven years, some of the best years of my life. They watched me grow up. They encouraged me to stand for ordination, which I did. The Christian Church (Disciples of Christ) received me into their fold on St. Patrick's Day (March 17), 2002—by far one of the most important days of my life. They put on their work clothes and helped us move our belongings to a house near the church. One of the members, an accountant, freely assisted us with our extremely complicated taxes from two nations. They taught us that in Canada you are supposed to bring wine to people's homes when you visit them (certainly not something we were used to in Texas). They encouraged us to file for citizenship, which we did. Our status changed from "landed immigrants" to "citizens" of the great nation of Canada in 2005. They supported us financially, spiritually, and socially as we became part of them. They rejoiced when our twin babies were born in 2006. It was painful to leave them in 2007 when we moved back to the United States to take up a position teaching at Pepperdine University in California.

Once again we were migrants. Once again we were in a foreign place, at the mercy of another group of people to support us, to show us the ropes, to accept us, and to allow us into their personal lives. In California, I began to teach religious studies in the university and pastor a church in nearby Pasadena. As I reflect back on my life's migrations—from California (where I was born) to New Mexico (where I grew up) to Texas (college) to Canada and back to California, I am humbled by the amount of effort that has gone into supporting me and my family at various stages: a child, a college student, a minister, a professor, a husband and a father. I have received mercy and hospitality from countless faces and hands in my life, and I am grateful. None of the migrations would have happened without the support of others. And it was always people of deep Christian faith who welcomed us and lifted us onto our feet.

Reverse Flows and New Methods

As a professor in an American university, each semester I see many Korean and Chinese students who have come to my classroom to receive a coveted education in the United States. It is their key to a noble profession. That degree will enable them to hold their heads high in this life as they proudly return home to joyous cheers and praise. With degree in hand, and perfect English-speaking skills in their tool box, these foreign students will open up doors for their family members and friends. Many of these people are of deep Christian faith. Some will become Christians once in the United States, often because Christians offered them support during their hour of need. A few of them understand themselves as missionaries, combining their faith with their quest for a better life.

These are the new missionaries: "Guest workers, students, labor migrants, asylum seekers, family reunification migrants, political and economic refugees."[1] These world wanderers are rapidly changing the landscape of Christianity. The old days—when Western missionaries from Europe and North America went out to proclaim the gospel to the rest of the world—have passed. There are new flows now, both *to* the rest of the world and *from* the rest of the world.

Andrew Walls has written extensively about the Great European Migration—when Europeans moved all over the world for adventure, for their government, and for their faith.[2] They fanned out in all directions, settling in North America, South America, Oceania,

---

1. Jehu Hanciles, "Migration and the Globalization of Christianity," in *Understanding World Christianity: The Vision and Work of Andrew F. Walls*, ed. William Burrows, Mark Gornik, and Janice McLean (Maryknoll, NY: Orbis, 2011), 236.
2. This is a common theme in Walls's many works, but see the excellent speech "Christian Mission in a Five Hundred Year Context," located online at http://webcache.googleusercontent.com/search?q=cache:q15sGUDYvysJ:www.liverpoolcathedral.org.uk/642/ajax.aspx/download/193&cd=1&hl=en&ct=clnk&gl=us. See also Walls, "Mission and Migration: The Diaspora Factor in Christian History," in *Journal of African Christian Thought* 5, no. 2 (2002).

North Africa, sub-Sahara, India, Indonesia, the Middle East, and China. The Great European Migration began in the 1400s when southern European Catholics sailed out first. Northern European Protestants were delayed by a few hundred years, but they made an equally massive impact on the world's people and cultures. It was a colossal spreading of European values, economics, political interests, and, yes, religiosity. These two great migrations are precisely why Christianity is the largest religion in six of the world's eight cultural block. Only in the Middle East and in Asia is Christianity not the major religion. In the other cultural block—Africa, Oceania, Latin America, North America, Eastern Europe, and Western Europe—Christianity claims the allegiance of more people than any other religion.

The reasons these Europeans launched out are complex. Walls writes, "Some went under compulsion, as refugees, indentured laborers or convicts, some under their conditions of employment as soldiers or officials, some from lust of wealth or power. Most, however, were simply seeking a better life or a more just society than they found in Europe."[3] Europe began consolidating the world, politically. Maps were redrawn according to Europeans' ways of perceiving. Power was increasingly in the hands of Europe as new civilizations came into being such as the Americas and Australia. Muslims came under the scepter of Queen Victoria, who had "more Muslim subjects than the sultan ever had. By the 1920s it was hard to find an independent Muslim ruler who was not a client of a Western power."[4]

But suddenly, in the twentieth century, the Great European Migration "came to a halt and went into reverse." Thus began the "Great Reverse Migration."[5] The former European imperial satellite

---

3. Walls, "Christian Mission in a Five Hundred Year Context," 1.
4. Ibid., 2.

states began to move to Europe. They came from all of the places the Europeans had been: the Caribbean, Polynesia, North Africa, Latin America, and sub-Sahara. And many of these people are willing to risk their lives to get through the gates of Europe and North America.

Where does religion fit into this? Remarkably, the receiving nations became very religious during the half-millennium from 1500 to 2000, while the sending nations became secular. Walls comments on this most perplexing phenomenon:

> Here is the strangest development of the Great European Migration. The Christian faith declined sharply and so rapidly in what had long been its heartland, the apparent center of its strength, in lands where it had permeated culture and molded law and custom, while it spread into lands beyond. It was not the first time in Christian history that what seemed to be the heart of the Church wilted, and it may not be the last. Christian history is marked by such collapses in the locations of apparent Christian strength which has coincided with rapid growth at what seemed to be the margins. The majority of those who profess the Christian faith are now Africans, Asians, Latin Americans, and Pacific Islanders; and they substantially outnumber the professed Christians of Europe, the old Christendom, and its North American outcrop.[6]

The trends continue apace. Today, Christianity is migrating. As it leaves the Western world, especially the cities and the intellectual circles, it is increasingly attractive to Asians. Asia, with over half of the world's population, may one day become another great Christendom, after Latin America and sub-Sahara. Christianity has always shifted and moved. It is the parable of the sower in real time: one culture accepts the seeds of the gospel—and it flourishes, while another land loses the gospel due to its getting choked by other concerns. Or else the ground just hardens up. No more fertility in the soil.

5. Ibid., 1, 3.
6. Ibid., 8.

Short Term Missions

No longer is it in vogue for Western missionaries to go abroad for the duration of their lives, as in yesteryear. It is expensive business to fund people for that kind of work. Today, Westerners prefer the short-term mission model: go abroad for a week or two, make a few connections, and return home. It is almost a rite of passage for America's Christian youth: Guatemala to work with poor kids, Mexico for building a house, Kenya for street ministry, or Rwanda for reconciliation study.

According to Robert Wuthnow, billions of American dollars are spent on short-term missions. And the number of personnel involved is huge. Around 1.4 million Americans take a short-term mission trip each year.[7] But the jury is still out on whether these trips are good investments of time and money. Wuthnow provides myriad statistics showing how popular short term missions have become for American Christians. But the history of the movement is foggy. He writes, "Nobody knows exactly when amateur volunteers started thinking of themselves as short-term missionaries, but studies of the phenomenon generally locate its origins in the 1950s and 1960s and suggest that it experienced a dramatic increase in popularity during the 1980s and 1990s" due to groups such as Youth with a Mission.[8] Teen Missions International has sent over 40,000 youth to foreign countries. The Southern Baptist Convention sends out 150,000 members each year, and the United Methodists send out over 100,000 annually. Since 2000, around 12 percent of high school youth group members have gone overseas on a short-term mission trip.

Short-term missions is today the way to go. But it is not without its detractors. Wuthnow writes,

7. Robert Wuthnow, *Boundless Faith: The Global Outreach of American Churches* (Los Angeles: University of California Press, 2009), 23.
8. Ibid., 166–67.

The growing popularity of short-term mission trips has generated considerable debate among church leaders themselves. On the one hand, proponents argue that short-term volunteers greatly expand the work of Christianity. . . . On the other hand, critics contend that short-term volunteers are often poorly trained or organized and are essentially a drain on the busy schedules of full-time workers and on the scarce resources of those who provide hospitality. Gospel tourism, the pejorative term some critics use, can be a substitute for more serious engagement.[9]

Good or bad, they have become extremely popular, and there is no doubt that awareness has increased: of other cultures, other ways of life, and the systemic problems related to poverty.

But the point here is this: "Short-term missions reflect a new paradigm that is replacing old-style missionary programs."[10] In the old days of worldwide missions, especially before air travel, a missionary made a lifetime commitment. She took a coffin to hold her belongings, and when she died she was buried in it, in the land of her work. Many missionaries, especially in tropical Africa, died within a few years of arrival. Old European cemeteries in the former colonial lands make that point clear. What is amazing is that missionaries knew the risks, and decided to go anyway.

But perhaps the old missionary model made sense in a world without cell phones, airplanes, and Skype. Besides, all along, the goal of the missionaries was to create churches that were self-sufficient. It makes little sense to keep a missionary in the field if she is not really needed anymore. Why should a mission board continue to pay a missionary family when the community is already Christianized? It would be money better spent to bring the missionary home and funnel resources straight to the African or Asian church that is in need of help. It is not cheap to support a missionary family: plane tickets for

9. Ibid., 167–68.
10. Ibid., 169.

furlough, salary, pension, and education for their children—usually back in the Western world.

Reverse Missions

"Reverse missions" are now happening, yet they are different from the previous waves of missionaries sent by the West to the rest. The missionaries are now coming to North America and Europe for education, refuge, and employment. But their patterns of faith are unpredictable. For example, my colleague Rebecca Kim studies Korean college students in the United States and why they tend to stick together when it comes to faith, rather than branching out and interacting with non-Koreans.[11] Asians, especially Koreans, account for a good percentage of the evangelicals in America's most prestigious schools. She provides the following snapshots:

- 80 percent of evangelicals at University of California Los Angeles and University of California Berkeley are Asian-American.

- 70 percent of Harvard Radcliffe Christian Fellowship's members are Asians.

- Yale's Campus Crusade for Christ chapter is 90 percent Asian. Twenty years ago it was 100 percent white.

- At Stanford, InterVarsity Christian Fellowship is nearly entirely Asian.

- Over the last fifteen years, InterVarsity Christian Fellowship saw its Asian-American numbers grow by 267 percent.[12]

11. Rebecca Kim, *God's New Whiz Kids?: Korean American Evangelicals on Campus* (New York: NYU Press, 2006).
12. Ibid., 1–2.

Kim calls these Asian Christian students "God's New Whiz Kids." They are a new breed of missionaries. And while Kim argues that in the vast majority of cases their mission efforts are directed at fellow Koreans, or perhaps other Asians, the fact remains that they are missionaries nonetheless. As these Koreans interact more with whites, blacks, Latinos, and others, it is likely that at some point the ethnic lines will get crossed.

As the West continues to diversify ethnically, there is no doubt that these zealous evangelicals with roots in Asia will make a lasting impact on the religious terrain of American universities and cities, and, ultimately, its culture. Perhaps secularization will be confronted, or stymied, or even reversed in the United States. The path to secularization is not inevitable. However, another possibility remains: perhaps the missionaries themselves will become secularized.

In the year 2000, there were thirty-three thousand foreign missionaries working in the United States.[13] However, a common paradigm—as described above—is the tendency to serve one's own. Abundant research shows that Asian missionaries reach out most effectively to Asians, African missionaries reach out mainly to African migrants, and Latinos establish Spanish-speaking churches.[14] Just because someone serves as a missionary does not necessarily mean that person is crossing ethnic or cultural lines.

The various national Orthodox churches have struggled with this issue for years. When they establish churches in other lands they do so as a service to their own people with whom they share the

13. Wuthnow, *Boundless Faith*, 56.
14. For Korean missionaries tending to reach out rather exclusively to Koreans, see Rebecca Kim, *God's New Whiz Kids?*. For Latinos reaching out mainly to Latinos, see Daniel Rodriguez, *A Future for the Latino Church* (Downers Grove, IL: IVP Academic, 2011). On African churches establishing ethnic or nationally linked churches in the Western world, see Afe Adogame, *The African Christian Diaspora: New Currents and Emerging Trends in World Christianity* (London: Bloomsbury, 2013) and Mark Gornik, *Word Made Global: Stories of African Christianity in New York City* (Grand Rapids, MI: Eerdmans, 2011).

national and religious identity. Their churches serve as cultural hubs where they can help one another adjust to a new society. Orthodox churches are not established in foreign nations for purposes of missionizing the *other*; rather, the primary concern is to missionize their own ethnicity in a foreign country. This arrangement is rooted in the very tightly knit church-state relationship that exists in Orthodox countries. Ethnicity has always been tied to religion. Greeks are Greek Orthodox. Russians are Russian Orthodox. Armenians are Armenian Orthodox. There is an expectation that those who attend understand the liturgy, language, and creeds of the motherland.[15]

Fortress Europe

What people from the Global South often encounter in the West is overwhelming secularization, changing laws against immigrants, cold receptions, and an overall "fortress mentality." Afe Adogame, a Nigerian scholar who teaches world Christianity at the University of Edinburgh, has called attention to the plight of the African immigrant in Europe.[16] He is able to speak from experience as he has lived in Germany and the United Kingdom. For two decades he has researched migratory trends from Africa to Europe, and he does not like what is happening: after decades of flourishing immigration from Africa to Europe, the doors are now closing, if not closed already.

African immigrants to Europe search for a better life, but they encounter many obstructions. Ceuta and Melilla, Spain's North African enclaves, hem themselves in with barbed wire that rip open the hands and feet of desperate Africans who in record numbers risk

---

15. On the almost exclusively Armenian identity in Armenian Orthodox churches in Southern California, see Dyron Daughrity and Nicholas Cumming, "Finger on the Pulse: Armenian Identity and Religiosity in Southern California," in *Armenian Christianity Today: Identity Politics and Popular Practice*, Alexander Agadjanian (Farnham, UK: Ashgate, 2014).
16. See Adogame, *African Christian Diaspora*.

life and limb to get into the promised land of Europe. Some make it. Many others drown. On March 19, 2014, five hundred migrants scaled that fence. Once on European soil, they can make their claims for asylum. Immigrants using simple boats to access the island of Lampedusa, Italy, were up 300 percent between 2013 and 2014. In spring 2014, around three hundred thousand hopefuls were "waiting in Libya to board dangerously unsafe smuggling boats."[17] Italy and Spain rescue thousands of Africans each year as treacherous sea trips fail. They come from Senegal, Central African Republic, Cameroon, all over Africa, hoping to get a taste of the prosperity that Europeans enjoy. The average lifespan of an African is the lowest in the world: fifty years. The average lifespan of a Western European is the highest in the world: eighty years.[18] It is enticing. By scaling that fence, an African will extend his life by thirty years. It is a race against life's clock . . . with measurable rewards. It is easily worth the risk.

Immigration is an extremely complex phenomenon. Some do it because they want to. Others because they have to in order to survive, such as in cases of famine, war, and poverty. People who emigrate out of their homeland are in a liminal state, having to place a foot in two worlds: the homeland, and the new world. And in many cases, religious networks are the most logical point of entry into a new land. A Ghanaian who migrates to Brussels or Amsterdam can attend a Ghanaian church and feel right at home. There is a built-in structure for immigrants when they find "their" people in an immigrant church. Often these church networks are like countercultural societies that have little to do with the surrounding culture, a bit like an Amish person in America's Midwest. They might

17. Paul Schemm, "African Migrants Risk Lives to Reach Europe," *The World Post*, April 9, 2014, located at http://www.huffingtonpost.com /2014/04/09 /african-migrants-europe_n_5117035.html.
18. For statistics on life expectancy, see Dyron Daughrity, *The Changing World of Christianity: The Global History of a Borderless Religion* (New York: Peter Lang, 2010), 3.

work in an American factory, but their life is on the compound. The factory is simply a job for them, and it has little to do with their chosen way of life. And their cultural enclaves can withstand centuries of assimilation pressures, as evinced by Amish and Hutterites scattered all over North America.

Jesus speaks tenderly toward the immigrant in the Gospels. One of the powerful scriptures is in Matt. 25:34–36:

> Then the king will say to those on his right, "Come, you who are blessed by my Father; take your inheritance, the kingdom prepared for you since the creation of the world. For I was hungry and you gave me something to eat, I was thirsty and you gave me something to drink, I was a stranger [also translated "immigrant" or "alien"] and you invited me in. I needed clothes and you clothed me, I was sick and you looked after me, I was in prison and you came to visit me."

Hunger, thirst, a stranger in need of clothes, sick and needing medical care, imprisoned for illegally scaling the wall . . . these are all rather apt descriptions of the life of an immigrant who makes it over or through the barricade, from Africa to Europe, from Latin America to North America.

Once the migrant slips through a crack in the fortress, she is vulnerable indeed. Adogame discusses the life of the immigrant who happens to make it inside: mountains of paperwork, filed and refiled. Punishing fees. Random checks. Rude interrogation. Being slapped on the wrist by the law for completely illogical reasons. Racist and ethnically insensitive jokes. Dehumanizing comments abound.[19] Some immigrants stare at the ceiling, wondering—like the Jews after escaping from Egypt—why they left home in the first place. One of Adogame's interviewees expressed this regret:

> I hold a Masters Degree in Economics and Banking Management. I was Assistant Manager in a branch of the New Nigeria Bank PLC

19. Adogame, *African Christian Diaspora*, 23.

before I came over to Germany in 1992. . . . Today, I really regret taking such an action, but what can I do to unmake this? Would anyone at home believe that I clean toilets in a shopping center here in order to survive? What I am paid in a month is barely enough to pay rents in the one-room apartment I share with a friend. . . . If my country was good I would not have come over here nor taken up these dehumanizing jobs. It is really a shame but what can I do? After all, shit money does not smell. When things get better at home, I will definitely return, get married, raise a family and assist my younger ones with their education.[20]

These are the unfiltered words of a conflicted and despairing immigrant. But they are not unique. Europe's fortress mentality has led many immigrants to feel like "guinea pigs and scapegoats" as "public venting of anger on immigrants and foreigners" ratchets up all the time.[21] Even Switzerland—known for its openness and progressiveness—has voted to curtail immigration significantly . . . and this for a nation "where almost one in four of the population are immigrants."[22]

Given the insecurity and vulnerability of an immigrant, it is no wonder that churches have come to the rescue, often establishing little cultural enclaves where people can feel a sense of familiarity. They can hear the comforting liturgy they grew up with. They can sing the songs that reach deep into their hearts. They share potlucks that inevitably feature a taste of home. And, importantly, they can be a *somebody* in their church—a preacher, a deacon, an officer—rather than a nobody who cleans toilets in the shopping mall. Ethnic churches provide a home away from home. On Sundays it is common for these immigrants to speak the language of the

---

20. Ibid., 54.
21. Ibid., 55.
22. Ian Traynor, "Switzerland Backs Immigration Quotas by Slim Margin," *The Guardian*, February 9, 2014, located at http://www.theguardian.com /world/2014/feb/09 /swiss-referendum-immigration-quotas.

motherland before, during, and after services. Spanish-speaking churches in America work hard to combat this proclivity because they realize they will never be able to reach out to the culture around them if they simply exist for their own culture, whether Mexican, Guatemalan, or El Salvadoran.[23]

The New Missionaries of Latin America

The new face of the missionary is a refugee, a student, or a domestic worker who brings her faith as "hand baggage."[24] The Middle East, for example, is witnessing massive hemorrhaging of Christians as the pressure on Christian minorities gets worse all the time. Iraq's Christian population has been reduced by more than half in the last decade, and the decline continues unabated.[25] Egypt's and Syria's Christians are experiencing brutal persecution as the various "Arab Springs" have led to more havoc than reform. In these unstable, highly religious societies such as the Middle East, minorities often receive the wrath of frustration. A century ago, Christians made up 20 percent of the Middle Eastern population.[26] That number is now around 2 percent.[27] Where did they go? In most cases they moved West, to Europe or America. And they took their faith with them. These are the modern missionaries.

---

23. For the best analysis of this phenomenon in the USA, see Rodriguez, *Future for the Latino Church*.
24. Adogame, *African Christian Diaspora*, 86.
25. See "A Rock and a Hard Place," *The Economist*, July 14, 2014, located at http://www.economist.com/blogs/erasmus/2014/07/iraqi-christians-and-west. See also Daniel Williams, "Christianity in Iraq Is Finished," September 19, 2014, located at http://www.washingtonpost.com/opinions/christianity-in-iraq-is-finished/2014/09/19/21feaa7c-3f2f-11e4-b0ea-8141703bbf6f_story.html.
26. See Christa Case Bryant, "What the Middle East Would Be Like Without Christians," *Christian Science Monitor*, December 22, 2013, located at http://www.csmonitor.com/World/Middle-East/2013/1222/What-the-Middle-East-would-be-like-without-Christians.
27. See Daughrity, *Changing World of Christianity*, 3.

Today, Latin Americans are getting in on the action. While American short-term missionaries go south for a week or two, Latinos move north for life—like the old missionary model, except in reverse. Often they are illegal, or perhaps categorized under the fuzzy umbrella term of *undocumented workers*. But in other cases they are highly organized, strategically plotting out how to evangelize their increasingly secularized neighbors to the north. Since the 1970s, Latinos "began sending their own," and what we are now witnessing are Latino-based transcultural Christian movements connecting people all over the Americas.[28]

Pew Research's statistics on Hispanics in the United States reveal that the United States is being dramatically shaped by a great south-to-north flow. In 1970, only one million Mexican migrants lived in the United States. Mexicans now account for 11 percent of the US population—that is around 33.7 million people. This migration is "one of the largest mass migrations in modern history."[29] Today, Mexico is by far the most common country of origin for Latinos in the United States—around 64 percent. According to Pew Research, "The United States has about as many immigrants from Mexico alone (more than 12 million, including both legal immigrants and unauthorized ones) as any other nation has received *from all sources combined.*"[30] And with a higher than average fertility, the Hispanic population in the United States will continue to surge. In 2014 Latinos surpassed whites as the largest racial group in California, America's most populated state. Similar trends are occurring in other

---

28. Todd Hartch, *The Rebirth of Latin American Christianity* (Oxford: Oxford University Press, 2014), 185.

29. Ana Gonzalez-Barrera and Mark Lopez, "A Demographic Portrait of Mexican-Origin Hispanics in the United States," May 1, 2013, PewResearch, located at http://www.pewhispanic.org/2013/05/01/a-demographic-portrait-of-mexican-origin-hispanics-in-the-united-states/.

30. "Faith on the Move—The Religious Affiliation of International Migrants," March 8, 2012, located at http://www.pewforum.org/2012/03/08/religious-migration-exec/. Italics are theirs.

states, particularly in the Southwest and Florida. According to Pew Research, Texas—America's second-most populated state—will be next. As of 2012 Texas residents were 38 percent Hispanic and 44 percent white, but "the Hispanic population is growing more quickly than the non-Hispanic white population."[31]

In 2003, Hispanic-Americans surpassed African-Americans as the largest ethnic minority group in the United States.[32] In 2012, America was 63 percent white, 17 percent Latino, 12 percent black, 5 percent Asian, and 1 percent Native American.[33] What does this mean for religion in America? It means the future of Christianity should be very well endowed. Statistics show that Latin Americans are the most Christianized people group in the world. Around 93 percent of them are Christians, overwhelmingly (83 percent) Catholic. And Mexico is even more Christian; around 96 percent of Mexico's citizens are Christians, again, overwhelmingly (90 percent) Catholic.[34] As Latinos make their way into the United States, they are making America even more Christian than it already is.

Todd Hartch has written about the extensive missionary flows originating in Latin America. They missionize their own people, they missionize Central and South America, they missionize *norteamericanos*, and they now launch out "to the ends of the earth."[35] He cites the 1976 missionary congress of the University Biblical

31. Mark Lopez, "In 2014, Latinos Will Surpass Whites as Largest Racial/Ethnic Group in California," PewResearchCenter, January 24, 2014, located at http://www.pewresearch.org/fact-tank/2014/01/24/in-2014-latinos-will-surpass-whites-as-largest-racialethnic-group-in-california/. For an excellent analysis of how Latinos are impacting the American church, see Rodriguez, *Future for the Latino Church*.

32. Lynette Clemetson, "Hispanics Now Largest Minority, Census Shows," *New York Times*, January 22, 2003, located at http://www.nytimes.com/2003/01/22/us/hispanics-now-largest-minority-census-shows.html.

33. Lopez, "In 2014, Latinos Will Surpass Whites," cited above.

34. Dyron Daughrity, *Church History: Five Approaches to a Global Discipline* (New York: Peter Lang, 2012), 243, 247.

35. Hartch, *Rebirth of Latin American Christianity*, chapter 10 is called "Universal Christianity: From Latin America to the Ends of the Earth," 184.

Alliance in Curitiba, Brazil, as the pivotal point when Latin Americans began to think strategically about how to send missionaries rather than just to receive them. The conference participants, largely from Brazil, expressed regret that Latin Americans were not sufficiently involved in the mission of God. Attendees were impacted profoundly, and several committed to missionary work, both in Latin America and abroad. This conference "started a boom in Latin American missions that sent over 1000 Protestant missionaries to other regions of the world by 1982."[36]

Hartch discusses a 1986 conference in Switzerland where Manuel Arenas, a Christian convert from the Totonac Indians of Mexico, gave his testimony and then discussed his impressive mission work to his own people. After the lecture he was confronted by a Swiss man who asserted that all religions are the same and therefore it was wrong to try to convert his people out of their indigenous religion and into Christianity. Arenas had encountered this mindset before, and due to his extensive academic training in Canada, the United States, and Germany, he was able to offer a ready defense. Arenas explained why he started the Totonac Cultural Center in the Mexican state of Puebla. He discussed the improved agricultural technology he had introduced. He discussed the array of health services and pastoral training taking place. And finally he outlined, philosophically and practically, why Christianity is superior to the previous religion of the Totonacs—a religion that emphasizes fearing evil spirits that are all around. Rather, Jesus Christ is the truth, and "only he can take away fear and give hope and peace, for this life and for the life to come." The Swiss man was so moved that he accepted Jesus Christ as Lord and Savior right there on the spot.[37]

36. Ibid., 186.
37. Ibid., 169–70, 185.

In the last few decades, Latin America's missionary mindset, especially among Protestants, has changed dramatically. No longer were they simply receiving cultures. They wanted to send. And they did. Brazilians, in particular Brazilian Pentecostals, picked up the challenge and planted churches all over the world. For example, by 2004, the God is Love denomination had planted churches in 136 different countries. The IURD—the Universal Church of the Kingdom of God (Igreja Universal do Reino do Deus)—has around five thousand churches in Brazil and over one thousand churches in ninety-six countries.[38] In 2012 they had 161 churches in the United States and 314 in the nation of South Africa, and hundreds more all over the world. In Portugal they "have become a permanent part of the religious landscape."[39] Their mission work is global, media savvy, ambitious, and, importantly, the church now has "the financial means to carry out its plans."[40] One scholar comments, "No Christian denomination founded in the Third World has ever been exported so successfully and so rapidly."[41]

Conclusion: "The Great New Fact of Our Time"

Andrew Walls wrote the following: "The great new fact of our time—and it has momentous consequences for mission—is that the great migration has now gone into reverse. There has been a massive movement, which all indications suggest will continue, from the non-Western to the Western world."[42] But the more things change, the more they stay the same. Walls points out that migration has

---

38. See the UCKG website at http://www.uckg.org.au/about-us.aspx. See also Hartch, *Rebirth of Latin American Christianity*, 187.
39. Hartch, *Rebirth of Latin American Christianity*, 189–90.
40. Ibid., 189.
41. Paul Freston, in ibid. 190.
42. Walls, "Mission and Migration: The Diaspora Factor in Christian History," in *Journal of African Christian Thought* 5, no. 2 (2002): 10.

a long, human history going back to Adam and Eve being driven out of the Garden of Eden. He contrasts "Adamic" migration with "Abrahamic" migration. "Adamic migration means disaster, deprivation and loss. But there is another model, which we may call 'Abrahamic', where migration stands for escape to a superlatively better future."[43] As this chapter has discussed, migrants make their way from everywhere to everywhere. And today, many "sending" nations are just as likely to be "receiving" nations as well. Christians from everywhere go everywhere, and their faith travels with them.

According to Pew Research, today there are well over 200 million people living as migrants, around 3 percent of the world's population.[44] Around half of them are Christians. In other words, there are over 100 million Christian migrants. The top "sending" nations are Mexico, India, and Russia. The top "receiving" nations are the USA, Russia, and Germany. According to the Pew Report, "Migrants come from every inhabited part of the globe, and no one continent or region is the source of a majority."

Many of these migrants are "Abrahamic": they are moving to a place of refuge, or to a place that offers more opportunity—just as I migrated to Canada for my education. However, many of these migrants are Adamic. They were driven out of their homeland. Or they were forced to move because of religion, politics, or catastrophe. And "the great new fact of our time" is that these people bring faith with them. And in the case of 100 million of them, they bring Christian faith.

These 100 million Christian migrants are the faces of the new missionaries. The old missionary image—"a white person sent to a distant land"—remains entrenched in the minds of many.[45] But that is

---

43. Ibid. 4.
44. This paragraph looks at the research from Pew entitled "Faith on the Move."
45. Jehu Hanciles, "Migration and the Globalization of Christianity," 229.

not the reality any more. There are still white missionaries, of course. But increasingly, as Christianity continues its southern shift, those old stereotypes will give way. The far more typical white missionary today is that of a teenager or young college student on spring break, framing a house or visiting an orphanage in Guatemala. The far more typical nonwhite missionary is a Nigerian on a student visa in London, or a Filipino domestic worker in Saudi Arabia, or a Mexican working the fields of southern California.

A Christian with a heart for missions cannot help but to cheer for the Christian immigrant, for many reasons. They are our faith's new missionaries. As they seek a better life, they are taking their faith to the ends of the earth, like the apostles in times of old. But, perhaps, Christians should also cheer for the non-Christian immigrants, especially if they happen to land on Christian shores. Studies show that when immigrants enter the United States, even if they are from non-Christian backgrounds, there is a decent likelihood they will convert to Christianity. For example, sociologist Jerry Park has discovered that "44 percent of all Asian-Americans are Christian."[46] That is remarkable, considering that only about 10 percent of Asians overall are Christian. Either the American government is recruiting Christian Asians or else Asians are choosing to be Christian once they get here. Similar trends show up with Vietnamese immigrants to America. While Vietnam is only about 9 percent Christian, fully one in three Vietnamese-Americans are Christian.[47] Could it be that the most effective missionary strategy America could take in years to come would be to welcome the non-Christian immigrant?

But shouldn't the Christian also cheer for migrants simply out of obedience to Christ? Jesus said, "I was a stranger [or immigrant] and

---

46. Jerry Park's research is cited in Wesley Granberg-Michaelson, *From Times Square to Timbuktu: The Post-Christian West Meets the Non-Western Church* (Grand Rapids, MI: Eerdmans, 2013), 89.
47. For statistics of Asia in general and Vietnam in particular, see Daughrity, *Church History*, 234, 238. See also Granberg-Michaelson, *From Times Square to Timbuktu*, 89.

you invited me in, I needed clothes and you clothed me, I was sick and you looked after me, I was in prison and you came to visit me." People do not tend to make the perilous journey of a migrant without a good reason. But many of them will not make it. They will get stuck in the system, languishing in a holding center or a jail. Some will get snatched up and funneled into the wretched, diabolical world of sex trafficking. Others will get exploited for organ transplants, for child soldiering, or forced labor without pay.[48]

Surely the Christian must respond to issues of migration. Not only for the expansion of Christian faith, but also for the basic dignity of the migrant, the stranger. It seems rather obvious that Christ would sympathize with their plight. After all, he was an immigrant. The core of the gospel message is that God sent his son to our land. The Messiah was an immigrant. Yet he was despised and rejected and cruelly killed by the host country. For Christ's sake, his disciples must respond to these tragic stories.

---

48. See World Council of Churches report, "Human Trafficking Brings Shame to Humanity," *World Council of Churches*, April 7, 2014, located at https://www.oikoumene.org/en/press-centre/news/human-trafficking-brings-shame-to-humanity-un-special-rapporteur-tells-an-ecumenical-consultation.

PART IV

Contemporary Themes

11

Marriage and Sexuality

1 Corinthians 5:11–13

I am writing to you that you must not associate with anyone who claims to be a brother or sister but is sexually immoral. . . . What business is it of mine to judge those outside the church? Are you not to judge those inside? God will judge those outside. "Expel the wicked person from among you."

I was once lecturing on marriage in different cultural contexts when somehow *Fifty Shades of Grey* came up. When I asked the students about the book several urged me not to read it, in spite of the fact that 90 million people already had. One student warned, "Don't read it professor; we don't want you to become corrupted." I reminded them I have children of my own. I then asked this student if she had read the book. She said yes, all three of them in fact (there is a *Fifty Shades* trilogy), and she planned to see the movie. Indeed, several students in class had read the books. I was led to believe *Fifty Shades* was exploitative, masochistic, even misogynistic. Their response: "Yes, but in the end they get married."

I walked away from that conversation bemused, but I also began to realize that a class on Christianity probably should come up to speed and engage students where they are at, instead of pretending that religion and sexuality have nothing to say to each other. Topics pertaining to marriage and sexuality are featured regularly on television: polygamous reality shows, MTV's popular *16 and Pregnant*, and news outlets are regularly abuzz with stints by Miley Cyrus and others twerking their way into our living rooms. If culture is saturated with sexuality, shouldn't my course on Christianity and Culture say something to all that?[1]

"The Ultimate Test"

.Sexuality, especially homosexuality, has become the lightning rod issue of our time. In the 1980s the hot-button topic was abortion. While abortion is still potentially incendiary—America's Affordable Care Act is a case in point—homosexuality may be the more combustible topic today. As early as 1998, sociologist Alan Wolfe described homosexuality as "the ultimate test" of religious tolerance in the United States:

> No other issue taps into such a potential conflict more than the issue of homosexuality. The question of gay rights is important to a discussion of religious toleration, for it is over this question that the more liberal and more conservative religious believers have had their most persistent clashes. From specific congregations to whole denominations such as the Episcopalian Church . . . a seemingly unbridgeable gulf has opened between those who believe that the Bible's condemnation of homosexuality as an abomination must be taken as a moral injunction versus those who believe that Christianity requires the love and acceptance of everyone.[2]

---

1. One of the best available resources on the history of Christian sexuality is Merry Wiesner-Hanks, *Christianity and Sexuality in the Early Modern World: Regulating Desire, Reforming Practice*, second edition (London: Routledge, 2010).
2. Alan Wolfe, *One Nation, after All* (New York: Penguin Books, 1998), 72.

Wolfe's words are as relevant today as they were then.

The Episcopal Church has experienced deep fissures over homosexuality, and the controversies are far from over. In 2004 Bishop Gene Robinson became the first person in a major American denomination to be elevated to the bishopric while living in an openly gay relationship. And this was after he had divorced his wife of fourteen years, with whom he had two children. Although he retired in 2013, the fallout continues. The Anglican Realignment movement is a repercussion of the tumultuous decision to consecrate Gene Robinson as bishop of New Hampshire. Some churches and even dioceses have tried to put themselves under the authority of a more conservative hierarch. Several of these churches have established relationships with bishops in Africa, resulting in quarrels over theology, succession, and property.[3] Who owns the church building and its assets: the members, the diocese, or the denomination?

The controversy has pummeled the Episcopal Church, leading to losses in members and in morale. Hundreds of churches have split or left the denomination. The *Wall Street Journal* reported on one very odd case. After disagreeing with the denomination on "what the Bible says about sexuality," a congregation made an offer to purchase the church property. The Episcopal Church, however, seized the building and sold it for a fraction of the previously offered price "to someone who turned it into a mosque."[4] Tens of millions of dollars have been spent in litigation, but *hundreds* of millions of dollars are at stake. For example, the breakaway Diocese of South Carolina is

3. See Kathleen Reeder, "Whose Church Is It, Anyway? Property Disputes and Episcopal Church Splits," *Columbia Journal of Law and Social Problems* 40, no. 2 (2006). Reeder writes that US parishes have joined churches in Nigeria, Rwanda, Uganda, and "various provinces in Latin America." See 169n186.

4. Mollie Ziegler Hemingway, "Twenty-First Century Excommunication," *The Wall Street Journal*, October 7, 2011, located at http:// www.wsj.com / articles /SB10001424053297020347 680457661493230830 2042.

fighting to keep its buildings and grounds, which are estimated to be worth $500 million.[5]

While the vitriol concerning homosexuality continues in both directions, statistics have changed markedly in recent years. In 2010 Robert Putnam and David Campbell's important work *American Grace* examined this shift:

> Twenty years ago, virtually everyone opposed gay marriage. . . . All of this evidence points to one unmistakable trend: Homosexuality is increasingly acceptable, especially among young people. . . . Gay characters are common in TV programs and movies and many prominent gay celebrities project an image of respectability. . . . Pop culture, though, is not the whole story . . . Young people are also the least religious age group. Since religiosity is such a strong predictor of attitudes toward same-sex marriage, and homosexuality more generally, it comes as no surprise that the most secular cohort of the population is the most accepting of gay marriage. As young people become a larger portion of the population, overall approval of homosexuality, including but not limited to gay marriage, will rise.[6]

According to Pew Research, 49 percent of Americans supported same-sex marriage in 2013. In their conclusion they wrote, "The rise in support for same-sex marriage over the past decade is among the largest changes in opinion on any policy issue over this time period."[7] Leading voices among Catholics, Mormons, and Evangelical churches continue to hold the conservative line, but the more progressive churches and the secular crowd have moved decisively to the left. Some churches are in the early stages of either making

---

5. Valerie Bauerlein, "Church Fight Heads to Court," *The Wall Street Journal*, April 16, 2013, located at http:// online.wsj.com / news / articles / SB10001424127887324010704578418983895885100.

6. Robert Putnam and David Campbell, *American Grace: How Religion Divides and Unites Us* (New York: Simon and Schuster, 2010), 404.

7. See "Growing Support for Gay Marriage: Changed Minds and Changing Demographics," March 20, 2013, located at http://www.people-press.org/2013/03/20/growing-support-for-gay-marriage-changed-minds-and-changing-demographics/.

the switch or of splitting their ranks, such as the Mennonites and the new Presbyterian denomination ECO (Evangelical Covenant Order).[8] Reform and Conservative Jews generally accept same-sex marriage.[9] In more recent years, two widely publicized incidents clearly demonstrated that the culture war continues to rage on this issue: the fallout over "homosexual offender" comments made by an actor on one of America's most popular TV shows, *Duck Dynasty*; and the commotion surrounding Chick-fil-A's support of "the biblical definition of the family unit."[10] Both of those incidents provoked widespread reactions, illustrating America's deep ambivalence over homosexuality.

A Voice From the East

While America moves left on homosexuality, it is a very different story in much of the East and in Africa. During the 10th General Assembly of the World Council of Churches in South Korea in 2013, I witnessed a bombshell lecture that was, in my view, the most memorable of the entire ten-day conference.[11] The lecture was delivered by Metropolitan Hilarion of Volokolamsk, one of the leading hierarchs in the Russian Orthodox Church. Hilarion is an extraordinary figure on the scene of world Christianity today. He is

8. See Elizabeth Evans, "Mountain States Mennonites Take Step Toward Gay Ordination," *Religion News Service*, February 3, 2014, located at http://www.religionnews.com/2014/02/03/denver-mennonites-take-first-step-toward-gay-ordination/; and Daniel Burke, "New Presbyterian Body Aims for Orthodoxy with Less Bureaucracy," *Christianity Today*, January 23, 2012, located at http://www.christianitytoday.com/gleanings/2012/january/new-presbyterian-body-aims-for-orthodoxy-with-less.html.

9. See "Overview of Same-Sex Marriage in the United States," December 7, 2012, located at http://www.pewforum.org/2012/12/07/overview-of-same-sex-marriage-in-the-united-states/.

10. See Greg Braxton, "A&E reverses suspension of 'Duck Dynasty's' Phil Robertson," *LA Times,* December 28, 2014, located at http://www.latimes.com/entertainment/tv/showtracker/la-et-st-duck-dynasty-phil-robertson-20131228,0,7784571.story#axzz2sIKoJt7N; and Kim Severson, "Chick-fil-A Thrust Back into Spotlight on Gay Rights," *New York Times*, July 25, 2012, located at http://www.nytimes.com /2012/07/26/us /gay-rights-uproar-over-chick-fil-a-widens.html?_r=0.

11. The WCC 10th Assembly Conference website is located at http://wcc2013.info/en.

a respected theologian, a gifted musician (his orchestral compositions are performed globally), a former soldier, a monk, and one of the most prolific bishops in Orthodoxy today. Hilarion holds a PhD from the University of Oxford, a credential that has earned him legitimacy in the Western world.[12] His years studying in the West gave him the opportunity to understand the Western mind, both theologically and socially. Here is a rare person: deeply respected in the East but also deeply aware of Western culture. And he is not an old man; he was born in 1966, and he understands the culture of today's youth. Perhaps most importantly, his voice is taken seriously by the 250 million Orthodox Christians in the world, and especially the 100-plus million members of the Russian Orthodox Church—the world's second-largest Christian denomination.

Hilarion's lecture caught many by surprise. Some simply rolled their eyes at this Russian hierarch from a bygone Byzantine era. Some were clearly offended by his lecture, and proceedings that day at the WCC were put on hold after he stepped away from the microphone. Personally, I was shocked. I am familiar with the World Council of Churches, having served it in the past, and having dedicated part of my career to researching and observing its work.

Hilarion's lecture was entitled "The Voice of the Church Must Be Prophetic."[13] His lecture began by discussing the WCC—how it was a good idea originally, but its effectiveness is today questioned. Churches continue to split; unity has yet to be achieved in any clear way; and the WCC's finances are in serious trouble. Many blame the world economic crisis for the WCC's financial woes, but, Hilarion

12. Hilarion's biography is available on the Russian Orthodox Church website: https://mospat.ru/en/decr-chairman/.
13. See Metropolitan Hilarion of Volokolamsk, "The Voice of the Church Must Be Prophetic," *The Ecumenical Review* 65, no. 4 (December 2013). It is also located online at http://www.oikoumene.org/en/resources/documents/assembly/2013-busan/plenary-presentations/address-by-metropolitan-hilarion-of-volokolamsk?set_language=en. I have used the lecture as it was distributed to the media at the general assembly.

argued, "I cannot agree . . . funding can often be found for noble goals."

After making these initial, trenchant critiques, he laid out his objectives for the lecture:

> I would like to focus on two fundamental challenges which the Christian world today faces . . . The first is that of the militant secularism which is gathering strength in the so called developed countries, primarily in Europe and America. The second is that of radical Islamism that poses a threat to the very existence of Christianity in a number of regions of the world.

What was so striking about his agenda was its brazen political incorrectness, and its seeming inappropriateness. After all, this was the World Council of Churches, an organization frequently critiqued for its championing of progressive issues.[14] The room went silent as Hilarion talked about Soviet history, when "godlessness was elevated to the level of state ideology," while "the so called capitalist countries, they preserved to a significant degree the Christian traditions which shaped their cultural and moral identity." Then came his assessment: "Today these two worlds appear to have changed roles."

Hilarion spoke of the exuberant return of Christianity in Eastern Europe. His statistics were breathtaking to all of us present:

> An unprecedented religious revival is underway. In the Russian Orthodox Church over the past twenty five years there have been built or restored from ruins more than twenty five thousand churches. This means that a thousand churches a year have been opened, i.e. three

---

14. For example, see "A Crisis of Motivation," *TIME* 92, no. 3 (July 19, 1968). That anonymous article describes the Fourth General Assembly in Uppsala, Sweden: "The scene at Uppsala smacked more of a New Left 'demo' than of a religious body in pious conference." In the 1980s the World Council of Churches made headlines when the popular *Reader's Digest* "unfairly linked the group to leftist political and social programs," for example WCC involvement in African and Latin American liberation movements. See, for example, Charles Austin, "National Council of Churches Faces New Type of Critic," *New York Times*, November 3, 1982, located at http://www.nytimes.com/1982/11/03/us/national-council-of-churches-faces-new-type-of-critic.html.

churches a day. More than fifty theological institutes and eight hundred monasteries, each full with monks and nuns, have been opened.

He then contrasted the situation in Eastern Europe with the one in Western Europe, where we witness

a steady decline of the numbers of parishioners, a crisis in vocations, and monasteries and churches are being closed. The anti-Christian rhetoric of many politicians and statesmen becomes all the more open as they call for the total expulsion of religion from public life and the rejection of the basic moral norms common to all religious traditions.

Hilarion spoke of the "battle between the religious and secular worldview." Then came the bombshell:

One of the main directions of its activity today is the straightforward destruction of traditional notions of marriage and the family. This is witnessed by the new phenomenon of equating homosexual unions with marriage and allowing single-sex couples to adopt children. From the point of view of biblical teaching and traditional Christian moral values, this testifies to a profound spiritual crisis.

Hilarion was methodical in his critique. He argued that those who argue for homosexual marriage are operating "under the pretext of combating discrimination." He deplored the rising number of nations that are granting legal status to single-sex unions, describing it as "a serious step towards the destruction of the very concept of marriage and the family."

Hilarion's critiques were against all manner of sexuality outside the traditional teachings of the church. He railed against rising divorce rates, declining birthrates, increasing abortions, prevalence of sexual relations outside of marriage, and the degradation of traditional family values,

The female mother is losing her time-honored role as guardian of the domestic hearth, while the male father is losing his role as educator of his children in being socially responsible. The family in its Christian understanding is falling apart to be replaced by such impersonal terms as "parent number one" and "parent number two." All of this cannot but have the most disastrous consequences for the upbringing of children.

Hilarion sounded the alarm of a "demographic crisis," and a "demographic abyss." Western societies are "pronouncing upon their peoples a death sentence."

He then explained that this controversy is usually "linked to the division of Christians into conservatives and liberals." However, "We are not speaking about conservatism but of fidelity to Divine Revelation which is contained in scripture. And if the so called liberal Christians reject the traditional Christian understanding of moral norms, then this means that we are running up against a serious problem in our common Christian witness." Hilarion addressed the fact the liberals and conservatives interpret the Bible very differently. However, he argued, "We all possess the same Bible and its moral teaching is laid out quite unambiguously." He lamented those churches that cannot muster the courage to go "against that which is fashionable" in an increasingly secular society.

Hilarion held up the Orthodox churches as exemplary on these issues, refusing to capitulate to "headlong liberalization." He cautioned against reducing the Orthodox churches to simply "conservatism" because "the faith of the Ancient Church which we Orthodox confess is impossible to define from the standpoint of conservatism and liberalism. We confess Christ's truth which is immutable, for 'Jesus Christ is the same yesterday, and today, and forever' (Heb. 3:8)." The bishop then came back to the theme of his lecture: being prophetic. He questioned whether the "prophetic" voice of the church today was actually a proclamation of God's truth or simply "rhetoric of the secular mass media and non-governmental organizations." He then implored the WCC to "find its own special voice" that refuses to capitulate to "aggressive secularism and ideological atheism."

It is important to note that the WCC has no policy on issues surrounding homosexuality, and it is difficult to know with any quantifiable certainty where the churches stand. The Orthodox churches in particular, however, remain united in their opposition to the specific issue of gay marriage. For example, in 2013 the prominent Greek Orthodox Bishop Seraphim threatened to excommunicate members of parliament who might choose to vote in favor of gay marriage. The European Union has warned that Greece is in violation of human rights by taking such a stance.[15] This issue has been very thorny in Greece, particularly since the release of the controversial American play *Corpus Christi* depicting Jesus Christ and his apostles as being homosexual men from Texas. In the play Jesus performs a gay marriage.[16] Bishop Seraphim's campaign successfully thwarted the play from being shown in Greece in 2012.[17]

Interpreting Marriage

The painful debate over gay marriage in the Western world is only the latest in a longstanding attempt within Christianity to figure out what marriage should look like. It has never been a clear issue. For centuries, the church has struggled with whether to allow clergymen to marry. The Orthodox churches allow their priests to marry, but not their bishops. Since the First Lateran Council of 1123, the Roman

---

15. Helena Smith, "Bishop Threatens to Excommunicate Greek MPs Who Vote for Gay Unions," *The Guardian*, December 4, 2013, located at http://www.theguardian.com/world/2013/dec/04/greek-bishop-threatens-excommunicate-gay-unions.

16. See Sharon Green, *Corpus Christi* (performance review), *Theatre Journal* 51, no. 2 (1999).

17. Karolina Tagaris, "Blasphemy Charges Filed over Gay Jesus Play in Greece," *Reuters*, November 16, 2012, located at http://www.reuters.com/article/2012/11/16/entertainment-us-greece-blasphemy-idUSBRE8AF0MU20121116.

Catholic Church requires clerical celibacy with a few exceptions. That council concluded in Canon 21,

> We absolutely forbid priests, deacons, subdeacons and monks to have concubines or to contract marriages. We adjudge, as the sacred canons have laid down, that marriage contracts between such persons should be made void and the persons ought to undergo penance.[18]

Thirteen years later, at the Second Lateran Council of 1139, the Roman Catholic Church's stance against marriage became even more strict and the rules more explicit in Canons 6–8:

> 6. We also decree that those in the orders of subdeacon and above who have taken wives or concubines are to be deprived of their position and ecclesiastical benefice. For since they ought to be in fact and in name temples of God, vessels of the Lord and sanctuaries of the Holy Spirit, it is unbecoming that they give themselves up to marriage and impurity.
>
> 7. Adhering to the path trod by our predecessors, the Roman pontiffs Gregory VII, Urban and Paschal, we prescribe that nobody is to hear the masses of those whom he knows to have wives or concubines. . . . We decree that where bishops, priests, deacons, subdeacons, canons regular, monks and professed lay brothers have presumed to take wives and so transgress this holy precept, they are to be separated from their partners. For we do not deem there to be a marriage which, it is agreed, has been contracted against ecclesiastical law. Furthermore, when they have separated from each other, let them do a penance commensurate with such outrageous behavior.
>
> 8. We decree that the selfsame thing is to apply also to women religious if, God forbid, they attempt to marry.[19]

And since 1139 these laws have been in force. Catholic theologian Hans Küng condemns the history of these developments:

---

18. Documents of the First Lateran Council, A.D. 1123, located at http://www.papalencyclicals.net/Councils/ecum09.htm.
19. Documents of the Second Lateran Council, A.D. 1139, located at http://www.papalencyclicals.net / Councils / ecum10.htm.

There were revolting witch hunts of priests' wives in the clergy houses. . . . Indeed priests' children officially became the church's property as slaves. There was furious mass protest by the clergy, especially in northern Italy and Germany, but to no avail. Henceforth there was a universal and compulsory law of celibacy, though in practice up to the time of the Reformation this was observed only with qualifications, even in Rome.[20]

In 2009, Pope Benedict XVI made headlines when he made allowance for men in other denominations, such as in the Orthodox Church and the Church of England, to become ordained in the Roman Catholic Church without having to dismiss their wife.[21]

Further complicating the issue of celibacy in the Roman Catholic is the fact that the apostle Peter—traditionally the first pope—was married in all likelihood, according to passages in the Gospels that mention Peter's mother-in-law.[22] The apostle Paul seems to have been annoyed by Peter's married state when he wrote, "Don't we have the right to take a believing wife along with us, as do the other apostles and the Lord's brothers and Cephas [that is, Peter]?"[23]

Marriage among the clergy is as confounding today as it was in the days of Peter and Paul. Clearly, Paul was committed to Jesus's ideal of celibacy:

Now to the unmarried and the widows I say: It is good for them to stay unmarried, as I do. But if they cannot control themselves, they should marry, for it is better to marry than to burn with passion.[24]

20. Hans Küng, *The Catholic Church: A Short History*, trans. John Bowden (New York: The Modern Library, 2003), 92–93.
21. See for example Jonah Dycus, "Former Anglican priests Begin Formation to Be Ordained Catholic Priests," *National Catholic Reporter*, February 17, 2012, located at http://ncronline.org/news/spirituality/former-anglican-priests-begin-formation-be-ordained-catholic-priests. See also Cindy Wooden, "Pope Establishes Structure for Anglicans Uniting with Rome," *Catholic News Service*, October 20, 2009, located at http://www.catholicnews.com/data/stories/cns/0904673.htm.
22. Matt. 8:14 and Luke 4:38.
23. 1 Cor. 9:5.
24. 1 Cor. 7:8–9.

However, he realized that marriage was necessary for some, including leaders, such as in his qualifications for elders and deacons: "An overseer, then, must be above reproach, the husband of one wife."[25]

Plural Wives

One question that arises here is whether plural wives may be allowed in a Christian marriage. Nothing in the New Testament explicitly forbids polygamy, and patriarchs in the Old Testament embraced it, leading to various interpretations, including the early Mormon movement that championed the practice with gusto. On one occasion Brigham Young—the proud husband to fifty-five wives—chastised those in his movement who might disagree with him, on the grounds that he might not have any living children had God not granted him plural wives:

> Suppose that I had had the privilege of having only one wife, I should have had only three sons, for those are all that my first wife bore, whereas, I now have buried five sons, and have thirteen living. It is obvious that I could not have been blessed with such a family, if I had been restricted to one wife, but, by the introduction of this law, I can be the instrument in preparing tabernacles for those spirits which have to come in this dispensation. . . . .
>
> Now if any of you will deny the plurality of wives, and continue to do so, I promise that you will be damned; and I will go still further and say, take this revelation, or any other revelation that the Lord has given, and deny it in your feelings, and I promise that you will be damned. . . . And do not sneer nor jeer at what comes from the Lord, for if we do, we endanger our salvation.[26]

In 1904, the largest branch of the Mormon Church banned plural marriage, although several other Mormon groups hold on to the

---

25. 1 Tim. 3 and Titus 1.
26. Brigham Young, "Plurality of Wives—The Free Agency of Man," delivered in Provo, July 14, 1855, located at http://jod.mrm.org/3/264.

practice.[27] At several isolated places in the North American West, particularly in the Rocky Mountains, the practice continues, even inspiring television shows such as *Big Love, Sister Wives,* and *The 19th Wife.*

It is a bit ironic that while the LDS mainline abandoned polygamy in the early 1900s, the Anglican churches resolved to recognize it—with conditions—a century later. At the 1988 Lambeth Conference, the bishops voted in favor of its acceptance in Resolution 26, "Church and Polygamy."[28] In that document, "a polygamist who responds to the Gospel and wishes to join the Anglican Church may be baptized and confirmed with his believing wives and children on the following conditions":

1. That the polygamist shall promise not to marry again as long as any of his wives at the time of his conversion are alive;
2. That the receiving of such a polygamist has the consent of the local Anglican community;
3. That such a polygamist shall not be compelled to put away any of his wives, on account of the social deprivation they would suffer.

Is there a "Polygamy in Yorkshire" reality show on the BBC's horizon? Probably not, since it is not the English who have to contend with this issue on a daily basis; it is their Anglican sisters and brothers in the old colonies.

---

27. See the 1904 official statement of Mormon President Joseph F. Smith at http://archive.org/stream/conferencereport1904a/conferencereport741chur#page/74/mode/2up. It reads, "I, Joseph F. Smith, President of the Church of Jesus Christ of Latter-day Saints . . . hereby announce that all such marriages are prohibited, and if any officer or member of the Church shall assume to solemnize or enter into any such marriages he will be deemed in transgression against the Church and will be liable to be dealt with, according to the rules and regulations thereof, and excommunicated therefrom." See 75.
28. See The Lambeth Conference website. See 1988 Resolution 26, "Church and Polygamy," located at http://www.lambethconference.org/resolutions/1988/1988-26.cfm.

Marriage outside the West

Plural marriage outside the Western world is not uncommon, especially in African societies, where polygamy was a thorn in the side of Western missionaries for generations. It also must be remembered that around 40 percent of Africa is Muslim, and in Islam plural marriage is completely acceptable when practiced in accordance with the Quran. However, defining marriage and plural marriage is a very complicated undertaking. If marriage is defined as a man and a woman becoming "one flesh," then Westerners just might be the most polygamous of all due to serial monogamy, premarital sex norms, and the relatively common practice of divorce and remarriage. In some non-Western societies, however, these practices are unacceptable. Sexual intercourse before marriage is seen in many cultures as one of the most scandalous activities one can participate in. It can have dreadful consequences for women who are viewed as polluted, even expendable, in the eyes of the community once they lose their virginity outside the confines of marriage. This is one reason the raping of virgins in India has caused so much outrage—those women's lives are ruined.[29] Marriage is not really an option for them after they have been violated. The entire family is shamed in these situations.

Historically, India's answer to this problem has been to have arranged marriages, where families take charge of the process in order to safeguard the reputation of the woman. If a young lady is already spoken for, there is more protection. And, crucially, it minimizes the chances of that woman getting raped since once she has been promised, there are two extended families involved. A potential rapist would think twice in this situation, whereas a woman who had

---

29. See E. J. Graff, "Purity Culture Is Rape Culture," *The American Prospect*, January 4, 2013, located at http://prospect.org/article/purity-culture-rape-culture.

not been claimed by anyone would appear more available, more vulnerable.

Most of my students react viscerally when the topic of arranged marriage comes up in class. Asian students, however, do not share that reaction. Arranged marriage does not comport with the Western mind because it comes across as forced. Parents making significant, life-long decisions for the children violates the sacred cow of Western society—the freedom to choose. However, in the Indian context and contexts like it, one is hard-pressed to argue against it. As immigration continues, Westerners will continue to come face to face with arranged marriage since it often gets imported. The 2007 film *Arranged* is a wonderfully humanizing look at arranged marriage through the lives of two young women schoolteachers in America—an Orthodox Jew and a Syrian Muslim—whose families are in the process of finding them a suitable mate. It is an important look into how arranged marriage, particularly when transferred to the West, is often a middle path between love marriage and the stricter forms of arranged marriage. Yes, the parents make the ultimate decision, but in each case the young woman rejects multiple men before the right one comes along. Arranged marriage is often a delicate dance that includes the woman's right to choose, the parents' right to help, and the religious community's right to chime in from time to time.

These values do not translate very well in the West, where anything other than the typical love marriage is seen as restrictive. The *New York Times* published a pretty condescending review of the film, calling it "doctrinaire," and dismissing it as a "Father always knows best" tale where "patriarchy can't help but prevail."[30] The reviewer laughs at a "hilarious scene" where the Orthodox Jewish

---

30. Jeannette Catsoulis, "Teachers United," movie review of *Arranged, New York Times*, December 14, 2007, located at http://www.nytimes.com/2007/12/14/movies/14arra.html?_r=0.

woman gets offered a drink and a dance by a young man present, and she heads for the door, as if she was stupid for not participating in the revelry of the party. The film is ridiculed as being "well-meaning but oblivious"; however, I would argue that any reviewer who is this oblivious to the consequences of violating sexual taboos in Muslim and Orthodox Jewish culture needs to stick to reviewing *Fifty Shades of Grey* and *Spring Breakers*.

On the other hand, a much more sensitive understanding of arranged marriage was published in the *New York Times* in 2013.[31] The article looks at the research of Robert Epstein, a psychologist who studies arranged marriage in many different societies. Epstein's findings go against the grain of Western expectations. For example, the best arranged marriages involve parents earlier rather than later, since the parents serve as a "screen for deal breakers" before a romance begins. They also "remove so much of the anxiety about 'is this the right person?'" The "right" person is a very subjective decision to make. It makes sense to have people involved in the decision who have tread these paths before, and who typically have their own child's best interests in mind.

Arranged marriage is based on a very different model, one that repulses but intrigues Westerners. It is not based exclusively on *individual* choice, as typical in the West, but more of a *collective* choice that includes the individual, along with people who have a vested interest in the marriage turning out well, such as in honor-shame societies where extended families stick together. Indeed, in these societies, extended families often live together, multiple generations

---

31. Ji Hyun Lee, "Modern Lessons from Arranged Marriages," *New York Times*, January 18, 2013, located at http://www.nytimes.com/2013/01/20/fashion/weddings/parental-involvement-can-help-in-choosing-marriage-partners-experts-say.html?pagewanted=all. See the study by Robert Epstein, Mayuri Pandit, and Mansi Thakar, "How Love Emerges in Arranged Marriages: Two Cross-cultural Studies," *Journal of Comparative Family Studies* 44, no. 3 (May/June 2013). The article looks at arranged marriage in twelve different countries and includes participants from six different religions.

under one roof. It is a model where the partners begin with obligation but learn the value of love over time, rather than starting with passion and working toward obligation later in life. Then there is the oft-quoted statistic that while 40–50 percent of American marriages fail, only 2–3 percent of Indian marriages end in divorce.

Of course buried within that statistic is much to contemplate and challenge, but in an age of globalization—where the East and the West often intermix and influence each other—arranged marriage may well emerge as an option for couples. If arranged marriages lead to a lower divorce rate in the West as they have in the East, then it would make good business sense to do whatever one could do—before the altar—to add another layer of security to their unions. After all, divorce can be very costly, both financially and emotionally. I suppose this high cost is what is motivating the recent proposal to transform "wedlock" into "wedlease"—where two people commit to a short period of time that can be renewed or canceled when the lease is up.[32]

Worlds Apart: Africa vs. the West

Issues of sexuality are interpreted in vastly different ways among the world's Christians, and often they are worlds apart. This was perhaps best demonstrated at the Anglican Communion's Lambeth Conference of 1998, where a divide over homosexuality became very public. Bishops from Africa led the charge to pass Resolution I.10 on human sexuality:

This Conference:

---

32. See Paul Rampell, "A High Divorce Rate Means It's Time to Try 'Wedleases,'" *Washington Post*, August 4, 2013, located at http://www.washingtonpost.com/opinions/a-high-divorce-rate-means-its-time-to-try-wedleases/2013/08/04/f2221c1c-f89e-11e2-b018-5b8251f0c56e_story.html.

b) In view of the teaching of scripture, upholds faithfulness in marriage between a man and a woman in lifelong union, and believes that abstinence is right for those who are not called to marriage. . . .

d) While rejecting homosexual practice as incompatible with scripture, calls on all our people to minister pastorally and sensitively to all irrespective of sexual orientation and to condemn irrational fear of homosexuals. . . .

e) Cannot advise the legitimizing or blessing of same sex unions nor ordaining those involved in same gender unions.[33]

The African bishops were strongly united: homosexuality violates scripture. However, they cautioned, gays and lesbians must not be persecuted or avoided for their sexual orientation. Rather, they should be ministered to, "pastorally and sensitively."

Some Western bishops were appalled by the resolutions, such as John Shelby Spong—a well-known liberal theologian in the US Episcopal Church. Spong condemned the African bishops' resolutions as being backward and archaic. In his view, the context of the New Testament is worlds removed from the church of today. Christianity must evolve beyond the world of first-century Palestine, or, as stated in the title of one of his celebrated books, Christianity must change, or die![34] To stay locked in the past is a terrible mistake. We must not forget about the great gains by the Enlightenment and by human reason. Christian faith must be adapted to a new context, enriched with new and improved knowledge. We must modernize. Otherwise we run the risk of sinking into the abyss of barbarism.

On the other hand, the conservative bishops, led by Bishop Emmanuel Chukwuma of Nigeria, were repulsed at the thought of sanctioning same-sex unions. At the conference, Bishop Chukwuma tried to exorcise the demons of homosexuality out of Rev. Richard

---

33. See The Lambeth Conference website. Resolutions from 1998 are located at http://www.lambethconference.org/resolutions/1998/1998-1-10.cfm.

34. John Shelby Spong, *Why Christianity Must Change or Die* (New York: HarperCollins, 1998).

Kirker, a gay priest who founded the Lesbian and Gay Christian Movement. Citing Leviticus's death penalty for homosexuals, he accused Kirker of "killing the Church." He was joined by Bishop Gbonigi, also of Nigeria, who said listening to homosexuals "would be a sheer waste of time . . . it is against the word of God. Nothing can make us [African bishops] budge because we view what God says as firm."[35] This controversy is ongoing and could potentially result in an outright split in the global Anglican Communion in coming years.

Conclusion: Who's Welcome?

To whom does Christianity belong? Are practicing gays and lesbians welcome? How about those who "hook up" or those who cohabitate before marriage? Are polygamists able to practice their Christian faith without prejudice or fear? What about the asexual and celibate members in the church—either by nature or by choice—have they lost their once-vital presence in the church? And what kind of relationships may the church sanction? Serial monogamy? Remarriages after divorce? Homosexual couples? Clearly, these are among the most potent challenges facing world Christianity, and how Christians deal with them today will indelibly shape the church of tomorrow.

---

35. Frank Kirkpatrick, *The Episcopal Church in Crisis* (Westport, CT: Praeger, 2008), 5.

12

Women

Galatians 3:23, 25–29

Before the coming of this faith, we were held in custody under the law. . . . Now that this faith has come, we are no longer under a guardian. So in Christ Jesus you are all children of God through faith. . . . There is neither Jew nor gentile, neither slave nor free, nor is there male and female, for you are all one in Christ Jesus . . . and heirs according to the promise.

During the last few decades, discussions of women and Christianity in the Western world have revolved around the notions of feminism, subordination, liberation, and equivalency with men.[1] This discourse is still very much alive in the West, but its fervor is not what it once was. There are reasons for this. First of all, major gains have been made. For example, since the 1980s, far more women are enrolled in colleges than men, causing what some have called the "gender

---

1. See, for example, the pioneering work of Rosemary Radford Ruether. A good introduction to her ideas is her chapter "Christianity," in *Women in World Religion*, ed. Arvind Sharma (Albany, NY: State University of New York Press, 1987).

gap" in higher education. In 2010 the *Chronicle of Higher Education* reported, "Women now account for a disproportionate share of the enrollments of higher-education institutions at every degree level and are likely to become an even more dominant presence on campuses over the coming decade."[2] Some refer to it as a "man-cession."[3] Today in America, more women are admitted, more finish their programs, and more continue on to graduate school. They also make better grades than men and they drop out less.[4] My own institution struggles to enroll enough men to create a balance; in a typical year, 60 percent of the student body is female. Without doubt, women in the United States have found their place in the academy, and the trends show no signs of reversing.

Female Clergy in America

Seminaries are not exempt from these trends, either. In 2006, the *New York Times* reported, "Women now make up 51 percent of the students in divinity school."[5] And changes are trickling down into the clerical ranks as women take their seats in the upper echelons of several denominations. Katharine Jefferts Schori is the presiding bishop of the Episcopal Church. Sharon Watkins is the general minister and president of the Christian Church (Disciples of Christ). Elizabeth Eaton is the presiding bishop of the Evangelical Lutheran Church in America. Perhaps the most influential female African-American church leaders today are Cynthia Hale—founding pastor of

---

2. Peter Schmidt, "Men's Share of College Enrollments Will Continue to Dwindle, Federal Report Says," *Chronicle of Higher Education*, May 27, 2010, located at http://chronicle.com/article/Mens-Share-of-College/65693/.

3. Associated Press, "In a First, Women Surpass Men in College Degrees," *CBSNews*, April 26, 2011, located at http://www.cbsnews.com/news/in-a-first-women-surpass-men-in-college-degrees/.

4. Alex Williams, "The New Math on Campus," *New York Times*, February 5, 2010, located at http://www.nytimes.com/2010/02/07/fashion/07campus.html?pagewanted=all.

5. Neela Banerjee, "Clergywomen Find Hard Path to Bigger Pulpit," *New York Times*, August 26, 2006, located at http://www.nytimes.com/2006/08/26/us/26clergy.html?th&emc=th.

Ray of Hope Christian Church (Disciples of Christ) in Georgia, and Bishop Vashti McKenzie of the African Methodist Episcopal Church.

Some of America's female megapastors transcend denominational and national boundaries, reaching out through television, conferences, and publications. Joyce Meyer's ministry is probably the most prolific, and certainly the most entrepreneurial. She is revered all over the Christian world and is a constant presence on Christian television, both in the United States and abroad. Paula White is a charismatic, globetrotting pastor based in Florida. In a nation where Sunday mornings are largely segregated, White is as comfortable preaching to black audiences as white ones. Beth Moore is another notable figure here, although she is known mainly for her Bible studies; they have made her a household name in evangelical circles. Several times per year influential women evangelists pool their talents together for the highly successful *Women of Faith* conferences that have reached five million attendees since 1996.[6]

Women Pastors: The Historical Background

Globally, Christians are conflicted over the issue of women in positions of religious leadership. The Roman Catholic and Orthodox churches do not allow women priests. Considering Catholics comprise half the world's Christians and the Orthodox about ten percent, that leaves only forty percent left, who are the Protestants, but Protestants are all over the map on whether women can pastor churches. As we have seen, in the United States, there are high-profile examples of female pastors, but there are also many denominations that do not allow females in key roles.

Where do these restrictions come from? Why wouldn't a church allow a woman to be pastor or priest? After all, Paul wrote, "There is

6. See "5 Million Women of Faith," October 28, 2013, located at http://www.womenoffaith.com/2013/10/five-million-women-faith/.

neither Jew nor gentile, neither slave nor free, nor is there male and female, for you are all one in Christ Jesus" (Gal. 3:28). The problem is that while Paul seemed open to women in certain leadership roles, he is rather closed in others:

> Women should remain silent in the churches. They are not allowed to speak, but must be in submission, as the law says. If they want to enquire about something, they should ask their own husbands at home; for it is disgraceful for a woman to speak in the church. (1 Cor. 14:34–35)

These two apparently contradictory passages are atop an entire corpus of scriptures referenced by scholars to make their case of whether churches should allow women to lead their flocks. And while the traditional position—that pastors should be men—has dominated church history, in recent decades, especially in the Western world, this conversation has been utterly recast.

It is too simple of an explanation to insist that the feminism of the 1960s changed everything, although it was significant. First of all, feminism's roots go back further than that, even into the Old Testament with its notion of prophetesses. Second, it is naive to assume that feminism did not go on during the history of Christianity. Women often held positions of leadership in church history, for example in the running of convents. Third, it is clear from a cursory reading of the New Testament that women were very much involved in the leadership of the church from early on. The apostle Paul cites Euodia, Syntyche, Junia, Priscilla, and Phoebe as but a few of the females who held important roles. Whether they presided during the assembly is not clear. What is clear is that Paul identified them as leaders in their churches.

About a century after the Reformation, various churches began to entertain the idea of women pastors. The early Quaker community was a trailblazer here with the career of Margaret Fell (1614–1702), 'one of its earliest members, and the wife of its founder, George Fox. She argued that since women and men were both created in the image of God, they were equals.[7] Anne Hutchinson (1591–1643), a Puritan leader in Massachusetts Bay Colony, was another key figure. She argued against clerical ordination and against patriarchy in the churches, putting her at odds with the religious establishment. She and her family, along with a group of supporters, were banished from the colony on charges of heresy. Hutchinson later relocated to Dutch territory where she and most of her family were massacred by Indians in 1643. She remains an important figure in early American feminism.[8]

The American Shaker movement, which reached "its apogee from 1810 to 1860," was an institutional experiment in male-female equality.[9] Shakers attempted to abolish the nuclear family since it perpetuated patriarchy. Sexual intercourse was forbidden and seen as the "main root of evil." Their founder, Ann Lee (1736–1784), "lost all of her four children at birth or during infancy," leaving her "scarred by her ordeals."[10] The movement attracted women mainly, but men were welcomed and were allowed positions of leadership. It seems the theological motivation for Shakers was to achieve salvation, but there were also socioeconomic reasons for a movement such as this. Many of the members came from broken homes, were widows with children, or were children who had been neglected, abandoned, or orphaned. Some Shaker communities were essentially orphanages or retirement communities. While eventually the movement faded, it

---

7. Fell's classic treatise on the topic is *Womens Speaking Justified, Proved and Allowed of by the Scriptures* (1667). See Mary Anne Schofield, "'Womens Speaking Justified': The Feminine Quaker Voice, 1662–1797," *Tulsa Studies in Women's Literature* 6, no. 1 (Spring 1987).

8. See Elaine Huber, "Anne Hutchison," in the *American National Biography Online*, located at http://www.anb.org/articles/01/01-00437.html.

9. See D'Ann Campbell, "Women's Life in Utopia: The Shaker Experiment in Sexual Equality Reappraised—1810 to 1860," *The New England Quarterly* 51, no. 1 (1978): 24.

10. Ibid., 28.

is remembered as "an historical American example in which women functioned as the political, economic, and social equals of men."[11]

There was a much larger context to the Shaker movement. At the time Shakerism was in its heyday, the American feminist movement was coalescing, usually in conjunction with the abolitionist movement. Women such as Sarah and Angelina Grimke, Lucretia Mott, Elizabeth Cady Stanton, and Susan B. Anthony perceived inequality among races as well as sexes, spawning the Seneca Falls Convention in 1848, a key moment in the history of women's rights. During the convention, it was resolved and passed that there should be a "speedy overthrow of the male monopoly of the pulpit." Just a few years later, in 1853, Antoinette Brown was ordained as a Congregationalist minister. She had been educated at Oberlin College, "the first theological seminary to admit women."[12]

It is important to note the high point of Protestant missions was happening during the age of Christian feminism. Many women became missionaries and assumed roles of leadership in the field that would have been denied them in the Western world. Feminist ideas, while gaining great traction in the West, were planted into the Global South, sometimes strategically, sometimes unconsciously. Missionaries took the gospel into the fields of Asia, Africa, and Latin America, but often embedded in their religious teachings were values considered avant-garde, if not objectionable, back home.

In the Catholic world, the profile of women is increasing at a rapid rate. This is a story not often reported. John Allen Jr., the veteran American journalist who covers all things Catholic, tells a fascinating story. In the United States, women occupy 80 percent of lay ministry roles, half of the diocesan-level administrative posts, and 27 percent of senior executive positions in the dioceses. Female representation

11. Ibid., 37.
12. Ruether, "Christianity," 231.

242

in the high-earning positions within America's Roman Catholic Church outperforms other American industries such as business, law, and the military. These facts cause him to wonder *not* why there are so few women in high positions in the church, but why so many? His suspicion is that because women are denied the priesthood, the bishopric, and virtually any influence in the Vatican, they have been welcomed and encouraged at most other levels in the church's structure. And while he does not see women's ordination occurring any time soon, he makes an effective argument that pastoral care in parishes, hospitals, and schools will be increasingly feminized.[13]

Dana Robert, an authority on Christian missions, drives home the point that women play a vital role in the world church today:

> Around the globe, more women than men are practicing Christians. . . . Christianity is a women's religion. The ratio of female to male Christians is approximately two to one. Within Catholicism, sisters outnumber brothers and priests by more than 50 percent. . . . In the late nineteenth and the twentieth centuries, in both Catholicism and Protestantism, the majority of missionaries were women. However, until recently overview histories of mission have scarcely analyzed women's roles or acknowledged that women typically make up the majority of active believers.[14]

There is a common theme occurring here: Christianity would be a shadow of itself without the contribution of women, both throughout history and in the present.

African Women

Overall, women in Africa have been denied positions of leadership in the church. "By the time a woman has spent her energies struggling to be heard, she barely has the energy left to say what she wanted

---

13. John L. Allen Jr., *The Future Church* (New York: Doubleday, 2009), 195–98.
14. Dana Robert, *Christian Mission: How Christianity Became a World Religion* (Oxford: Wiley-Blackwell, 2009), 118.

to say," writes Mercy Oduyoye. Similarly, Isabel Phiri writes, "With only a few exceptions, African churches have resisted including women in leadership positions. The most common argument is no longer theological but cultural: African cultures do not allow women to lead men."[15] This is changing on several fronts due to the work of courageous women who have built bridges with each other across the African continent. For example, the Circle of Concerned African Women Theologians was begun in Ghana in 1989 to facilitate communication, offer support, and serve as a forum for innovation and change. The World Council of Churches has taken a leading role in engaging women's issues, notably in its special program "The Decade of Churches in Solidarity with Women," which lasted from 1988 to 1998. That initiative attracted much awareness to women's issues.

Historically, African women were shamans, priestesses, mediums, and healers. That cultural legacy has not vanished. As Africans continue to embrace Jesus as Lord, their cultures make indelible impacts on the church, and the process of inculturation leads to new Christian outlets for women. A couple of examples will illustrate the point: the lives of Kimpa Vita and Alice Auma.

The Case of Kimpa Vita

In the late fifteenth century, Portuguese missionaries had great success evangelizing the great Kingdom of Kongo. The baptism of Kongolese King João I triggered a mass movement. The form of Christianity that began to mushroom was not precisely what the Portuguese anticipated, however. It was intertwined with ancestor veneration, infusing Christian theology into local culture in a way that preserved much of what the Kongolese held dear, such as their

---

15. See Mercy Oduyoye, "African Women Theologians," in *Twentieth-Century Global Christianity* (Minneapolis: Fortress Press, 2008), 84, 88.

holy places. The Portuguese were offended by what they perceived to be syncretism to the point of heresy.

Beatriz Kimpa Vita (1684–1706) was born during a time of upheaval.[16] The Kongo had erupted into civil war, food was scarce, and social stability was threatened on all sides. Roman Catholic Christianity had been successfully implanted for about two centuries by the time of her birth, but the society was as unstable as ever. Beatriz was born into the church and grew up Catholic. Twice she married, but both marriages failed. Like many women in similar circumstances, without children, she had nowhere to turn but the church.

Around 1704 Beatriz began to have visions of the beloved thirteenth-century Portuguese monk St. Anthony of Padua. She claimed his spirit had taken residence within her; thus she was speaking on his behalf, with the authority of a saint and a prophet. She spoke out against idolatry, war, and pagan practices. She taught that Jesus was actually Kongolese in origin. She declared that a new era of wealth was coming to the Kongo since—according to her claims—the Europeans had buried treasure all around and she knew how to access it. She argued for black saints rather than only white ones. Many commoners and even some nobility followed her, leading to a movement known as Antonianism. While at first peaceful, it later provoked the authorities and morphed into an all-out insurgency, even occupying the capital São Salvador for a time.

Beatriz's revolution was short-lived, however. She was arrested for sedition, declared a heretic, and burned publicly on July 2, 1706. While originally they intended to burn her infant son, at the last minute the child was taken from her arms and spared due to the intervention of a priest. Another priest carefully recorded the

16. See John Thornton, *The Kongolese Saint Anthony: Dona Beatriz Kimpa Vita and the Antonion Movement, 1684–1706* (Cambridge: Cambridge University Press, 1998).

execution, sarcastically adding, "The poor Saint Anthony, who was accustomed to dying and reviving, this time really died and never again revived."[17]

Alice Auma's Holy Spirit Movement

Alice Auma (1956–2007) was from an entirely different time and place.[18] Her name is associated with the Holy Spirit Movement in Uganda, where several political and religious rebellions rose up protesting Yoweri Museveni's rise to power in the aftermath of Idi Amin's brutal dictatorship in the 1970s. The post-Amin era was chaotic and left a political vacuum. Many local charismatic leaders filled the gap using spirit possession and divination. These diviners and mediums routinely connected themselves to Christianity for greater legitimacy.

Auma was raised Anglican and had only seven years of primary school for education. Her father was born Catholic, converted to Anglicanism, but eventually declared himself a prophet and founded his own church.

Alice married twice but in both cases the marriage failed due to infertility. Disgraced, she returned home to her father at age twenty-three to sell fish and flour for a living. During her twenties she joined the Roman Catholic Church. At age twenty-nine she went into the wilderness for forty days and emerged with supernatural stories, claiming she had met with animals and various spirits. She began to channel many of the spirits, most importantly an Italian World War II captain whom she called Lakwena. Like Kimpa Vita, she began speaking out on many different issues. Her message was

17. Ibid., 184.
18. See Tim Allen, "Understanding Alice: Uganda's Holy Spirit Movement in Context," *Africa* 61, no. 3 (1991); Heike Behrend, *Alice Lakwena and the Holy Spirits: War in Northern Uganda 1986–1997* (Athens, OH: Ohio University Press, 1999); and Emmanuel Twesigye, *Religion, Politics, and Cults in East Africa: God's Warriors and Mary's Saints* (New York: Peter Lang, 2010).

that her people—the Acholi of northern Uganda—needed to abandon their sins and turn to God. Many people believed in her and took her message seriously.

Alice also drew liberally from biblical imagery. She made several important claims, such as she would part the Nile, that her Acholi people were God's "chosen," and that the spirit of Lakwena living inside her was actually the Holy Spirit. She routinely invoked the Ten Commandments.

At age thirty, Alice and her followers attracted international attention for taking up arms against Museveni's National Resistance Army. She recruited exsoldiers, peasants, and even some people of influence in order to fight against what she perceived to be an evil regime. Professor Isaac Newton Ojok, a former minister of education, joined her cause, adding to her legitimacy. In the early months, Alice's Holy Spirit Battalion (or, Holy Spirit Mobile Forces) had success using very unorthodox methods. Her men would march shirtless, singing hymns and holding Bibles, covered in oil, believing they would be protected from bullets. Legends of her miraculous powers spread throughout Uganda and beyond. Her army grew into the thousands and eventually they adopted more conventional war tactics. Their string of victories ended when they came within fifty miles of Kampala in October 1987 and were crushed. Alice escaped, however, and lived out her remaining twenty years in a Kenyan refugee camp.

Alice's army fragmented into several groups, the most famous being the Lord's Resistance Army, led by her alleged cousin—the infamous Joseph Kony. Kony's atrocities became highly publicized through a short film entitled *Kony 2012* that was a viral sensation in the United States. Alice's father also took a leadership role in her movement both before and especially after her escape. Some followers declared Alice, her father, and Joseph Kony as a new Trinity.

The Holy Spirit Movement's members took copious notes documenting their movement. Their faith was syncretistic, and Alice wielded tremendous authority as one connected to both the political and divine realms. Spiritual mediums, who tended to be Catholic and almost always women, integrated the teachings of the church into the highly developed, complex milieu of African spirit possession.

Asian Women

In 1998 the World Council of Churches wrapped up its Churches in Solidarity with Women decade with a four-day festival. The project was deemed a success for bringing attention to issues confronting women. However, there was a gray cloud over the grand finale because of the huge problems that were made manifest to all participants, problems that were as big as ever—just better known after a decade of scrutiny.

A Lutheran delegate from India, Rev. Deenabandhu Manchala, spoke passionately about the "widespread prevalence and escalation of violence against women."[19] His statistics were extremely disturbing. Year after year, India tops the list in nearly every category of violence committed against women. Every year in India,

- 15,000 women are raped

- 15,000 women are kidnapped or abducted

- 7,000 brides are killed for not bringing enough dowry

- 30,000 women are tortured

- 30,000 women are molested

19. See Rev. Deenabandhu Manchala, "Violence against Women," Document No. DE 3, located at http://www.wcc-coe.org/wcc/assembly/decpl-e.html.

- 15,000 women are harassed

- 15,000 girls and women are used for sex trafficking

That was in 1998. Unfortunately the statistics have only gotten worse due to more awareness of these crimes. For example, UNICEF claims 24,270 rape cases were *reported* in 2011, 30 percent of them against children. They claim that number is only the tip of the iceberg in a culture where even mentioning rape can prove devastating for an unmarried girl's future. How many rapes went unreported? India has taken steps to address the problem such as featuring its most important celebrity—actor Amitabh Bachchan—in its "Time to Sound the Red Siren" initiative, but the scale of the problem is daunting.[20]

In India, Christianity is a small minority, around 3 percent. However, Christianity has a disproportionate impact due to the large number of educational institutions and hospitals founded by North American and European missionaries. A Christian movement in India could certainly mobilize the youth—many who graduate from prestigious Christian schools and immigrate to the West for work or education.

In his lecture, Manchala chastised the churches for doing too little to combat the problem. "During our visits, we have found that, by and large, the churches seem to view this as a given cultural phenomenon. . . . Unfortunately, the responsibility of having to safeguard the traditions of the institutional Church seems more a faith imperative than to hunger and thirst for justice and peace, to many a Christian today." There was a silver lining, however:

But amidst this gloomy reality, we have seen signs of hope. We have

20. Priyanka Pruthi, "It Is Time to Sound the Red Siren against Violence against Girls and Women in India," *UNICEF*, August 26, 2013, located at http://www.unicef.org/infobycountry/india_70237.html.

sensed a growing consciousness among women. They are getting organized to resist, to fight for equality, justice and fair treatment. They are breaking the culture of silence. . . . Here lies the challenge: Does the Church wish to remain a custodian of a culture of violence or catalyst of a culture of life?

In more recent years the situation has become direr still. Several recent, high-profile cases have attracted worldwide attention to the problem. These cases have sparked a national outcry and a light is being shone into the darkness.[21] The light is showing the world, however, just how awful the situation has become.

In spite of the difficulties faced by some Asian women, there are many encouraging stories as well.

- In South Korea's Yoido Full Gospel Church—the largest single Christian congregation in the world—women typically lead their nearly ten thousand cell groups.[22]

- One of the great Indian Christian intellects of the twentieth century was Pandita Ramabai (1858–1922), a convert from Hinduism, revered for her expertise in the Sanskrit scriptures and facility with languages. She became a passionate reformer in Indian society and established an impressive array of ministries for women, children, the poor, blind, exploited, elderly, and the outcaste at her large Mukti ("freedom") Mission compound.

- One of the great hymn writers of our time is Xiao Min, a Chinese woman living in Henan province. Featured in the fascinating documentary The Cross: Jesus in China, she is the author of over

21. I am here referring to the 2012 gang rape of a twenty-three-year-old medical student in New Delhi, the 2013 gang rape of a twenty-two-year-old photojournalist in Mumbai, and the 2014 gang rape and hanging of two teenage girls in Uttar Pradesh.
22. According to a publication given to me at Yoido when I was a guest in November 2013, the church reported having 9611 cell groups as of March 2013. The sixty-page booklet is entitled "Yoido Full Gospel Church." See also the Yoido website for a discussion on the role of women in the cell groups. See "History," located at http://english.fgtv.com/a1/a1_062.asp.

1300 songs, known to Chinese Christians as the Canaan Hymns. They are sung all across the nation in underground and registered churches alike. She has no training—she dropped out of school in junior high. She is a common field worker and has been imprisoned for her Christian activities. While in prison she converted many others to Christ. Her husband scoffed at her for thirteen years until her prayers for him were answered and he too followed Christ.[23]

Latina Women

In Latin America, women take a leading role in church and society, in spite of the patriarchal reputation of the continent. The Virgin Mary is revered in Latin America to heights rarely encountered elsewhere. The Virgin of Guadalupe is a national symbol in Mexico and in the southwestern United States, where she is seen in apparitions, prayed to, and given homage by millions of pilgrims at the Basilica of Our Lady of Guadalupe in Mexico City. Most Latin American nations have their own version of the Virgin, showing the centrality of the feminine role in the cultures. She is upheld as the Queen of Heaven, but also serves as the pillar of the Holy Family while they were on earth. And she maintains a uniquely close relationship with her son Jesus, causing many Latin Christians to look first to Mary for grace and sustenance in daily living. She is the heavenly icon for Christian virtue, strength, and self-sacrifice in the Latin American home.

---

23. There is not much published on Xiao Min. The second disk in The Cross: Jesus in China (Petaluma, CA: China Soul for Christ Foundation, 2003) is the best source available on her life. Liao Yiwu mentions her in his highly popular God is Red (New York: HarperOne, 2011), 71. There are several websites that briefly discuss her work. See "Xiao Min on Preparing for the Lord's Return," November 21, 2012, located at http://chinesechurchvoices.com/2012/11/21/xiao-min-on-preparing-for-the-lords-return/; and "The Canaan Hymns," located at http://waysoflife.info/CanaanHymns.html.

As religious freedom continues to unfold in Latin America—challenging its centuries-long, staunchly Catholic culture—many women are turning to Pentecostalism to meet their spiritual needs.[24] There is also a concomitant payoff when a woman converts her husband to Pentecostalism—he "abstains from investing money and energy in drinking, womanizing, and betting." This is obviously a stereotype of Latin men, but it is something routinely addressed by scholars because of the "sweeping reconfiguration of family life" that tends to occur when Pentecostalism is embraced. While the patriarchal hierarchy of the family remains in place—a pattern set forth in several New Testament passages—"the shape of masculine behavior is nonetheless substantially reconfigured. The patriarchal household code acquires a benevolent aspect." [25]

Another reason women have turned to Pentecostalism is because of its emphasis on physical and emotional healing. Todd Hartch writes, "Because of their location in poor and even desperate neighborhoods, where the lack of sanitation services made disease more likely and where people's poverty put expensive medical treatment out of reach, Pentecostal churches put a special emphasis on divine healing, which often served as a decisive factor in attracting potential converts."[26] Pentecostal Christianity emerged among the poor in Latin America, due largely to the shortage of Catholic priests. Thus in the shanty towns there were only two organizations that had any effectiveness: Pentecostalism and organized crime.[27] And what mother would want her son in the mafia? The result was a quick and vast expansion of a

---

24. See Paul Sigmund, ed., *Religious Freedom and Evangelization in Latin America: The Challenge of Religious Pluralism* (Maryknoll, NY: Orbis, 1999).

25. Luis Rivera-Pagan, "Pentecostal Transformation in Latin America," in *Twentieth-Century Global Christianity* (Minneapolis: Fortress Press, 2008), 192. Rivera-Pagan cites the following New Testament passages: 1 Cor. 14:34, Eph. 5:22, Col. 3:18, 1 Tim. 2:11–12, and 1 Pet. 3:1.

26. Todd Hartch, *The Rebirth of Latin American Christianity* (Oxford: Oxford University Press, 2014), 101.

27. Ibid., 103.

new form of Christianity that promised health, healing, and a more stable family life.

While women in Latin America's Pentecostal churches are by and large denied the pulpit, they serve a very strategic role since recruitment to the faith occurs within families, and women play the central role. Research shows that women are more likely to be religious, and much more likely to lead the people around them to Christ. Andrew Chesnut writes, "Men work, play, and die in the street . . . more attuned to the drama unfolding outside their front door than to the scene inside their home. . . . Women, by contrast, were proselytized in the culturally constructed female domain of the household."[28] When reaching out with the gospel, women look first to their own kin. Only later do they look beyond the front door.

Conclusion: The Hand That Rocks the Cradle

To whom does Christianity belong? In a strictly numerical sense we could venture to say that Christianity belongs more to females than males. This dichotomy obviously breaks down in light of Paul's injunction that for those who have been baptized into Christ, there is no male or female. "You are all one in Christ Jesus. If you belong to Christ, then you are Abraham's seed, and heirs according to the promise" (Gal. 3:28–29).

However, it does seem to be the case that women—particularly mothers—play a uniquely significant role in Christianity. Somebody must take the children to church, catechize them, and generally pass on the faith. And that job will usually fall on mothers. This is not to downplay the role of fathers; obviously their role is meaningful in building a family in faith. However, a deep connection of mother and

---

28. R. Andrew Chesnut, "Exorcising the Demons of Deprivation: Divine Healing and Conversion in Brazilian Pentecostalism," in *Global Pentecostal and Charismatic Healing* (Oxford: Oxford University Press, 2011), 172.

child begins at conception, and mothers exercise a unique influence over the decisions of their offspring, and often that influence lasts a lifetime. Indeed, as the proverb goes, "The hand that rocks the cradle rules the world."

The big concern facing the future of Christianity in the Western world, however, has to do with the numerical decline of motherhood in the second half of the twentieth century. Fertility rates are way down from past generations, families begin much later, and sexual relationships are formed regularly outside the bounds of wedlock and childbearing. Scholar Mary Eberstadt believes she has found the culprit for the weakening of Christian faith in Western Europe and North America: the Pill. She writes,

> The Pill and its associated movement, the sexual revolution, contributed to the weakening of family bonds as no other single technological force in history—which explains as no other single factor why the 1960s are the linchpin of the change in Western religiosity. . . . More Pill equals less time in a family. More time in a family equals more time in church. Therefore more Pill equals less God.[29]

Citing the research of Robert Wuthnow, she claims the sexual revolution's tidal wave is far from over. It continues to crash against the family and—as a consequence—against religiosity. "With more children growing up in one-parent (typically fatherless) homes, fewer parents had the resources, or, for some, the motivation to be sure the children made it to religious instruction classes or church."[30]

Compounding the dire outlook in Western Europe is the extremely low fertility rate: it is currently at 1.5 children per woman. In other words, Western Europeans do not replace themselves. For every couple in Western Europe, only one or two children will result.

---

29. Mary Eberstadt, *How the West Really Lost God* (West Conshohocken, PA: Templeton Press, 2013), 135–36.
30. Ibid., 136.

The fertility rates in Eastern Europe are even lower, at 1.38 children per woman. Some have called this alarming trend a "slow-motion autogenocide."[31] It would be the first documented case in history where a society of humans made the decision not to flourish, but rather to reduce. At these rates, the civilizations of both Eastern and Western Europe would end in extinction.[32]

In the Global South it is a different situation. In Africa, for example, fertility rates remain high. On average, every single woman in Africa has five successful pregnancies during her childbearing years. Likewise, Latinas have much more robust fertility rates than their *norteamericana* counterparts, and they have their children earlier. While white fertility rates are down in the United States, the nation's Hispanic population continues to rise. And the women in Asia's most Christian nation—the Philippines—have a fertility rate of 3.32 children per woman. These fertility trends are not simply interesting as social phenomena, they correlate directly with religiosity. As Eberstadt has stated repeatedly, "Beyond question, being married and having children is linked to higher levels of churchgoing. . . . Children drive parents to church."[33]

Women have a major say in a religion's vibrancy or decay, simply by the number of children they are willing to have. More children translate into more energy, more resources, and a more sustainable future. Without children, institutions become aged, irrelevant, and unable to afford the demands of the institution: aging clergy, expensive structures, and top-heavy programs. A new generation that is larger than the previous one naturally takes care of those problems.

31. Philip Jenkins, *God's Continent: Christianity, Islam, and Europe's Religious Crisis* (Oxford: Oxford University Press, 2007), 6.
32. See my research on fertility trends in Dyron Daughrity, *Church History: Five Approaches to a Global Discipline* (New York: Peter Lang, 2012).
33. Eberstadt, *How the West Really Lost God*, 93, 95.

Christian women hold the future of Christian faith in their hands, whether they realize it or not. For all the talk of patriarchy, the power of women to shape a faith community is, in my view, vastly underestimated.

In a perfect world, Christian women from all over the globe would have a venue where they could come together to discuss the Christian faith, its future, its strengths and weaknesses. They could pool their knowledge and resources, and come up with solutions for how to aid their own communities in the name of Christ. However, this might be overly idealistic. Women in the Global South cannot typically afford a trip of that nature. Besides, in a household that includes five or six children, they would probably have a hard time getting away for a conference. Christian women in the Western world would have to bear much of the cost. However, moving forward, it is not altogether clear how long women in the Western world plan to remain connected to Christianity, or even raise their children in church.

13

——

Music

Ephesians 5:18b–20

Be filled with the Spirit, speaking to one another with psalms, hymns, and songs from the Spirit. Sing and make music from your heart to the Lord, always giving thanks to God the Father for everything, in the name of our Lord Jesus Christ.

In 2010 I had the privilege of visiting the holy rock-hewn, cruciform churches of Lalibela, Ethiopia. I witnessed worship services drastically different from my own, drastically different from anything else I had ever seen. Everything about it was ancient, transporting me back to the fourth century. I was in a Christian church, but it was so unfamiliar to me. A priest solemnly rubbed a large, gold cross on a woman as she shrieked and convulsed. I was told she was being exorcised of a demon. Worshipers were covered from head to toe in white cloths, looking like they were wrapped in cocoons. They were spellbound as the priest slowly, methodically paced around, censing all the believers. My nose was filled with foreign, exotic incense that dried my sinuses and throat. The floors were covered in worn carpets, providing a thin layer between my bare feet and the cool, rock foundation. The labyrinthine worship spaces were devoid of sunlight. What was lacking in sight was abundantly compensated in sound.

Ethiopia's Jewish Christians

Ethiopian Orthodox music is haunting, highly symbolic, and palpable. It feels closer to ancient Judaism than to Christianity. Evidence of Judaism is all around. Even the name of the prayer shawl around their bodies—the *shamma*—bears a close resemblance to the Jewish *Shema*: "Hear, O Israel: The Lord our God, the Lord is one" (Deut. 6:4).

The Ethiopian Orthodox Tewahedo Church is often recognized as the second oldest national church in the world after the Armenian, dating to the early 300s.[1] It claims around 45 million members and is the largest of the non-Chalcedonian, or Oriental Orthodox traditions.[2] The term *Tewahedo* means "one united nature," in reference to Christ having one nature—rather than the more typical Christian view that Christ had two united natures.

Ethiopia has many connections to Jewish history and culture, notably through Ge'ez and Amharic, both Semitic languages. A hallowed Ethiopian text, the *Kebra Nagast*, describes how the Ethiopian people were grafted in to the Israelites through a romantic encounter between Queen Makeda of Sheba and Solomon when she visited him in Jerusalem. She was greatly impressed by the king,

---

1. For overviews of the Ethiopian Orthodox Church, see Jacques A. Blocher and Jacques Blandenier *The Evangelization of the World: A History of Christian Missions*, trans. Michael Parker (Pasadena: William Carey Library, 2013); Dale Irvin and Scott Sunquist, *History of the World Christian Movement*, vol. 1 (Maryknoll, NY: Orbis Books, 2001); Elizabeth Isichei, *A History of Christianity in Africa* (Grand Rapids, MI: Eerdmans, 1995); and Ogbu Kalu, ed., *African Christianity: An African Story* (Trenton, NJ: Africa World Press, 2007).
2. The non-Chalcedonian churches include the Coptic, Jacobite Syrian, Malankara (Indian) Orthodox, Armenian, Ethiopian, and Eritrean.

adopting his religion and becoming pregnant with his child, Menelik—the first Jewish emperor of Ethiopia. Ethiopian Christians believe Menelik eventually returned to Jerusalem to meet his father, who received him warmly and sent him back with the ark of the covenant—a most sacred symbol in Ethiopia today. According to the Ethiopian Church, the ark is housed in the Chapel of the Tablet adjacent to the Church of Our Lady Mary of Zion in Axum. This story is etched deeply into Ethiopian Orthodoxy; every Tewahedo church contains a *tabot*—a replica of the ark. The church claims the dynasty created by the Solomon-Makeda union lasted up to Emperor Haile Selassie's death in 1974.

In Acts 8:27 (NIV), an Ethiopian eunuch, "an important official in charge of all the treasury of Kandake (which means "queen of the Ethiopians") traveled to Jerusalem to worship. This story is significant on a number of levels. It illustrates the ancient Ethiopian-Jewish connection, it reveals a pilgrimage culture to Jerusalem by Ethiopians, and it shows the Ethiopian man was acquainted with the Jewish scriptures—he was reading the book of Isaiah. It is also one of the first biblical accounts of a gentile converting to Christianity.

Ethiopia's embrace of Christianity is documented in royal inscriptions and coins minted in the Axumite Kingdom during King Ezana's reign in the fourth century. Throughout history, Ethiopian Christianity has evinced a much more Jewish ethos than the Roman Catholic and Eastern Orthodox churches. The church architecture and arrangements of the sanctuary are heavily dependent upon Jewish synagogues. The city of Lalibela—known as Ethiopia's New Jerusalem—was patterned after the holy city and was an attempt to replace it when it fell to Islam during Saladin's conquests over the crusaders in the twelfth century.

Ethiopians retain many Jewish elements in their life and faith: strong dietary restrictions such as proscription of pork, mandated circumcision for boys, restrictions on menstruating women, required head coverings for women in church, gender separation during worship, observance of both the Jewish Sabbath and Christian Sunday, and, historically, an allowance for polygamy. And for specialists who study the history of church music, the Ethiopians give us a glimpse of what music may have sounded like in the Jewish temple and in synagogues in earliest Christianity.

Ethiopian Christian Music

Historian of Christian music Andrew Wilson-Dickson writes, "The music of the Ethiopian Christians in particular is sufficiently old to have preserved the ancient Israelites' physical dimension of dance and the heartbeat of their rhythmic accompaniment."[3] He describes the Ethiopians as maintaining "remarkable links with the distant past."[4] Their traditions have hardly changed; rather, they move "at a glacier-like pace," preserving remarkable insights into early Christian worship styles.[5]

Wilson-Dickson argues that the Orthodox traditions have "preserved attitudes overturned in the West by the European Renaissance and Reformation."[6] In the Orthodox families of Christianity, there is very little emphasis on preaching to a group of individuals who need their weekly exhortation. Rather, emphasis is placed upon the great heroes of the Christian past. The liturgies are from the church fathers and are something to be preserved. Icons bring to mind important figures who shaped the beliefs and practices of the church. Nationalism gets bound up with Christian worship, as the churches and the state have not experienced the dramatic

3. Andrew Wilson-Dickson, *The Story of Christian Music: From Gregorian Chant to Black Gospel* (Minneapolis: Fortress Press, 2003), 167.
4. Ibid., 19.
5. Ibid., 245.
6. Ibid., 166–67.

separation so common in most Protestant and Catholic contexts. As the Western traditions have strived to be relevant, the Orthodox rejoice in their renunciation of the present order. They delight in conforming to the teachers of old. Relevance to present trends is suspect. It is the ancient and the apostolic that carries weight.

Music is vital to the Eastern traditions. However, when a Westerner hears Orthodox music the reaction is typically, "Why is this music so foreign, so ancient, so separated from current musical trends today?" Wilson-Dickson argues that the Orthodox churches give us a glimpse into the sacred music of medieval Western Europe. The big shift occurred in fifteenth-century Italy, when "the sanctity of personal rights, aspirations and freedom of expression" began to blossom due to the burgeoning "cult of the individual," which has "formed the cornerstone of Western culture since the Renaissance."[7] There was deep continuity between the early church and the late medieval church. However, the fractures that occurred in the West, separating Catholic and Protestant, also led to sweeping changes in church music.

But to worship in an Ethiopian church is to cut behind the Protestant-Catholic wars. It takes us to a place way back, where we hear echoes of Judaism in the first Christian centuries. All Ethiopian Orthodox clergy—priests, deacons, monks, and the mysterious debteras—are trained in music. Debteras are music specialists in the Ethiopian Orthodox tradition. They are revered for their long and arduous education in dance, music, chanting, and poetry. However, they are also feared because of their at times ecstatic behavior and association with traditional practices such as black magic, astrology, and divining. They work in close cooperation with the church, but have a reputation for regularly straying outside the bounds of Christian orthodoxy. They are, however, essential to Ethiopian

7. Ibid., 166.

Orthodoxy because of their great understanding of the holy texts, liturgy, and music. In many ways they are the great preservers of this ancient and proud tradition of worship.

The debteras are associated with an important sixth-century saint named Yared. In the Ethiopian tradition, Yared is the father of the church's sacred chant. They claim he was carried away by three birds into heaven in order to listen and to learn from twenty-four heavenly priests. However, Wilson-Dickson notes, the music of the Ethiopian Orthodox Church is far older than the hagiography of Yared suggests. Rather, "It is probably that some direct link exists with the temple music of Jerusalem."[8] The evidence he uses to support this idea relies heavily on architecture, dance, ritual, and language. For example, the Ethiopians refer to the innermost chamber as *keddusa keddusan,* evidently connected to the Hebrew *kodesh hakkodashim,* or, "holy of holies." Another example is how the Ethiopians venerate and transport the tabot (ark of the covenant) in solemn procession. They sing and dance, beating their staffs onto the ground making a thud. They rattle their sistra and sound their instruments in a way reminiscent of 2 Samuel 6, when David and his men brought the ark of God to Jerusalem using castanets, harps, lyres, tambourines, rattles, trumpets, and cymbals. "The entire spectacle, its substance and its atmosphere, has caused all who have witnessed it to feel transported into the times of the Old Testament."[9]

I asked my guide to explain aspects of the liturgy and its instrumentation. He handed me a sistrum, an instrument I had never seen before traveling to Ethiopia. It was used by the ancient Egyptians, but it is very common in the Ethiopian church today due

---

8. Ibid., 163–64.

9. Michael Powne, *Ethiopian Music, an Introduction: A Survey of Ecclesiastical and Secular Ethiopian Music and Instruments* (Oxford: Oxford University Press, 1968), 98–99. Quoted in Wilson-Dickson, *Story of Christian Music,* 165.

to the close ecclesial connection between the Coptic Christians and the Ethiopian Orthodox. It is basically in the shape of an upside-down *U* with a handle, and has three crossbars with thin pieces of moveable iron on them. It makes a high metallic jingle sound as the metal pieces crash together. I was told the sound represents the whipping of Jesus before the crucifixion. It also represents Jesus getting pushed to the ground by the crowds, a scene emulated in the church's intricate dance. The sistrum is rich in symbolism. The metal pieces represent the nails put into Jesus's body. The frame brings to mind many things for Ethiopian Christians: the Bible, Jacob's ladder, angels, and the church.

A second instrument is the prayer stick, a staff used by Ethiopian men in church, but also used to support their bodies while they stand and rest. During worship the movement of the prayer sticks is highly important, particularly when it hits the ground, a sound that brings to mind the incarnation of Jesus—from heaven to earth. Lifting up the prayer stick signifies the resurrection.

A third instrument is the drum. It represents the body of Jesus and the pounding of it is meant to remind believers of Jesus being struck in the face by those who condemned him and put him to death. The beating of the drum goes on and on during Ethiopian worship, pulsating to the point that when it stops there is great relief. The incessant pounding is meant to make the worshipers feel the punches into the face of the Lord. The two sides of the drum are an analogy for Jesus's two natures: human and divine. The cords and décor on the side of the drum represent the whips, thorn of crowns, and scars on Jesus's body. The drum's emptiness is a metaphor for the empty tomb.

Early Christian Music

Scholars do not fully understand early Christian music. The main reason for this lack of knowledge is simple: "Neither Jews nor Christians are known to have noted down any of the music they used for worship until at least the sixth or seventh century A.D."[10] We do have lyrics for some very old hymns, however. For example, "The earliest known Christian hymn recorded outside of the Bible" is the *Phos Hilaron*, or, "Hail Gladdening Light," still performed in the Eastern Orthodox Vespers service. It was written "in all probability in Cappadocia, the cradle of the 'early Christian' spirituality."[11] Identifying early Christian music in the textual record is a painstaking task, carried out by highly specialized scholars. There are other ways to approach the research, however. One fruitful method of recovery is to listen to the music of ancient traditions that have proven reluctant to change, such as the Ethiopians or the Yemenite Jews. These isolated, extremely conservative communities are then analyzed and compared.

Jesus and his apostles sang, according to Matthew's "Last Supper" account (26:30). The apostle Paul refers to singing in his epistles to the Ephesians (5:18–20) and Colossians (3:16). In Paul's day the Christians employed psalms, hymns, and spiritual songs (or, "songs from the spirit"). Paul mentions that he sings with his spirit as well as with his understanding, seemingly to illustrate that worship should be intelligible and orderly (1 Cor. 14:15). Paul and Silas sang hymns to God while incarcerated (Acts 16:25). James, the brother of the Lord, instructed believers to sing when they were happy (5:13).

That the early church sang songs comes as little surprise, since singing was a regular part of Jewish worship. Music enters the Bible

---

10. Wilson-Dickson, *Story of Christian Music*, 25.
11. Petros Vassiliades, "From the Pauline Collection to *Phos Hilaron* of Cappadocia," *St. Vladimir's Theological Quarterly* 56, no. 1 (January 2012): 9 and 5.

in the early chapters of Genesis (4:21) and continues throughout. The Psalms in particular are filled with music and singing. It only makes sense that the earliest Christians—being Jews—would have continued the practice. In a famous letter to Roman Emperor Trajan (ruled 98–117), written by an imperial official by the name of Pliny the Younger around the year 112, a few notable practices of the Christians are discussed, and it refers to them singing to Jesus Christ:

> On an appointed day they had been accustomed to meet before daybreak, and to recite a hymn antiphonally [call and response style] to Christ, as to a god, and to bind themselves by an oath, not for the commission of any crime but to abstain from theft, robbery, adultery and breach of faith, and not to deny a deposit when it was claimed. After the conclusion of this ceremony it was their custom to depart and meet again to take food; but it was ordinary and harmless food.[12]

Pliny then describes how "many persons of all ages and classes and of both sexes" are converting to Christianity, both in the cities as well as in the countryside. In order to gain more information he tried "applying torture to two maidservants, who were called deaconesses." After interrogating them he was convinced it was "nothing but a depraved and extravagant superstition."

Liturgical scholar Frank Senn writes that the early church fathers had real misgivings with music and dancing, concluding that "most of them disapproved of it most of the time."[13] However, they had to compete with the Greco-Roman religions and thus were in need of music. It was a conflicted situation. The apostle Paul seemed to prefer "rational worship" (Rom. 12:1) over the flutes, tambourines, and cymbals of the Greek styles of worship.[14] Paul's preferences seemed

12. Henry Bettenson, *Documents of the Christian Church*, second ed. (Oxford: Oxford University Press, 1963), 3–4.
13. Frank Senn, *The People's Work: A Social History of the Liturgy* (Minneapolis: Fortress Press, 2006), 114.
14. "Rational worship" is Senn's translation of Rom. 12:1. The NIV translates this phrase "proper worship."

to be similar to the philosopher Plato's (c. 428–348 B.C.)—proper sacrificial ceremonies to the gods excluded the use of instruments. And this view is the one that carried the day, for many centuries. Church music, by and large, became a cappella, a word that means "in the style of the church." Indeed, in the Eastern Orthodox Churches, the music is still unaccompanied. Timothy Ware writes, "In the Orthodox Church today, as in the early Church, all services are sung or chanted. . . . Singing is unaccompanied and instrumental music is not found, except among certain Orthodox in America—particularly the Greeks—who are now showing a penchant for the organ or harmonium."[15]

Why did this happen? How did the worship of God in the Jewish temple, resplendent with all manner of musical instrumentation (just read Psalm 150!) become something for voices only in the church? The blame can be placed partly on the shoulders of the powerful Archbishop of Constantinople John Chrysostom (347–407), one of the three holy hierarchs in Orthodoxy (with Basil the Great and Gregory Nazianzus). He is also considered the father of Orthodox Christian liturgy—the celebration of the Eucharist. Chrysostom was no friend of musical instruments in the worship of God.

In one of Chrysostom's fiery sermons he asked his congregants, "What is it that you are rushing to see in the synagogue of the Jews who fight against God? Tell me, is it to hear trumpeters?" He went on,

> Do you wish to see that God hates the worship paid with kettledrums, with the lyre, with harps, and other instruments? God said, "Take away from me the sound of your songs and I will not hear the canticle of your harps." . . . Do you run to listen to their trumpets? Do you wish to learn that, together with the sacrifices and musical instruments and the festivals and the incense, God also rejects the temple because of those

15. Timothy Ware, *The Orthodox Church* (New York: Penguin, 1997), 268.

who enter it? He showed this . . . when he gave it over to barbarian lands, and later when he utterly destroyed it.[16]

Chrysostom's name means "golden-mouthed." And anyone who ran afoul of his eloquence could pay dearly for it, as the case of the instrument-loving Jews during his day. He was notoriously hard on them in his speeches, presumably because he wrote during a time when Christian identity was being defined in contrast to Judaism and paganism. Senn writes, "Thus, the condemnation of the use of musical instruments by the church fathers was not an aesthetic criticism, but a matter of staking out Christian identify and morality."[17]

Early Christian music was very basic for hundreds of years. "What is clear is that the Christian public worship came to make use of unaccompanied monophonic chant."[18] However, the Ethiopians used basic instrumentation, as did the Coptic Christians of Egypt who used triangles and cymbals. Chanting of the Psalms was the most common method of worship, however, and it mirrored what took place in the synagogues. Chanting is still common in more ancient Christian traditions, as well as in Islam—which freely adopted aspects of Christian faith in the seventh century and beyond. In both of these religions, the chanting became complex and required a high level of expertise. Timothy Ware writes, "Until very recent times all singing in Orthodox churches was usually done by the choir; today, a small but increasing number of parishes . . . are beginning to revive congregational singing."[19]

---

16. Quoted in Senn, *People's Work*, 118. The source is Chrysostom's *Discourses against Judaizing Christians*, preached in 386 and 387. The quotation comes from discourse 4.

17. Senn, *People's Work*, 117–18.

18. David Melling, "Music," in *The Blackwell Dictionary of Eastern Christianity*, ed. K. Parry, D. Melling, D. Brady, S. Griffith, and J. Healey (Oxford: Blackwell, 2001), 328–31. Quotation is from 329.

19. Ware, *Orthodox Church*, 268.

Equally complex is the music of the other ancient Christian traditions. Both the Armenians and the Ethiopians have their "own systems of notation."[20] Movements are precise and nuanced. There is no way an outsider could understand the divine liturgies of these older traditions without being educated beforehand. "Byzantine notation and chant developed through the middle ages, becoming increasingly complex, until by the fall of the city [1453] only experts could master them."[21]

In the West, church music remained monophonic well into the medieval period. In the eleventh and twelfth centuries the Western church began to integrate polyphony (multiple parts) into the liturgy, for example in a descant part sung above the plain chant melody.[22] The liturgical chant in the West was known as "Gregorian chant" in memory of Pope Gregory the Great (reigned 590–604) although it has "minimal if any association with him."[23] Music had limited changes in the West until the thirteenth century, when "there is clear evidence of the organ being used regularly; it replaced the singing of some liturgical texts in the late fourteenth century."[24]

Protestant Ambivalence

When the Western church split in the sixteenth century due to the Reformation, music culture followed suit. Luther was responsible for transforming music dramatically, proclaiming "next to the Word of God, music deserves the highest praise."[25] Luther became well known for his musical compositions, including his enduring paraphrase of Psalm 46, "A Mighty Fortress Is Our God," which is still sung

20. Melling, "Music," 329.
21. Ibid., 330.
22. Everett Ferguson, *Church History*, vol. 1: *From Christ to the Pre-Reformation* (Grand Rapids, MI: Zondervan, 2013), 463.
23. Ibid., 321.
24. Ibid., 464.
25. Carter Lindberg, *The European Reformations*, second ed. (Oxford: Wiley-Blackwell, 2010), 372.

worldwide. In 1620 a Jesuit claimed, "Martin Luther destroyed more souls with his hymns than with all his writing and preaching."[26] Luther wanted the entire congregation to sing, and his "own hymn-writing set the highest of standards."[27] Luther loved medieval church music; he just wanted to baptize it with Protestant convictions such as vernacular language and congregational participation. The pinnacle of Lutheran music is to be found in the choral masterpieces of Johann Sebastian Bach (1685–1750), considered by many to be the climax of sacred music, period. The former archbishop of Canterbury, Rowan Williams, once described Bach as one "who somehow does a great deal more theology in a few bars of music than most do in many words."[28]

Other Protestants were not so keen, particularly those in the Reformed churches. In Zurich, Ulrich Zwingli "closed all the organs" in 1524 and banned all forms of chant, arguing that "music distracted from worship." Calvin was not quite that harsh, but he prohibited instrumental music in the Geneva churches.[29] He allowed a chanting of the Psalms. Hymn writing was inherently pompous because it implied the word of God was somehow inadequate for worship services. At a time when church music was reaching new heights, early Reformed churches were a throwback to the earlier Roman Catholic and Orthodox outlook, "not unlike the plainchant of medieval monasteries."[30] However, they had to paraphrase many of the Psalms in order to make them work metrically. While accuracy was not exactly adhered to, this practice made memorizing the Psalms

26. Ibid., 372.
27. Diarmaid MacCulloch, *The Reformation: A History* (New York: Penguin, 2003), 589.
28. Rowan Williams, *Where God Happens* (Boston: New Seeds, 2007), 49.
29. Lindberg, *European Reformations*, 372–73.
30. Alister McGrath, *Christianity's Dangerous Idea: The Protestant Revolution* (New York: HarperOne, 2007), 297.

much easier. And that's what Protestants really cared about. They wanted people to know their Bibles.

English Protestantism reached its high watermark in the work of Isaac Watts (1674–1748), known affectionately as the father of English hymnody. Watts, a Nonconformist (Congregationalist) pastor, was able to innovate musically without compromising the Bible. His solution was ingenious. He argued that if the Psalms were the source for music, then New Testament teaching gets shortchanged. It was thus very necessary for the church to sing the gospel rather than exclusively the Psalms, as most of the English churches were doing. Nonetheless, Watts did not have a major impact on the English and Scottish churches early on. Alister McGrath writes, "Watt's breakthrough was generally ignored by Anglicans and Presbyterians."[31] He did have a huge impact on the brothers Wesley, however, in the eighteenth century. And the Wesleys, particularly Charles, indelibly shaped Christian hymnody in ways that come down to the present, especially the "warming of the heart" phenomenon so closely associated with the early Methodist movement and subsequent holiness churches. Wesley's song "Jesus, Lover of My Soul" is a good example of the intimacy between humans and God that music facilitated.

Protestants remained ambivalent about music for some time. But as pipe organs were integrated into church services, those who held onto plainchant were becoming smaller in number. In general, Americans lagged behind the Europeans in the embracing of hymnody and instrumentation. However, when the Americans finally caught up, they really made church music their own. Prominent American preacher Dwight Moody (1837–1899) toured with a musician named Ira Sankey. Sankey's singing attracted audiences and then Moody preached to them. They wrote hymns

31. Ibid., 300.

together that instructed in the essentials of theology and practical discipleship. Probably the most prolific hymn writer of the era, however, was Fanny J. Crosby (1820–1915), a blind Methodist woman who had unparalleled success. She authored thousands of hymns, many of which are still with us, such as "Blessed Assurance" and "To God Be the Glory." Crosby and Sankey were close friends, and their style, known as the "gospel song," cast a long-lasting spell over American Protestantism. Ultimately this style found its heartiest proponents in the African-American churches.

African-American Music

> It is impossible to "have church" without good music. In the African-American community, music is to worship as breathing is to life . . . A good sermon ain't nothing but a song.[32]

African-Americans have had a significant influence on American music since claiming church music as their own. With highly participatory styles, call-and-response patterns, exuberant choirs, and a constant stream of remarkably gifted soloists, black gospel music is a vital part of American Christianity. Many of the great African-American singers were first church vocalists, such as Mahalia Jackson, Marvin Gaye, and Whitney Houston.

Rooted in the slave experience, black gospel is a vivid reminder that America was not "the beautiful" for an entire race, for a very long time. While European-Americans enjoyed the promised land in the Americas, for many Africans it was a living hell. However, the church provided a refuge, and over time it became an "invisible institution" that fostered black leadership, a unique liturgy, and a

---

32. Pedrito Maynard-Reid, *Diverse Worship: African-American, Caribbean & Hispanic Perspectives* (Downers Grove, IL: InterVarsity Press, 2000), 69. I am indebted to Maynard-Reid's excellent book for this section. I am also indebted to the wonderful documentary *Rejoice and Shout: A Jubilant Journey through Gospel Music History* (Magnolia Pictures, 2011) a tour de force that should be seen by anyone interested in the topic.

form of Christianity that even still non-blacks know little to nothing about.[33] This is the black church experience, and it is one reason the black churches are nearly all black. It is difficult for an Asian, or Latino, or Caucasian to understand the collective identity of what it means to be black. But the traditions, songs, and collective memory are passed down in the church like in no other place.

An important aspect of the black church experience is that there is not a neat and clean dividing line separating the sacred from the profane. Christopher Partridge has described this phenomenon as one of "liminality," with a "mild transgressive appeal."[34] There is porousness between the church and the club. This is why Whitney Houston could sing the party anthem "Queen of the Night" and the solemn, tender "Jesus Loves Me" back to back on the *Bodyguard* film soundtrack. It is why Smokey Robinson could move so fluidly into gospel music after a sensational career on the Billboard charts. It is why Andraé Crouch—called the father of modern gospel music—could join forces with Michael Jackson in the studio during the weekday and on weekends pastor his Christ Memorial Church of God in Christ in Pacoima, California.

I must share a relevant story here. In my courses, I require students to go on "field research trips" where they visit churches unfamiliar to them. I often send students to the West Angeles Church of God in Christ—pastored by Bishop Charles Blake—to experience a black Pentecostal church service. Bishop Blake, his staff, and members have proven to be extremely hospitable to my students through the years. On one occasion, however, a student of mine said, "Professor, I need to go home for the weekend. May I attend a Church of God in Christ in my hometown?" I gave him permission. The student returned

---

33. For "invisible institution," see Maynard-Reid, *Diverse Worship*, 54.
34. Christopher Partridge, *The Lyre of Orpheus: Popular Music, The Sacred, and the Profane* (Oxford: Oxford University Press, 2014), 242.

the following week and said, "I had a very successful trip, and the preacher was amazing! He is an incredible musician. I mean, this man is really talented. I couldn't believe how well he sang and played the piano. He talked with me after services for a long time, and he was so warm."

I asked the student where he went for the field research trip, and he said, "Pacoima, California." I immediately clued in. I asked, "Is there any chance the pastor's name was Andraé Crouch?" Indeed it was. I told the student he had just enjoyed a private meeting and interview with one of the most important musicians living today, attested by his many Grammy and Dove awards and 1998 induction into the Gospel Music Hall of Fame.[35] The student had no idea. But now he does.

In American history, some of the greatest leaders among African-Americans were men and women of the church. Naturally, Martin Luther King Jr. comes to mind here. As a Baptist pastor, his speeches were always laced with theological themes, undergirded by theological motivations. This same process has occurred in the black music scene.

There is no border separating R&B, hip-hop, and jazz from the collective experience of the black church. They bleed together. One of the most important and best-selling songs of my lifetime is Puff Daddy's "I'll Be Missing You"—a tribute to rapper Notorious B.I.G. Laced throughout the song is the melody from the gospel classic "I'll Fly Away." Clearly a rap song, it is infused with gospel. It held massive crossover appeal as it integrated "Every Breath You Take," a hit by the Police in the 1980s. The haunting lyrics evince a deep faith, a firm belief in life after death, a commitment to prayer, and a conviction that they will reunite in heaven one day. It is a powerful and most religious song. One scholar writes, "It was, and

---

35. See the GMA Gospel Music Hall of Fame entry for Andraé Crouch at http://www.gmahalloffame.org/site/andrae-crouch/.

still is, typical for a black composer to take a song written by a white composer, reshape it and improvise it in a folk-like manner, or 'blackenize' it, giving it new life. This is the genius of worship in the African-American experience."[36] "I'll Be Missing You" is one of the finest examples of this process.

But the black community offers many more examples, due to its intensely spiritual worldview and its turning to religion for relief from intense suffering. These are themes that go deep into black gospel's roots; the collective unconscious does not soon forget the slave ships, the plantations, and the pain. Yet religion is always there. Even a rapper as troubled as Tupac Shakur is described by his biographer thus: "Tupac was obsessed with God. His lyrics drip with a sense of the divine."[37] His smash hit "So Many Tears" encapsulates the hopes, fears, and profound despair of a young black man struggling with existence. He describes himself as cursed, and in the song he foresees his death as being imminent. However, he welcomes death, because his intense pain and suffering will end. He reasons that he will end up in hell, but at least he won't have to deal with the profound sorrow that his life entails. And he won't have to lament his friends being killed with such brutal regularity. One way or another, his "many tears" will finally come to an end, for better or for worse.

Tupac's lyrics were prophetic. He joined his departed peers in the afterlife when he was killed in a drive-by shooting in 1996 at the young age of twenty-five. His legacy in the world of rap and hip-hop is unparalleled.

It has been enriching for me to encounter rap artists such as LeCrae and Trip Lee, artists who share the black experience but who are decidedly Christian. They represent uncharted territory on

---

36. Maynard-Reid, *Diverse Worship*, 71.
37. Michael Eric Dyson, *Holler If You Hear Me: Searching for Tupac Shakur* (New York: Basic Books, 2001), 202.

the Christian music scene. As the influence of American hip-hop continues to expand globally, especially into Asia, they will be on the cutting edge of Christian evangelization among the world's youth.

Conclusion: Global Christian Music

The world's Christian music is diverse and fascinating. And while it unites the followers of Christ, it also highlights the huge differences in collective identities. This is to be expected as music is part of the indigenization process that occurs when people claim Christianity as their own. Believers from the West and disciples of the Global South are in a constant dance together in this age of globalization. The cross-pollination process is on full display when it comes to music. For example, one of the most innovative bands today is Aradhna, a band whose music is a fusion of Hindustani with Christian-bhakti devotion. They sing mainly in Indian languages, but they are Caucasian.

Perhaps no other musical artist of the last generation has impacted American Christianity as deeply as Amy Grant, a teenager who burst onto the contemporary Christian music scene in 1978 at the age of seventeen. "Within a decade, Amy Grant changed the course of sacred music—and in the process, altered the way Christians worship God."[38] She sold millions of albums and crossed over into secular music, tearing down the parochial walls of Christian radio. Amy Grant's impact set in motion the situation we have today, where many churches base their architecture and services around the music, much like a stage or a concert hall.

The range of world Christian music is breathtaking, as it should be since Christianity is by far the most globalized of the religions.

---

38. David Murrow, "How a 17-Year-Old Girl Changed the Way We Worship God," April 29, 2014, located at http://www.patheos.com/blogs/churchformen/2014/04/how-a-17-year-old-girl-changed-how-we-worship-god/.

And the United States is the great nexus point for the various kinds of music today. America is also the great exporter of culture, and that includes music.

Thus while Casting Crowns and Chris Tomlin top the charts in the United States, it is inevitable that their music will go global. And when Africans, Asians, and Latinos immigrate into the West, they will bring their creative juices with them. Certainly these musicians from various parts of the globe will influence each other, creating a musical fusion. Andrew Walls has called this fusion "the Ephesian Moment," when two distinct cultures—Jewish and gentile—began to fuse, transforming both. The Ephesian Christians created a new cultural identity: "In union with him [Christ], you too are being built together with all the others to a place where God lives through his Spirit" (Eph. 2:22).[39]

Music has a unique ability to unite people. And as Christianity has expanded globally, music has served as an effective medium for transmitting the gospel. D. T. Niles, a Methodist theologian from Sri Lanka, put the point this way: "Now when missionaries came to our lands they brought not only the seed of the Gospel, but their own plant of Christianity, flower pot included! So, what we have to do is to break the flower pot, take out the seed of the Gospel, sow it in our own cultural soil, and let our own version of Christianity grow."[40] It could very well be that the musicians of the faith are the next great wave of Christian missionaries.

---

39. See Andrew Walls, "The Ephesian Moment," in his book *The Cross-Cultural Process in Christian History* (Maryknoll: Orbis, 2002), 72ff. The scripture reference is from 76.

40. D.T. Niles, cited in C. Michael Hawn, *Gather into One: Praying and Singing Globally* (Grand Rapids, MI: Eerdmans, 2003), 32.

14

Conclusion

If one were to put a date to the decline of Christianity's dominance in the Western world, the likeliest choice would be July 28, 1914—the beginning of the Great War, or World War I. Lamin Sanneh argues that this war ushered Europe into a period of "debilitating introspection," and was in many ways "the first sign of the transition of the modern West to a post-Christian phase."[1]

Some claim it is far too early to write off Christianity in Europe. Nevertheless, there is an unmistakable passing of the baton. Before the nineteenth century, Christianity was closely tied to Europe. This is simply not the case anymore. Sure, most Europeans still declare themselves Christian in surveys, but the reality on the ground is that the enmeshment of Christ with national identity barely exists anymore.

So if Christianity does not belong chiefly to the Western world anymore, then to whom does it belong? One way to approach an

---

1. Lamin Sanneh, *Disciples of All Nations* (Oxford: Oxford University Press, 2008), 273.

answer to the overarching question of this book is to look at the world's nations having the most Christians. A top-ten list from Pew Research in 2011 reveals a fascinating truth of twenty-first century Christianity: it is extremely widespread.[2]

- United States: 246 million Christians

- Brazil: 175 million

- Mexico: 107 million

- Russia: 105 million

- Philippines: 86 million

- Nigeria: 80 million

- China: 67 million

- DR Congo: 63 million

- Germany: 58 million

- Ethiopia: 52 million

Breaking this down further, we see three of the largest Christian nations are from Africa: Nigeria, DR Congo, and Ethiopia. Two are from Asia: China and the Philippines. And two are from Latin America: Brazil and Mexico. Thus, when scholars project that the future of Christianity is in Asia, Africa, and Latin America, statistics suggest the future is now.

Several questions seem pertinent to me as we envision the evolution of global Christianity over the course of the twenty-first century:

---

2. See Pew Forum, "Global Christianity: A Report on the Size and Distribution of the World's Christian Population," December 19, 2011, located at http://www.pewforum.org/2011/12/19/global-christianity-exec/.

- Will North America secularize like Western Europe has?

- Will Western Europe see a revival of Christian faith?

- What will Eastern Europe do? Will it continue to embrace Christianity in the aftermath of enforced atheism? Or will secularization trends win out?

- Will China continue its surprisingly Christian surge? Or will it reach a high point and plateau, much like what has happened in South Korea?

- Will Islamic terrorism provoke widespread antipathy toward all religion? Or will it feed a rising Christian zeal?

These are the questions that will, to a large extent, determine the expansion or contraction of global Christianity in the coming decades. The key stories to watch will be America and China. As the United States leads the Western world, and China the East, it makes sense to assume that how the citizens of these mammoth nations embrace or reject Christianity will impact billions of people in both hemispheres.

One important question that is difficult to talk about is Islamic terrorism, and how it might stir cultural tensions. In the wake of such events as September 11, the ISIS caliphate, and the *Charlie Hebdo* killings, it is unclear how leaders will respond. The Western world reacted to 9/11 with a decade of war. There is no way to know how long the ISIS caliphate will stand, or how far it will expand. And the aftermath of *Charlie Hebdo* will surely play out for decades, as freedom of speech is one of the Western world's sacred cows, and a point of deep sensitivity when it is aimed at Islam's hallowed icons.

In 1993 Samuel Huntington wrote the hugely influential article "The Clash of Civilizations." His argument was straightforward and bold:

> World politics is entering a new phase. . . . It is my hypothesis that the
> fundamental source of conflict in this new world will not be primarily
> ideological or primarily economic. The great divisions among
> humankind and the dominating source of conflict will be cultural. . . .
> The clash of civilizations will dominate global politics. The fault lines
> between civilizations will be the battle lines of the future.[3]

His thesis was provocative, and the events following September 11, 2001 seemed to play right into his projections. Two of his chief detractors, Edward Said and Noam Chomsky, claimed his thesis was overly simple, racist, and reckless.[4] They argued that Huntington created false distinctions between the world's cultures, and he brazenly assumed something as rich and complex as "Islam" can be stereotyped as one of seven or eight world civilizations. How can one and a half billion Muslims scattered all over the world possibly be reduced to "a culture"?, they asked.

Whether one agrees with Huntington or not, one thing is certain: how the world's Christians respond to these sporadic attacks—from ISIS, the Taliban, Al-Qaeda, Boko Haram, Al-Shabaab, and other jihadist groups—will go a long way in setting a world Christian agenda in the twenty-first century. Will Christians in New York, Paris, London, northern Nigeria, southern Sudan, Egypt, Iraq, and Syria simply "turn the other cheek?" Or will they don their war helmets and fuel up the drones, using Augustine's "just war theory" to rationalize counterattacks? Only time will tell, but for our purposes, it remains to be seen whether Christianity will belong chiefly to the oppressors or to the oppressed. Often throughout the history of Christianity, it has been a very fine line that separates the two.

---

3. Samuel Huntington, "The Clash of Civilizations?," in *Foreign Affairs*, summer 1993, located at http://www.foreignaffairs.com/articles/48950/samuel-p-huntington/the-clash-of-civilizations.
4. See Edward Said, "The Clash of Ignorance," in *The Nation*, October 22, 2001, located at http://www.thenation.com/article/clash-ignorance#. Chomsky has repeatedly argued against Huntington's thesis, although with less clarity than Said.

Another major issue that deserves careful investigation is how Christianity and economics will impact one another moving forward. For several centuries, Christianity has been associated with the relatively wealthy countries of the West. Christianity today, however, is much more a poor person's faith than a rich person's. Africa will soon pass Latin America as the cultural bloc with the most Christians. And compared to rest of the world, Africa is poor. A 2010 study concluded, "Today Sub-Saharan Africa . . . is the poorest part of the planet. For the first time in World history, due to the sustained economic growth which China and India have experienced over the past 20 years, the majority of the world's poor (living on $1 a day or less) are in Africa."[5] According to the study, the per-capita incomes of poor countries—for example, Ethiopia and Sierra Leone—and the prosperous countries of the world differ by a factor of about forty. People in Africa live about thirty years less than Westerners on average, their health care is pitiful, educational opportunities are restricted, and the economic outlook is grim due to authoritarian governments and perennial economic crises. There is little reason to think change will come any time soon.

What this means is that in the foreseeable future, Christianity will be a religion associated with the poorest of the poor. This does not mean that it will be associated *solely* with the poor. But it may cause the wealthier Christian nations to think a little harder when they realize it is their Christian brothers and sisters who are suffering so profoundly from famine, disease, and hopelessness.

On the other hand, we must ask, will Christianity lead to material improvement, economic advance, and social uplift? It certainly has in the past. In the early twentieth century, Max Weber argued that Protestantism was especially prone to material advancement because

---

5. Daron Acemoglu and James A. Robinson, "Why Is Africa Poor?," in *Economic History of Developing Regions* 25, no. 1 (2010): 21.

of the twin engines of working hard—as if laboring for God—and saving money. Spending selfishly and acquiring possessions was seen to contradict the teachings of Christ. The result was people who work hard but spend little. Capital accumulates. And this excess capital fuels investment that eventually leads to widespread social prosperity. Could it be that Christianity's influence will lead sub-Saharan Africa out of its grinding poverty? Although it is a strongly Roman Catholic bloc, it does seem to be the case that Latin America has finally turned a corner. The World Bank forecasts that "the middle class will comprise close to half of the total population [of Latin America] by 2030."[6] China's Christian population seems to be growing alongside its economic boom. And there are other Asian nations that have followed or are following a similar trajectory, such as South Korea and Vietnam. Thus there are arguments to be made that sub-Sahara could follow suit.

There is much more to Christianity, however, than economic and geopolitical concerns. The religion of Christ, in recent years, has been shaped largely by its desire to offer healing to a damaged world. Whether this healing comes in the form of Pentecostal charisma or modern science makes little difference to the overarching mission: Christians have a desire to help, to bind up wounds, to cure, and to reach out to others in the name of Jesus. We read of Christian medical personnel working selflessly to shut down Ebola in West Africa, or female church members in India courageously protesting violence against women. And we are reminded of the words of Jesus: "Whatever you did for one of the least of these brothers and sisters of mine, you did for me" (Matt. 25:40).

6. "Latin America: Middle Class Hits Historic High," *The World Bank*, November 13, 2012, located at http://www.worldbank.org/en/news/feature/2012/11/13/crecimiento-clase-media-america-latina.

For all of the critiques of a militant Christendom in the West, of an exploitative era of colonialism, or of a triumphalist period of global Christian missions, it is clear that disciples of Jesus Christ have, time and time again, worked to make their world a more just and humane place. From my vantage point at a university campus in California, I see students giving their spring breaks to teaching children in remote corners of Guatemala, their summers to encouraging orphans in Nairobi, and their postcollege years to teaching English (and, by the way, sharing the gospel) in Shanghai. Millennial Christians have been criticized for being self-entitled. But that's only part of the story. For every entitled one, there are several others eager to give up something in order to make a difference.

To whom does Christianity belong? This book showcased many examples of followers of Christ trying to make Christianity their own. African women, Latin American Catholics, American Evangelicals, disciples in the Chinese underground movements, European pastors, Rwandan genocide survivors . . . they are all embracing Christianity in their own way according to their own context. Some of them call upon the Lord to heal their lands, others put their hope in him to bring them prosperity, and hope, and a fighting chance to lift themselves out of despair. Some call upon Christ to vindicate them after being subjected to the kind of brutality that few Westerners will ever know. Many of them see in Christianity a reason to hope that the best is yet to come. That the injustices of the past will be made right. That darkness will be pierced by shafts of glorious light. That death will be overcome by resurrection.

These are the longings of all Christians who know pain, poverty, and exploitation. Jesus understood these things. And he addressed them. And every generation that encounters the risen Christ is filled with this marvelous hope that God pays special attention to bruised reeds, for "the Lord is near to the brokenhearted and saves those who are crushed in spirit" (Ps. 34:18).

Indeed, in the Sermon on the Mount, Jesus himself seemed to offer an answer to our central question, To whom does Christianity belong? He answered it thus: "Blessed are the poor in spirit. . . . blessed are those who are persecuted because of righteousness, *for theirs is the kingdom of heaven*" (Matt. 5:3, 10).

For Further Reading

Adogame, Afe. *The African Christian Diaspora: New Currents and Emerging Trends in World Christianity*. London: Bloomsbury, 2013.

Agadjanian, Alexander, ed. *Armenian Christianity Today: Identity Politics and Popular Practice*. Farnham, UK: Ashgate, 2014.

Aikman, David. *Billy Graham: His Life and Influence*. Nashville: Thomas Nelson, 2007.

———. *Jesus in Beijing*. Washington, DC: Regnery Publishing, 2003.

Alfeyev, Archbishop Hilarion. *Christ the Conqueror of Hell: The Descent into Hades from an Orthodox Perspective*. Crestwood, NY: St. Vladimir's Seminary Press, 2009.

Allen Jr., John. *The Catholic Church*. Oxford: Oxford University Press, 2013.

———. *The Future Church: How Ten Trends Are Revolutionizing the Catholic Church*. New York: Doubleday, 2009.

Anderson, Allan, and Edmond Tang, eds. *Asian and Pentecostal: The Charismatic Face of Christianity in Asia*. Oxford: Regnum, 2005.

Barker, Gregory, and Stephen Gregg, eds. *Jesus beyond Christianity: The Classic Texts*. Oxford: Oxford University Press, 2010.

Bebbington, David. *Baptists through the Centuries: A History of a Global People*. Waco, TX: Baylor University Press, 2010.

Bediako, Kwame. *Christianity in Africa: The Renewal of a Non-Western Religion*. Edinburgh: Edinburgh University Press, 1995.

————. *Jesus and the Gospel in Africa*. Maryknoll, NY: Orbis, 2004.

Bednarowski, Mary Farrell, ed. *Twentieth-Century Global Christianity*. Minneapolis: Fortress Press, 2008.

Behrend, Heike. *Alice Lakwena and the Holy Spirits: War in Northern Uganda 1986–1997*. Athens, OH: Ohio University Press, 1999.

Bell, Rob. *Love Wins*. New York: HarperOne, 2011.

Bettenson, Henry. *Documents of the Christian Church*. Second ed. Oxford: Oxford University Press, 1963.

Blocher, Jacques A. and Jacques Blandenier. *The Evangelization of the World: A History of Christian Missions*. Translated by Michael Parker. Pasadena: William Carey Library, 2013.

Boff, Leonardo. *Church, Charism and Power: Liberation Theology and the Institutional Church*. London: SCM, 1985.

Brackney, William. *Baptists in North America*. Oxford: Blackwell, 2006.

Brecht, Martin. *Martin Luther: The Preservation of the Church, 1532–1546*. Vol. 3. Minneapolis: Fortress Press, 1999.

Brown, Callum. *The Death of Christian Britain*. New York: Routledge, 2001.

Brown, Candy Gunther, ed. *Global Pentecostal and Charismatic Healing*. Oxford: Oxford University Press, 2011.

Burrows, William, Mark Gornik, and Janice McLean, eds. *Understanding World Christianity: The Vision and Work of Andrew F. Walls*. Maryknoll, NY: Orbis, 2011.

Cahill, Thomas. *Pope John XXIII*. New York: Viking, 2002.

Calhoun, Craig, Mark Juergensmeyer, and Jonathan Van Antwerpen, eds. *Rethinking Secularism*. Oxford: Oxford University Press, 2011.

Campolo, Tony. *Red Letter Christians: A Citizen's Guide to Faith and Politics*. Ventura, CA: Regal Books, 2008.

Carter, Jimmy. *Our Endangered Values: America's Moral Crisis*. New York: Simon & Schuster, 2005.

Charles, H. R. *Book of Enoch*. Oxford: Clarendon Press, 1917.

Chaves, Mark. *American Religion: Contemporary Trends*. Princeton, NJ: Princeton University Press, 2011.

Coward, Harold, ed. *Life after Death in World Religions*. Maryknoll, NY: Orbis, 1997.

Cox, Harvey. *Fire From Heaven: The Rise of Pentecostal Spirituality and the Reshaping of Religion in the Twenty-First Century*. Cambridge, MA: Da Capo Press, 1995.

Cox, James. *Critical Reflections on Indigenous Religions*. Farnham, UK: Ashgate, 2013.

Damascene, Hieromonk. *Father Seraphim Rose: His Life and Works*. Third ed. Platina, CA: St. Herman Press, 2010.

Daughrity, Dyron. *The Changing World of Christianity: The Global History of a Borderless Religion*. New York: Peter Lang, 2010.

———. *Church History: Five Approaches to a Global Discipline*. New York: Peter Lang, 2012.

Davies, Noel, and Martin Conway. *World Christianity in the 20th Century*. London: SCM Press, 2008.

Dawson, Lorne. *Comprehending Cults: The Sociology of New Religious Movements*. Oxford: Oxford University Press, 1998.

Donovan, Vincent. *Christianity Rediscovered*. Maryknoll, NY: Orbis, 1978.

Dyson, Michael Eric. *Holler If You Hear Me: Searching for Tupac Shakur*. New York: Basic Books, 2001.

Eberstadt, Mary. *How the West Really Lost God*. West Conshohocken, PA: Templeton Press, 2013.

Ferguson, Everett. *Church History: From Christ to the Pre-Reformation*. Grand Rapids, MI: Zondervan, 2013.

———, ed. *Encyclopedia of Early Christianity*. Second edition. New York: Routledge, 1999.

Gornik, Mark. *Word Made Global: Stories of African Christianity in New York City*. Grand Rapids, MI: Eerdmans, 2011.

Granberg-Michaelson, Wesley. *From Times Square to Timbuktu: The Post-Christian West Meets the Non-Western Church*. Grand Rapids, MI: Eerdmans, 2013.

Gutierrez, Gustavo. *A Theology of Liberation*. Maryknoll, NY: Orbis Books, 1973.

Haleem, M. A. S. Abdel. *The Quran*. Oxford: Oxford University Press, 2005.

Hanciles, Jehu. *Beyond Christendom: Globalization, African Migration, and the Transformation of the West*. Maryknoll, NY: 2008.

Hartch, Todd. *The Rebirth of Latin American Christianity*. Oxford: Oxford University Press, 2014.

Hawn, C. Michael. *Gather into One: Praying and Singing Globally*. Grand Rapids, MI: Eerdmans, 2003.

Irvin, Dale, and Scott Sunquist. *History of the World Christian Movement*. Vol. 1. Maryknoll, NY: Orbis Books, 2001.

Isichei, Elizabeth. *A History of Christianity in Africa*. Grand Rapids, MI: Eerdmans, 1995.

Jenkins, Philip. *God's Continent: Christianity, Islam, and Europe's Religious Crisis*. Oxford: Oxford University Press, 2007.

———. *The Next Christendom: The Coming of Global Christianity*. Oxford: Oxford University Press, 2002.

Jones, E. Stanley. *The Christ of the Indian Road*. London: Hodder and Stoughton, 1925.

———. *Gandhi: Portrayal of a Friend*. Nashville: Abingdon, 1948.

Kalu, Ogbu, ed. *African Christianity: An African Story*. Trenton, NJ: Africa World Press, 2007.

———. *African Pentecostalism: An Introduction*. Oxford: Oxford University Press, 2008.

Kelley, Dean. *Why Conservative Churches Are Growing*. Macon, GA: Mercer University Press, 1996.

Kim, Rebecca. *God's New Whiz Kids? Korean American Evangelicals on Campus.* New York: NYU Press, 2006.

Kirkpatrick, Frank. *The Episcopal Church in Crisis.* Westport, CT: Praeger, 2008.

Küng, Hans. *The Catholic Church: A Short History.* Translated. by John Bowden. New York: The Modern Library, 2003.

Küster, Volker. *The Many Faces of Jesus Christ.* Maryknoll, NY: Orbis, 1999.

Lewis, Nicola Denzey. *Introduction to "Gnosticism": Ancient Voices, Christian Worlds.* Oxford: Oxford University Press, 2013.

Lindberg, Carter. *The European Reformations.* Second ed. Oxford: Wiley-Blackwell, 2010.

MacCulloch, Diarmaid. *The Reformation: A History.* New York: Penguin, 2003.

Masumian, Farnaz. *Life after Death.* Oxford: Oneworld, 1995.

Maynard-Reid, Pedrito. *Diverse Worship: African-American, Caribbean & Hispanic Perspectives.* Downers Grove, IL: InterVarsity Press, 2000.

McConnell, Francis John. *Human Needs and World Christianity.* New York: Friendship Press, 1929.

McGrath, Alister. *Christianity's Dangerous Idea: The Protestant Revolution.* New York: HarperOne, 2007.

McLaren, Brian. *A New Kind of Christianity: Ten Questions That Are Transforming the Faith.* New York: HarperOne, 2010.

Meyers, Eric, and Mark Chancey. *Alexander to Constantine: Archaeology of the Land of the Bible.* New Haven: Yale University Press, 2012.

Meyer, Marvin, trans. *The Gospel of Thomas: The Hidden Sayings of Jesus.* New York: HarperSanFrancisco, 1992.

Migliore, Daniel. *Faith Seeking Understanding.* Grand Rapids, MI: Eerdmans, 1991.

Miller, Donald, Kimon Sargeant, and Richard Flory. *Spirit and Power: The Growth and Global Impact of Pentecostalism*. Oxford: Oxford University Press, 2013.

Miller, Donald, and Tetsunao Yamamori. *Global Pentecostalism: The New Face of Christian Social Engagement*. Berkeley: University of California Press, 2007.

Miller, Robert J., ed. *The Complete Gospels*. New York: HarperSanFrancisco, 1994.

Moody, Raymond. *Life after Life*. New York: Bantam, 1975.

Neill, Stephen. *Jesus through Many Eyes*. Philadelphia: Fortress Press, 1976.

Nietzsche, Friedrich. *The Gay Science*. Edited by Bernard Williams. Translated by Josefine Nauckhoff. Cambridge: Cambridge University Press, 2001.

O'Brien, Joanne, and Martin Palmer. *The Atlas of Religion*. Los Angeles: University of California Press, 2007.

Oden, Thomas C. *John Wesley's Teachings*. Vol. 2, *Christ and Salvation*. Grand Rapids, MI: Zondervan, 2012.

O'Malley, John. *A History of the Popes: From Peter to the Present*. New York: Rowman and Littlefield, 2010.

Osteen, Joel. *Break Out!* New York: FaithWords, 2013.

Pagels, Elaine. *Revelations: Visions, Prophecy, and Politics in the Book of Revelation*. New York: Penguin, 2012.

Parry, K., D. Melling, D. Brady, S. Griffith, and J. Healey, eds. *The Blackwell Dictionary of Eastern Christianity*. Oxford: Blackwell, 2001.

Partridge, Christopher. *The Lyre of Orpheus: Popular Music, The Sacred, and the Profane*. Oxford: Oxford University Press, 2014.

Pobee, John S., and Gabriel Ositelu II. *African Initiatives in Christianity: The Growth, Gifts, and Diversities of Indigenous African Churches*. Geneva: WCC Publications, 1998.

Pope-Levison, Priscilla, and John Levison. *Jesus in Global Contexts*. Louisville: Westminster/John Knox, 1992.

Powne, Michael. *Ethiopian Music, an Introduction: A Survey of Ecclesiastical and Secular Ethiopian Music and Instruments*. Oxford: Oxford University Press, 1968.

Putnam, Robert, and David Campbell. *American Grace: How Religion Divides and Unites Us*. New York: Simon and Schuster, 2010.

Robert, Dana. *Christian Mission: How Christianity Became a World Religion*. Oxford: Wiley-Blackwell, 2009.

Rodriguez, Daniel. *A Future for the Latino Church*. Downers Grove, IL: IVP Academic, 2011.

Rose, Fr. Seraphim. *The Soul after Death*. Platina, CA: St. Herman Press, 2009.

Rouse, Ruth, and Stephen Neill, eds. *A History of the Ecumenical Movement 1517–1948*. Philadelphia: The Westminster Press, 1967.

Rupp, E.G., and Benjamin Drewery. *Martin Luther: Documents of Modern History*. London: Edward Arnold, 1970.

Sanneh, Lamin. *Summoned from the Margin: Homecoming of an African*. Grand Rapids, MI: Eerdmans, 2012.

———. *Translating the Message: The Missionary Impact on Culture*. Maryknoll, NY: Orbis, 1989.

———. *West African Christianity: The Religious Impact*. Maryknoll, NY: Orbis, 1983.

———. *Whose Religion Is Christianity? The Gospel beyond the West*. Grand Rapids, MI: Eerdmans, 2003.

Senn, Frank. *The People's Work: A Social History of the Liturgy*. Minneapolis: Fortress Press, 2006.

Spence, Jonathan. *God's Chinese Son: The Taiping Heavenly Kingdom of Hong Xiuquan*. New York: W. W. Norton, 1996.

Sharma, Arvind, ed. *Women in World Religion*. Albany: State University of New York Press, 1987.

Shelby Spong, John. *Why Christianity Must Change or Die*. New York: HarperCollins: 1998.

Sigmund, Paul, ed. *Religious Freedom and Evangelization in Latin America: The Challenge of Religious Pluralism*. Maryknoll, NY: Orbis, 1999.

Stanley, Brian. *The World Missionary Conference, Edinburgh 1910*. Grand Rapids, MI: Eerdmans, 2009.

Stark, Rodney. *The Triumph of Christianity*. New York: HarperOne, 2011.

Stark, Rodney, and William Bainbridge. *Religion, Deviance, and Social Control*. New York: Routledge, 1997.

Street, Nick. *Moved by the Spirit: Pentecostalism and Charismatic Christianity in the Global South*. Los Angeles: Center for Religion and Civic Culture University of Southern California, 2013.

Sundkler, Bengt, *Bantu Prophets in South Africa*. Oxford: Oxford University Press, 1961.

Sutton, Matthew Avery. *Aimee Semple McPherson and the Resurrection of Christian America*. Cambridge, MA: Harvard University Press, 2007.

Synan, Vinson. *The Century of the Holy Spirit: 100 Years of Pentecostal and Charismatic Renewal*. Nashville: Thomas Nelson, 2001.

———. *The Holiness-Pentecostal Tradition: Charismatic Movements in the Twentieth Century*. Grand Rapids, MI: Eerdmans, 1997.

Thomas, V. V. *Dalit and Tribal Christians of India: Issues and Challenges*. Nilumbur Post, Kerala: Focus India Trust, 2014.

———. *Dalit Pentecostalism: Spirituality of the Empowered Poor*. Bangalore: Asian Trading Corporation, 2008.

Thornton, John. *The Kongolese Saint Anthony: Dona Beatriz Kimpa Vita and the Antonion Movement, 1684–1706*. Cambridge: Cambridge University Press, 1998.

Tillich, Paul. *Dynamics of Faith*. New York: Harper and Row, 1957.

Troeltsch, Ernst. *The Social Teachings of the Christian Churches.* Vol. 1. London: George Allen and Unwin, 1931.

Twesigye, Emmanuel. *Religion, Politics, and Cults in East Africa: God's Warriors and Mary's Saints.* New York: Peter Lang, 2010.

Verstraelen, F. J. *Missiology: An Ecumenical Introduction; Texts and Contexts of Global Christianity.* Grand Rapids, MI: Eerdmans, 1995.

Walls, Andrew. *The Cross-Cultural Process in Christian History.* Maryknoll, NY: Orbis, 2002.

———. *The Missionary Movement in Christian History.* Maryknoll, NY: Orbis, 1996.

Ware, Timothy. *The Orthodox Church.* London: Penguin, 1997.

Weber, Max. *The Protestant Ethic and the Spirit of Capitalism.* New York: Charles Scribner's Sons, 1958.

Weigel, George. *Evangelical Catholicism: Deep Reform in the 21st-Century Church.* New York: Basic Books, 2013.

Wellman, James. *Rob Bell and a New American Christianity.* Nashville: Abingdon, 2012.

White, Alma. *Demons and Tongues.* Bound Brook, NJ: The Pentecostal Union, 1910.

Wiesner-Hanks, Merry. *Christianity and Sexuality in the Early Modern World: Regulating Desire, Reforming Practice.* Second ed. London: Routledge, 2010.

Wijsen, Frans, and Robert Schreiter, eds. *Global Christianity: Contested Claims.* New York: Rodopi, 2007.

Williams, Rowan. *Where God Happens: Discovering Christ in One Another.* Boston: New Seeds Books, 2005.

Wilson-Dickson, Andrew. *The Story of Christian Music: From Gregorian Chant to Black Gospel.* Minneapolis: Fortress Press, 2003.

Wolfe, Alan. *One Nation, after All.* New York: Penguin Books, 1998.

Wright, N. T. *Surprised by Hope.* New York: HarperOne, 2008.

Wuthnow, Robert. *Boundless Faith: The Global Outreach of American Churches*. Los Angeles: University of California Press, 2009.

Xi, Lian. *Redeemed by Fire: The Rise of Popular Christianity in Modern China*. New Haven: Yale University Press, 2010.

Yiwu, Liao. *God Is Red*. Translated by Wenguang Huang. New York: HarperOne, 2011.

Yun, Brother, and Paul Hattaway. *The Heavenly Man*. Grand Rapids, MI: Monarch Books, 2002.

Zuckerman, Phil. *Society without God*. New York: New York University Press, 2008.

Index